The Shenandoah Valley's Interstates

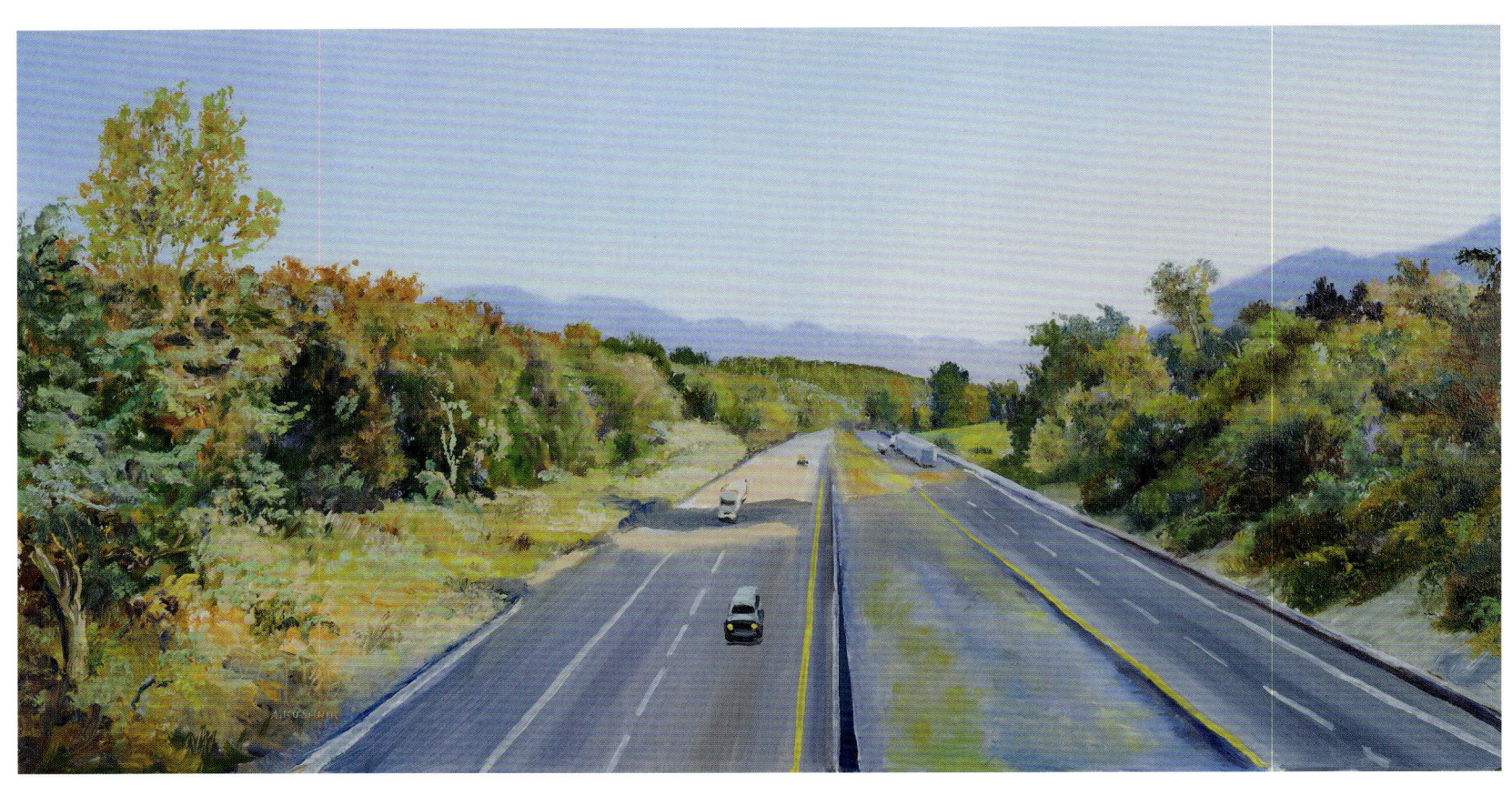

Southernmost View of the Shenandoah Valley and I-81 from the VA 608 Bridge, Indian Rock Road, MM 170.2, just north of Buchanan, oil on panel, 10¼" x 20¼" (height by width), September 25, 2020.

The Shenandoah Valley's Interstates

Plein-air Paintings along I-81, I-66, and I-64
by Andrei Kushnir

with an introduction by Warren R. Hofstra

George F. Thompson Publishing
in association with the
Center for the Study of Place

"The Interstate Highway System will never be finished because America will never be finished."

—FRANCIS C. TURNER, FEDERAL HIGHWAY ADMINISTRATOR (1969—1972)

CONTENTS

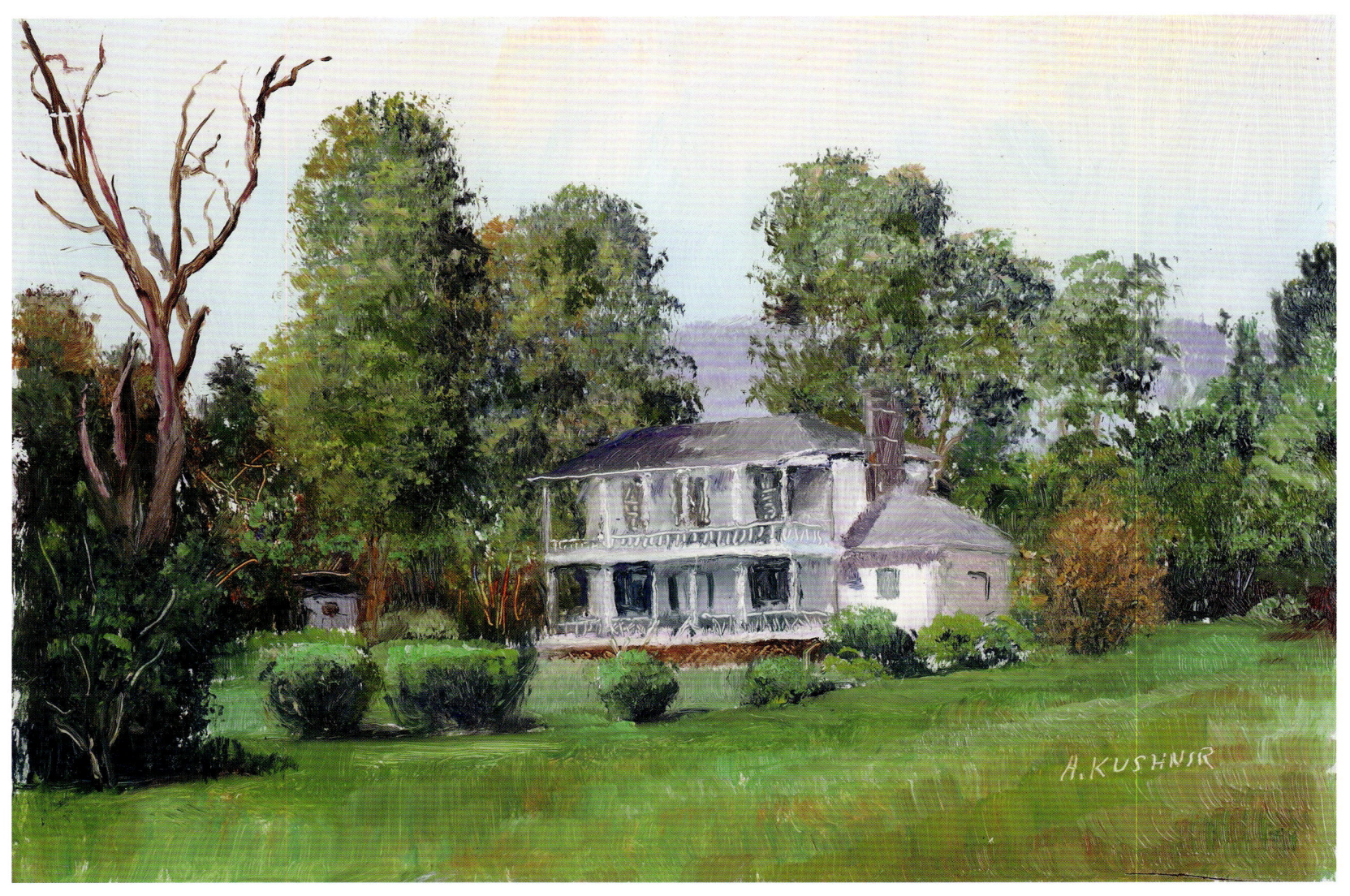

A Nineteenth-Century House on Purgatory Mountain Road along I-81 at Exit 168, Arcadia/Buchanan, oil on panel, 6"x 9," September 22, 2020. Buchanan, on the James River, is the self-proclaimed "Southern Gateway to the Shenandoah Valley."

The Evolving Valley Road:
From Indian Trail to the Modern Highway and Interstate

WARREN R. HOFSTRA

Andrei Kushnir is regarded as one of the most prolific and accomplished regional painters in the United States today. The Potomac Valley, the state of Maryland, the Florida Gulf Coast, Colorado, New Mexico, and seven other western states have been among the objects of his talents. His career has been honored by nearly a dozen one-artist shows. His works hang in the Commission of Arts & Humanities of Washington, D.C.; Museum of Florida's Art and Culture; Museum of the Shenandoah Valley in Winchester, Virginia; Virginia Museum of History and Culture in Richmond; University of Maryland galleries; and University Club in D.C. His genius has been widely praised. According to one Washington critic, "pure landscape painters like Andrei Kushnir . . . reach back to the way the earth was once and hold it dear."[1] "Admirably," a reviewer for *Maine Antiques Digest* asserts, "the directness of [his] plein-air painting yields undeniable freshness."[2]

Most notable among his achievements is a collection of 264 masterful paintings of the Shenandoah Valley completed over a ten-year period and celebrated with exhibitions at the Museum of the Shenandoah Valley in Winchester, Duke Hall Gallery of Fine Art at James Madison University, and the Virginia Museum of History and Culture in Richmond. The entire collection appears in Kushnir's 416-page book, *Oh, Shenandoah: Paintings of the Historic Valley and River* (page 16), published in 2016 by George F. Thompson, noted for creating award-winning books that integrate art, photography, geography, and history.

With these many accomplishments in view and a reputation as a leading painter of Shenandoah Valley landscapes, the question naturally arises: Why would Kushnir take on an art project incorporating congested, truck-strewn, environmentally toxic interstate highways that trespass upon one of America's legendary landscapes otherwise known and appreciated worldwide for its beauty and scenic grandeur? When, in 1853, the renowned American writer Washington Irving (1783–1859) first encountered the Valley after a lifetime of world travels, visiting many of the greatest landmarks of Western culture, he was breathless: "Here I am in the centre of the Magnificent Valley of the Shenandoah—the great valley of Virginia. And a glorious Valley it is—equal to the promised land for fertility; and far superior to it for beauty."[3] Is Kushnir channeling that trope of American landscape painters of the nineteenth century by objecting to the intrusion of railroads, commerce, and industry into the case they were making on behalf of the natural landscape as the foundation of autonomous national values and the idyllic tastes appropriate for the pastoral peoples of an independent republic? One thinks of Thomas Cole's "River in the Catskills" (1843), a portrayal of despoiled forests fallen to the axe of industrial necessity, or George Inness's "The Lackawanna Valley" (1855), with the railroad penetrating that valley, violating a pristine rural setting.

Or is Kushnir embracing change and progress, celebrating the city and its crowded commerce, factories, workers, and their gritty industrial pursuits? Has he joined the ranks of George Bellows, John Sloan, Robert Henri, or George Luks in candid portrayals of urban life in all its extensions? After all, the interstate highway system was created in 1956 to facilitate the flow of goods, people, and military necessities among America's cities. It was, to a large degree, an exploded view of urban America—a repudiation of the haphazard but familiar road system developed over centuries to deliver goods to and from rural households. Is Kushnir telling us that the engineering triumph of the interstate system has created new forms of modernist beauty in sinuous, intersecting curves, Escher-like visualizations at interchanges, or the dramatic remaking of mountain landscapes? Consider that mountain orogeny and continental plate tectonics represent the most massive construction projects known to Earth. Altering them inspires a truly sublime sense of awe and apprehension.

In turn, the American interstate system is likely the largest construction project undertaken by humankind. Fully extended, it is almost long enough to circle Earth twice at the equator. It contains sufficient concrete to pave a sidewalk to the moon and back two and a half times. Enough earth was moved in constructing it to cover the state of Connecticut knee deep, and it occupies enough property to consume Delaware.[4] But Kushnir's work is anything but an accolade for the engineering and aesthetic triumphs of the interstate system. Nor can his paintings be taken in irony as a condemnation of the interstate for its impact on the natural or historic resources of the Valley.

Instead, Kushnir's art is naturalism—New Naturalism—pure and simple. It is aesthetically profound and deeply emotional. As he says: "I have chosen to paint nature and my *plein air* surroundings as they are," no more, no less. In this he is consistent with the goals of nineteenth-century naturalists. Naturalism owes its origins to the practice of painting *en plein air* in Europe and America and the effort to depict what can be readily seen and felt in our natural surroundings along with the quotidian pursuits of ordinary people. Kushnir puts it extraordinarily well: "Whether it is a sylvan stream, an orchard, a diner, or a sight along an interstate highway, I want my paintings to capture our world, in all its beauty, earnestness, and contemporary truth." He emulates nineteenth-century artists; his subjects, however, are not theirs but ours: "I don't want to turn back time, I just want my work to convey a bit of *our* time."[5]

Regarding the (in)compatibility of an interstate highway and a natural landscape renowned for beauty,

Kushnir "took the idea on as a challenge to explore the effect of blending traditional scenic landscape painting with the incorporation of contemporary structures and infrastructure."[6] Here is a through line connecting Kushnir to New Naturalism throughout his career. Of a 2011 painting of a restored historic building in the Valley town of Martinsburg, West Virginia, Kushnir commented: "I don't want to do such an exact representation so that it looks like a photograph. . . . It's got real character and it looks historic. But I also like that it's obviously been used for modern purposes, so they have integrated the old and new while preserving a part of history so that it can continue on into the future. . . . My main goal is to reflect what a beautiful building this is."[7]

Sincerity, directness, and honesty are Kushnir's watchwords. But there's a mystery to his art as well. It's a romance with the visual world. "If you paint a lot," he comments, "you intuitively know what works and what doesn't. It takes constantly being aware of your surroundings and involved in your work."[8] The enchantment comes in his ability to involve us, the viewers, and bring us in—and into—his art. His paintings are visceral and immersive—we want to walk into them, to feel what it's like to be in this place he has chosen to paint. His art brings us pleasure, interests us, and uplifts in what is seen and also in what we otherwise would not see, only intuit. He organizes the visual world and renders it meaningful, much as music gives order to sound and makes meaning out of melody, rhythm, and harmony without the need for analysis. Kushnir's means are form, color, and composition.

What Kushnir accomplishes in *Shenandoah Interstates* is, then, to bring the power of New Naturalism to a region famed not only for its beauty, but also for scenic beauty made public by the artifice of an interstate.

Ask people about the Shenandoah Valley. And whether they have visited it or not, the likely answer is, "It's so beautiful there, isn't it?" Beauty, of course, can't be fully quantified, and natural beauty can be found worldwide. The Shenandoah Valley has no exclusive hold on it, but beauty and the Valley combine mimetically in our culture. Interstate 81, for instance, has been long known as one of America's most scenic interstate drives. Why? Is this what Kushnir captures in this book of paintings? The reason behind the reflexive association of beauty and the Valley belongs partly to Irving. He was arguably America's most popular writer in his day. He was in the Valley during the 1850s to visit the family of longtime friend and Virginia writer, John Pendleton Kennedy (1795–1870), and to research his new biography of George Washington. The resulting five-volumes became a publishing phenomenon when completed three years later. A great many Americans read about Washington's early days spent extensively in the Valley both as a surveyor and as the commander of the Virginia Regiment during the Seven Years' War. Irving relates Washington's first encounter with the Shenandoah Valley in the language of beauty he had himself embraced:

They entered the great valley of Virginia, where it is about twenty-five miles wide; a lovely and temperate region, diversified by gentle swells and slopes, admirably adapted to cultivation. The Blue Ridge bounds it on one side, the North Mountain, a ridge of the Alleghanies, on the other; while through it flows that bright and abounding river, which, on account of its surpassing beauty was named by the Indians the Shenandoah.[9]

Irving had much to draw upon because, in Washington's own words on March 13, 1748, the surveying party to which he was then attached "went through most beautiful Groves of Sugar Trees & spent the best part of the Day in admiring the Trees & richness of the Land."[10]

What attracted Irving to the Shenandoah Valley? Why did he find it so beautiful? It was not wild nature. The Shenandoah Valley was one of the most intensely farmed regions of the United States at the time Irving encountered it. The forest cover had been almost entirely removed. Revealed, however, was limestone soil of remarkable fertility. Improved by fertilizing and fallow rotations with clover, it yielded wheat corps in excess of forty bushels per acre when farmers elsewhere in the Mid-Atlantic settled happily for less than half that amount. Combined in an era of economic expansion with the mixed agriculture of raising livestock, dairying, and cultivating other small grains with byproducts such as whiskey and leather goods, wheat produced a halcyon age of high farming. The resulting prosperity was in turn invested in an infrastructure of substantial brick and stone houses, large banked barns, granaries, stables, and a host of other

support structures along with mills of all sorts, market towns, and paved turnpike roads interconnecting it all. It was the integration of natural beauty with the beauty of human improvement that rendered the Valley so magnificent for Irving and so many other visitors. Its history tells us why.

Wheat had been the staple mainstay of agricultural production since the last decades of the eighteenth century when independence, free trade, global markets, and the decline of Europe's capacity to feed itself in the course of imperial wars and the Industrial Revolution created a substantial demand for American foodstuffs. And wheat was profitable at any scale of production. Much of the Valley had been settled during the eighteenth century by independent farmers, many from southeastern Pennsylvania, New Jersey, and upstate New York with immigrant backgrounds in England, Ireland, and the Germanic states of the Rhine River Valley where tenant farming in small grains prevailed. They developed a small-farm, diversified agricultural economy and a community-based system of self-sufficiency. As market demand for American grains boomed by the end of the eighteenth century and American trade expanded throughout the Atlantic world, the men and women of this Valley world responded.

Meanwhile, republican political principles driving revolutions and conflicts in Europe impelled a flood of Enlightenment-minded exiles and travelers to the United States. For these sojourners the Shenandoah Valley and its peoples came to represent a republican social order expressing what ordinary people could

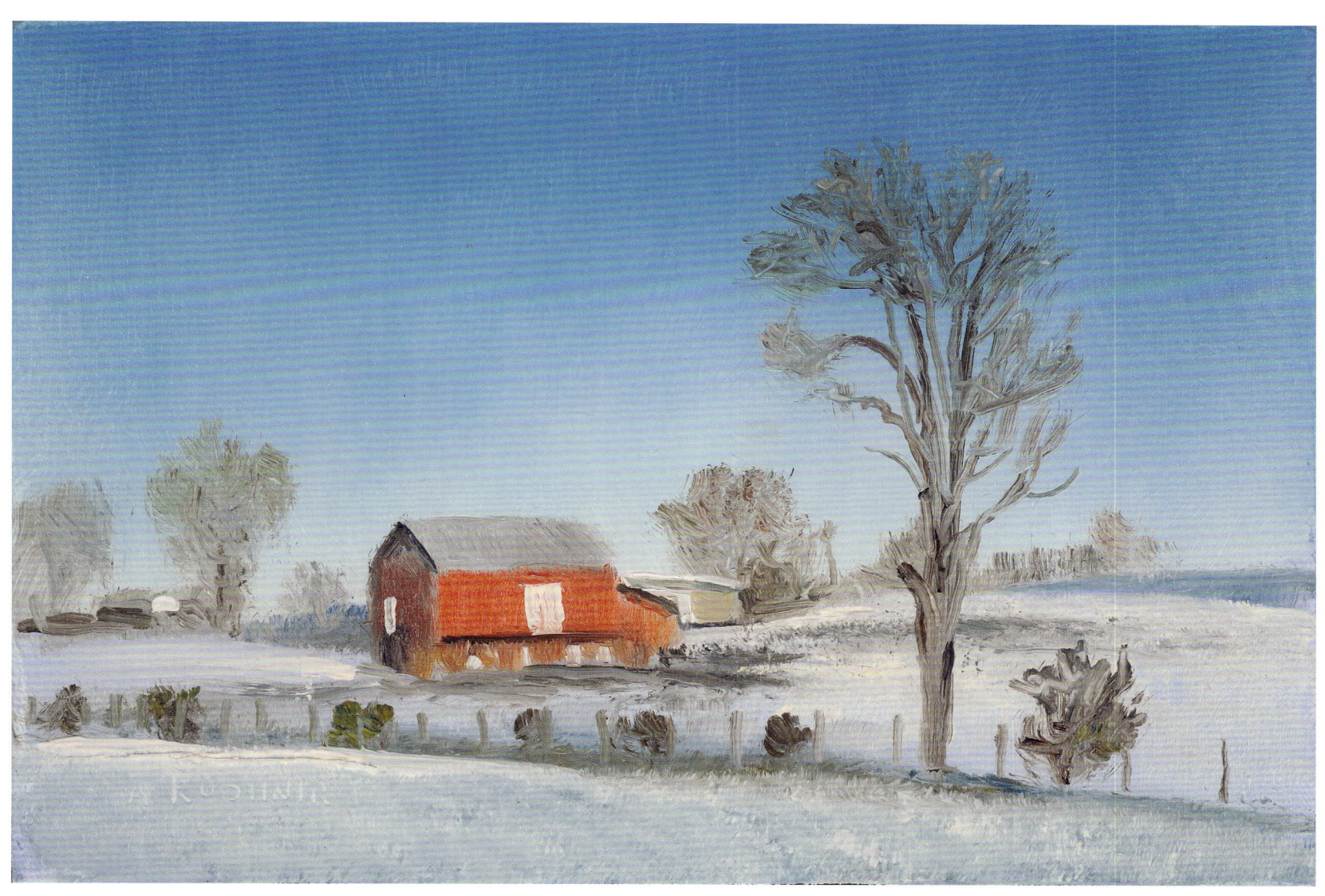

Winter View of a Nineteenth–Century Pennsylvania Bank Barn off I-81 at MM 229, north of Verona, oil on panel, 4" x 6," January 7, 2022.

accomplish when freed from the exploitative grasp of landed aristocracies and the crippling expropriations of taxes, rack rents, and the fees, fines, and obligatory labor of a feudal past. Visitors wrote about these people as if they embodied not only the moral virtue of grain production—the bread of life—but also the autonomous political values of an independent people uplifted by the invisible hand of self-interest freely pursued. These perceptions are key to what aesthetic Naturalism reveals in Kushnir's artistry: landscapes of a nature improved by the beauty of human endeavor inclusive even of a modern interstate.

It was Thomas Jefferson who set the tone. From Monticello, his home near Charlottesville, he visited parts of the Shenandoah Valley and wrote generally about the moral virtue of farmers who raised grains as compared to Virginia planters who produced tobacco with enslaved labor: "Those who labour in the earth are the chosen people of God, if ever he had a chosen people, whose breasts he has made his peculiar deposit for substantial and genuine virtue."[11] On a separate occasion in 1787, Jefferson wrote to George Washington from Paris, France, that "Agriculture . . . is our wisest pursuit, because it will in the end contribute most to real wealth, good morals and happiness."[12] Jefferson's encomiums to farming, free labor, and moral virtue must, of course, be set against the horror of the enslavement of peoples he and many Virginians, including Washington and James Madison, held in forced labor. This form of exploitation and human suffering was, however, not the primary lesson that late-eighteenth-century travelers carried away from visits to the Great Valley of Virginia where slavery was far less common than in Jefferson's or Washington's Virginia.

One visitor to the Shenandoah Valley in 1760 "could not but reflect with pleasure on the situation of these people. If there is such a thing as happiness in this life," he explained, "they enjoy it." All was owing to "the most delightful climate," the "richest soil imaginable," "majestic woods," and "beautiful prospects and sylvan scenes." Conclusion: "They live in perfect liberty."[13] Here was the republican social order for which European reformers and American revolutionaries yearned. "Cultivated lands," another observed, "are mostly parceled out in small portions. There are no persons here," he continued, "eminently distinguished by their education or knowledge from the rest of their fellow citizens. Poverty also is as much unknown in this country as great wealth."[14] It was in this nexus of a republican people, an improved and bountiful landscape of their own making, and a hard-wrought prosperity evident in all that they had built upon the land that visitors saw beauty emerge. By embodying a people's values and ambitions, this landscape inspired a sense of awe in the presence of the sublime. "The beautiful valley of Shenandoah is a fine country," waxed another visitor. It was "inhabited by an industrious and active people; a country, formed by nature to be rich."[15] Another extolled the "fine country" around Winchester, concluding: "The scene is worth a voyage across the Atlantic."[16]

Roads, of course, made possible agricultural productivity, prosperity, and the compellingly beautiful landscape of high farming. Farm-to-market roads connected to mills and towns, but long-distance roads had opened the markets of the world to the people of the Valley. Following Indian routes of continental travel forged partially for the commercial purposes of trade, the Great Wagon Road along the strike of the Great Valley of the Appalachians, from central Pennsylvania to upcountry Georgia, not only guided migration into the Shenandoah Valley during the eighteenth century, but also channeled the flow of goods, notably flour and livestock, northward to Philadelphia and later to Baltimore and Alexandria. Like many landscape features laid down during the first waves of European settlement, this route has persisted in governing the direction of trade and travel ever since. Improved as a series of interconnected turnpikes during the nineteenth century, it gave way to a new kind of Valley Road: U.S. 11, as part of the first federally planned national highway system during the 1920s.

So it is today. This continental routeway naturally influenced planning for the first wave of interstate highways under the Federal-Aid Highway Act of 1956. Completed in late 1966, Interstate 81 stands as a sign of historical continuity in the Shenandoah Valley, from the ancient age of Native American occupation and migration to the time of frontier settlement and wagon travel, from the turnpike era of high farming to the Automobile Age and creation of "Route 11." So when Andrei Kushnir applies the principles of New Naturalism to capture beauty and historical truth, its contemporary iterations, and a candid, honest, and inclusive perspective into the simple beauties of what we see around us, the Valley's interstate highways—I-81, I-66, and I-64—are no intruders but natural expressions of the pleasure and satisfaction that we, as viewers, can derive by journeying through the landscapes of Andrei Kushnir's magnificent art and artistry.

NOTES

1. Jim Magner, "Artist Profile: Andrei Kushnir," *Hill Rag* (August 2006): 94.

2. A.C.V. review of *Oh, Shenandoah: Paintings of the Historic Valley and River, Maine Antique Digest* (August 2017): 24-A.

3. Washington Irving to Sarah Irving, June 22, 1853, in Ralph M. Aderman, Herbert L. Kleinfield, and Jenifer S. Banks, eds., *Washington Irving: Letters*, 5 vols. (Boston, MA: Twayne, 1973–1982): Vol. 4, 413–14.

4. See Tom Lewis, *Divided Highways: Building the Interstate Highways, Transforming American Life* (New York, NY: Viking/ Penguin, 1997), ix.

5. Andrei Kushnir, personal communication, March 5, 2022.

6. Kushnir, personal communication, March 15, 2022.

7. As quoted in Jenni Vincent, "D.C. artist to feature local buildings," *The Journal* of Martinsburg, West Virginia (June 16, 2011): A1. This painting appears on page 134 of Kushnir's *Oh, Shenandoah*.

8. As quoted in Sherry Hamilton, "Outdoor landscape artist visits Pig Hill," *Gloucester-Mathews Gazette-Journal* (May 27, 2010): 5A.

9. Washington Irving, *The Life of George Washington*, 5 vols. (New York, NY: G. P. Putnam, 1855–1859), Vol. 1, 38–39.

10. George Washington, "Journal of My Journey over the Mountains Began Friday the 11th. of March, 1747/8," in Donald Jackson, ed., *The Diaries of George Washington*, Vol. 1, 1748–1765 (Charlottesville: University Press of Virginia, 1976), 7.

11. Thomas Jefferson, *Notes on the State of Virginia* (London, UK: J. Stockdale, 1787), 274.

12. Jefferson to Washington, Paris, August 14, 1787, in Julian P. Boyd, ed., *The Papers of Thomas Jefferson*, Vol. 12, Aug. 7, 1787 to March 1788 (Princeton, NJ: Princeton University Press, 1955): 36–38.

13. Andrew Burnaby, *Travels through the Middle Settlements in North America in the Years 1759 and 1760*, 3d ed. (London, UK: T. Payne, 1798; New York, NY: Augustus M. Kelley, 1970), 73–74.

14. Isaac Weld, *Travels through the States of North America*, 2 vols. (London, UK: John Stockdale, 1807; New York, NY: Johnson Reprint, 1968), Vol. 1, xix–xx, 232–33.

15. François Alexandre Frédéric, duc de la Rochefoucauld-Liancourt, *Travels through the United States of North America . . . in the Years 1795, 1796, and 1797*, 4 vols., 2d ed., translated by H. Neuman (London, UK: R. Phillips, 1800), Vol. 3, 197, 213–14, 216–18.

16. François Jean de Beauvoir, Marquis de Chastellux, *Travels in North America in the Years 1780, 1781 and 1782*, 2 vols., translated by Howard C. Rice Jr. (Paris, France: Prault, 1786; Chapel Hill: University of North Carolina Press for the Institute of Early American History and Culture, 1963), Vol. 1, 359.

The Shenandoah Valley's Interstates

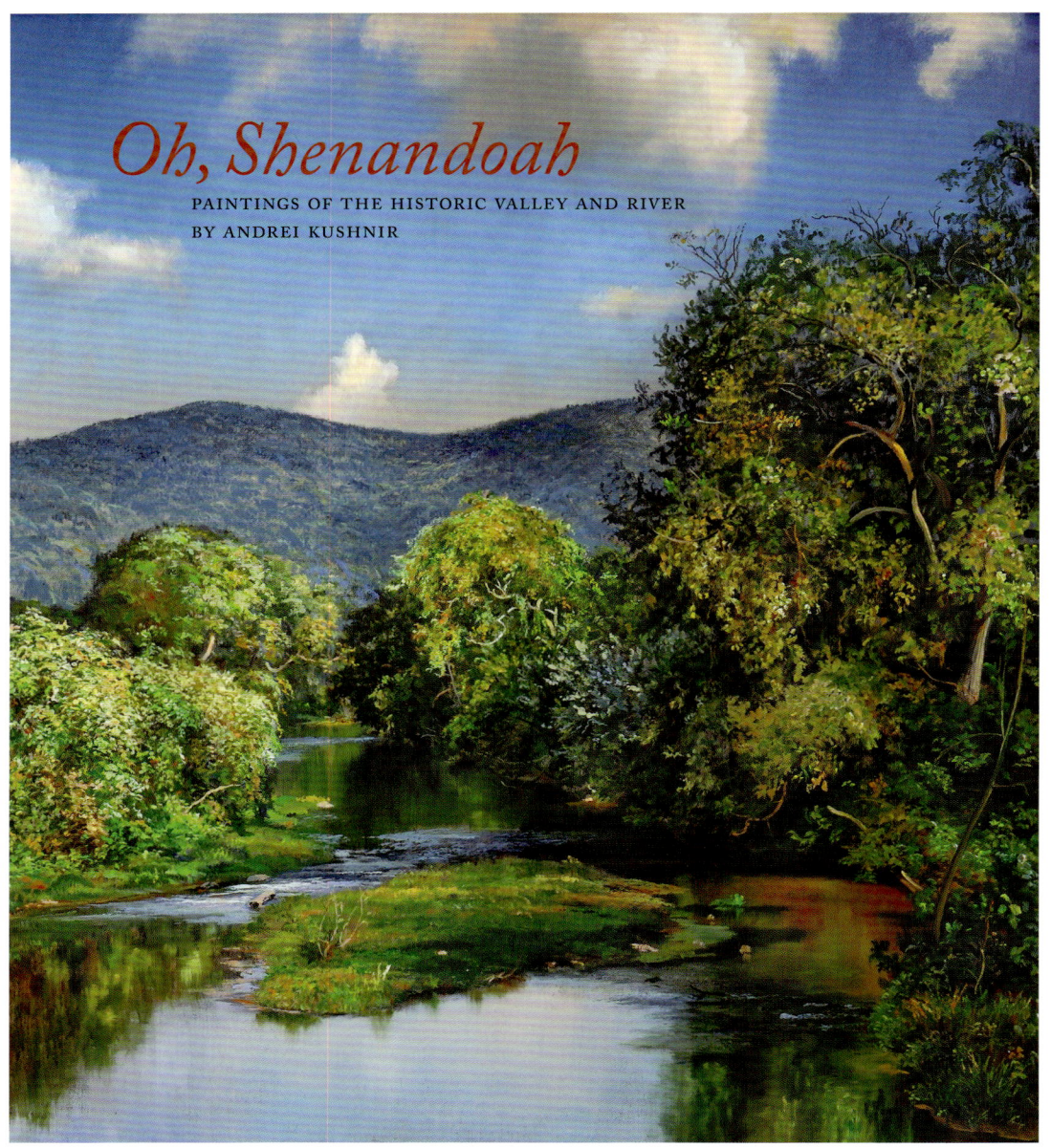

Oh, Shenandoah

PAINTINGS OF THE HISTORIC VALLEY AND RIVER
BY ANDREI KUSHNIR

In Oh, Shenandoah: Paintings of the Historic Valley and River, *Andrei Kushnir's 416-page magnum opus, 264 of his plein-air paintings are featured as well as a foreword by Dana Hand Evans, expansive historical vignettes by Jeffrey C. Everett, essays by Warren R. Hofstra and William M. S. Rasmussun, and an afterword by Edward L. Ayers. It was published in 2016 by George F. Thompson Publishing, in association with the Center for the Study of Place and Museum of the Shenandoah Valley. Thirteen paintings from Oh, Shenandoah reappear in this complementary volume, which features an additional seventy-two new paintings of and along the Valley's three interstates. No painter anywhere or at any time has rendered any region so completely as Andrei Kushnir has done with his 335 plein-air paintings of the beautiful, historic Shenandoah Valley. Both books are distributed by the University of Virginia Press.*

Painting the Shenandoah Valley's Interstates

ANDREI KUSHNIR

Many years ago, while driving west on I-66 from Washington, D.C., to deliver some of my paintings for an exhibit in Front Royal, Virginia, I noticed a very nice scene along the interstate to my right. A tree in a field rising up a hillside, surrounded by woods, almost screamed to be captured on canvas. I glanced quickly and fortunately noticed that the frontage road beside the interstate widened into a gravel access point and there was a gate to a dirt path. I also noted the location and returned later in glorious springtime to render that view (see page 88). Even as I was off the interstate, the cars and trucks noisily sped by, and even though they were yards away, they still seemed way too close for comfort!

A few years later, when working with George F. Thompson on the publication of my first book, *Oh, Shenandoah: Painting of the Historic Valley and River*, he remarked how some of the Valley's most beautiful landscapes and cultural sites are best or only seen from and alongside the Valley's three interstates: I-81, I-66, and I-64. He continued by saying that most drivers only see the Valley's landscapes while driving on the interstates. *Oh, Shenandoah* featured three lengthy "road portfolios" of my plein-air paintings along U.S. 11, U.S. 340, and

VA 42. Even back in 2016, George envisioned a companion book—the one you now hold in your hands—that would present an "interstate portfolio." And, George hoped, this book would also serve as an exemplary model for painters living elsewhere to render their home interstates *en plein air* (that is, outdoors).

The opportunity and challenge of such a task at first seemed overwhelming, but I soon got to work, especially with the arrival of the COVID-19 pandemic. I began by driving to old haunts in the Valley in search of (to my mind) more abstract subject matter—capturing scenes of and along I-81, I-66, and I-64 that might easily be missed by an intrepid (or simply hasty) traveler. Thankfully, I knew of Ed Ruscha's pop art paintings of the American road out West, and they were a preliminary point of reference as I considered my options. Of course it is illegal to stop along the interstate for any reason except for an emergency, so finding safe places to paint the Valley's interstate landscapes was an ever-present challenge, requiring extensive field research and some luck. Furthermore, as an artist who paints *en plein air*, I do not rely on a photograph that I can take back to my studio in order to paint a scene. My paintings are rendered live and reflect the light, weather conditions, and season and mood of the day I paint.

Painting *en plein air* on site is somewhat like any sport. One must have the right equipment and skills. Equipment can be purchased, but the skills are gained only through experience. And although there can be glorious days to be outside and paint, one must be ready to sweat, squint, and swear at the weather. Brain-melting heat and bone-crunching cold are pretty bad, but snow and rain are worse, and wind is worst of all (talk about stress!). A crack of thunder means it is time to pack up—fast. And the insects, especially those tiny flies that one can't even see and that seem to love taking needle-like bites in the most unmentionable areas on one's body. Ticks are also a serious health hazard, and long pants tucked into boots and organic repellents helped me avoid that danger. Regarding encounters, I have had little trouble with curious passersby, especially along the interstates where hitchhikers are illegal.

I must remark about the choking fumes and ear-splitting roar of passing trucks. Even when standing at a relative distance on a little road running alongside a highway, as described above, plein-air painting presents a sort of Hobson's choice: Wear a gas mask and insert earplugs and look like an oddball to locals. So one must painfully bear with the noise in order to be aware of the surroundings, which can turn dangerous and even deadly at any moment with cars and trucks ever present. I always remembered Dorsey Dixon's well-known country song, "Wreck on the Highway"

(1938), made famous by the cover versions of Bill Haley, Roy Acuff, George Jones/Gene Pitney, and Bruce Springsteen, among others.

I read somewhere that the American landscape painter Sanford Robinson Gifford (1823–1880) used to embark on a rigorous exercise program before engaging on a painting project, and that makes sense. A popular perception of an artist as someone with a paintbrush in one hand and a glass of wine in the other is way off the mark. The plein-air painter must simultaneously be able to envision the painting's design and color scheme, be in full control of pallet, brushes, rag, and medium, and have the fortitude to focus on the scene intently enough in all conditions to try to capture the artist's emotional or intellectual reaction to what meets the eye. All this, of course, while ENJOYING the process!

This particular project posed additional challenges, some of which I recount here. To paint on the grounds of a monastery in the Blue Ridge Mountains along I-66, permission could be obtained only by promising not to enter a fenced-in area, where the cloistered nuns walked. When it appeared there might be a slightly better view to paint on the other side of the fence, my asking the mother superior permission to go there was a big no-no, almost resulting in banishment from the grounds. Thus, humility toward and obedience of all rules are essential.

Sometimes, the only way to catch a good view of an interstate is to stand on the property of someone who lives or farms right next to the interstate. And being at

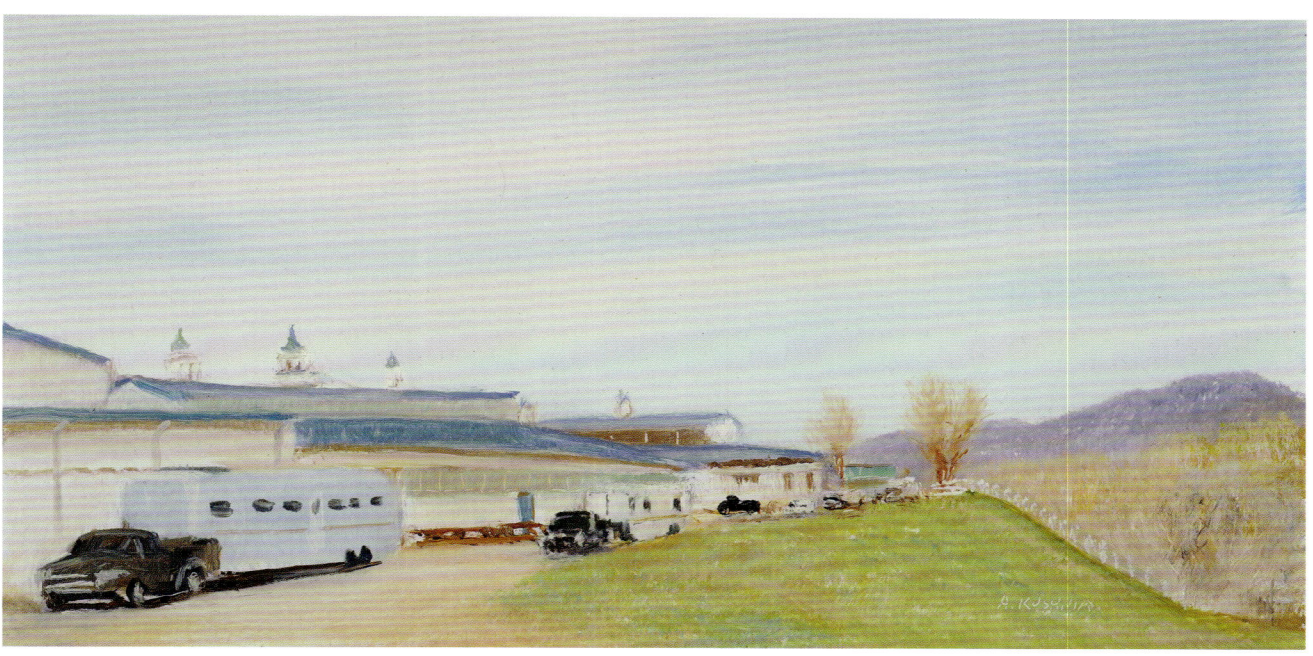

Virginia Horse Center near Exit 55 on I-64, west of Lexington, oil on panel, 6" x 12," March 1, 2020.

the right place at the right time helps. For instance, the owner of the site of ZOORAMA, the old zoo property near New Market (page 58) happened to be cutting grass on the site and gave me permission to paint anywhere I chose on the grounds. But if owners are unavailable, often relatives can be found nearby who are willing to assure the intrepid plein-air painter that it is OK to paint from the desired property to catch just the right view. This, in fact, was the case on I-64 west of Lexington. Still, I was a bit uneasy when the lady who gave me permission asked what day it was.

Sometimes, with a little advance planning, hardships can be avoided. George Thompson, for example, had discovered an "interstate view": an entrance with an allee of maple trees to a beautiful farm (Montvue) with an unencumbered view of Signal Knob in the background, but it was visible only from a tiny side road along I-66 just before it meets I-81. Upon learning of an upcoming blizzard and in need of some winter paintings for this collection, I drove to Front Royal on the Sunday morning right before a serious snowstorm hit the region. Arriving at the site, I was relatively comfortable, as I made these paintings (pages 94–96) from the passenger side inside my van. The trip home wasn't too bad, either, as I drove toward DC on I-66 East (slowly) behind three snow-plow trucks and arrived without much difficulty from the freezing snow and sleet.

A very good view (and commensurately good painting) can be had from uninhabited properties, such as deserted motels or abandoned gas stations. Two of my favorite paintings of this collection of interstate scenes resulted from such an instance. At the top of Afton Mountain, along I-64 east of Waynesboro where the Skyline Drive and Blue Ridge Parkway meet, are the remains of a gigantic defunct Holiday Inn with spectacular views (page 99). A guard obligingly allowed me to set up and catch the scene after noting my easel, paint box, and canvas. On another excursion, an iconic harvesting scene took place before my very easel along I-81 at Exit 180—as I stood on an outcropping of gas-station rubble overlooking the landscape (page 81). My plein-air experience dictated to paint the harvester and field first, before the rest of the landscape and sky.

This was a good decision, as the field was cleared and tractor long gone by the time I finished the rest of the painting! There were many more "adventures" on my journey to paint scenes along the three interstates of the Shenandoah Valley, but I will let the paintings tell their own stories.

One last comment regarding the three portfolios that follow. The paintings of and alongside I-81 are presented sequentially on I-81 South (technically from northeast to southwest), after crossing the Potomac River and entering the panhandle of West Virginia (some 183 miles/311 kilometers) to Buchanan, Virginia, at Exit 168; the paintings of and alongside I-66 and I-64 are both presented east to west.* Traditionally, from the early days during the mid-1700s when frontier settlement and commerce began in the Shenandoah Valley, most people discovered and entered the Valley on its general north-to-south and east-to-west roads. Regardless, the captions beneath each painting present exact locations that any actual driver or armchair reader can follow, no matter from which direction.

* I-64 West from Charlottesville and Richmond intersects with I-81 in Staunton (pages 68¬72) and joins I-81 South until reaching Lexington (pages 79¬80), where I-64 West continues toward West Virginia and Kentucky.

PORTFOLIO 1: Interstate 81

Note to the traveler:
All paintings in *Portfolio I* follow I-81 South, from page 23 to page 84. For those who are driving on I-81 North, your visual journey begins on page 84 and ends on page 23. I-66 intersects I-81 at pages 30–31, and I-64 intersects with and joins I-81, respectively, at Staunton (pages 68–72) and Lexington (pages 79–80).

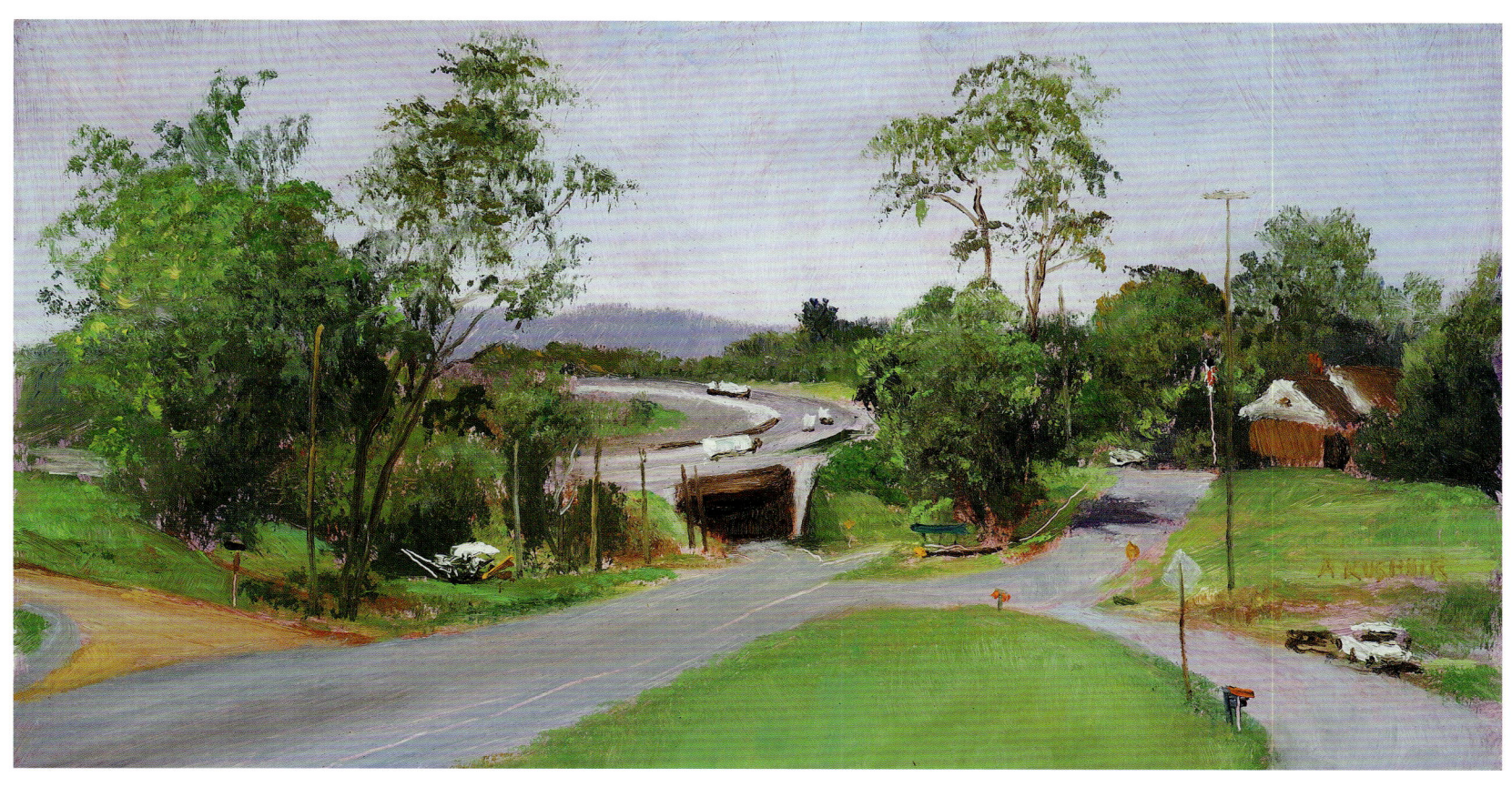

Overpass, I–81, and U.S. 11 near Falling Waters, West Virginia I, looking south, oil on panel, 6" x 12," September 15, 2020.

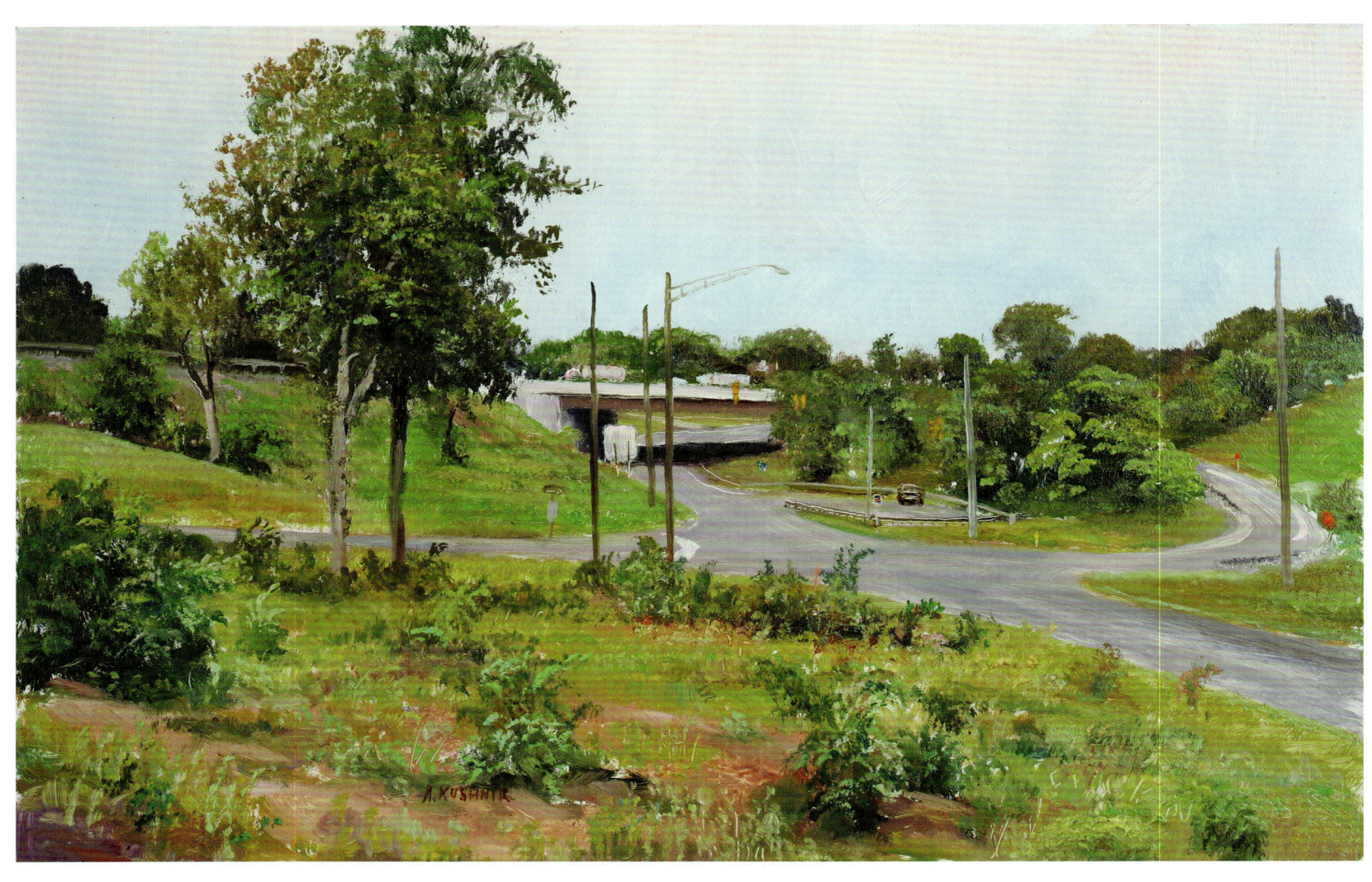

Overpass, I-81, and U.S. 11 near Falling Waters, West Virginia II, oil on panel, 10" x 16," September 15, 2020.

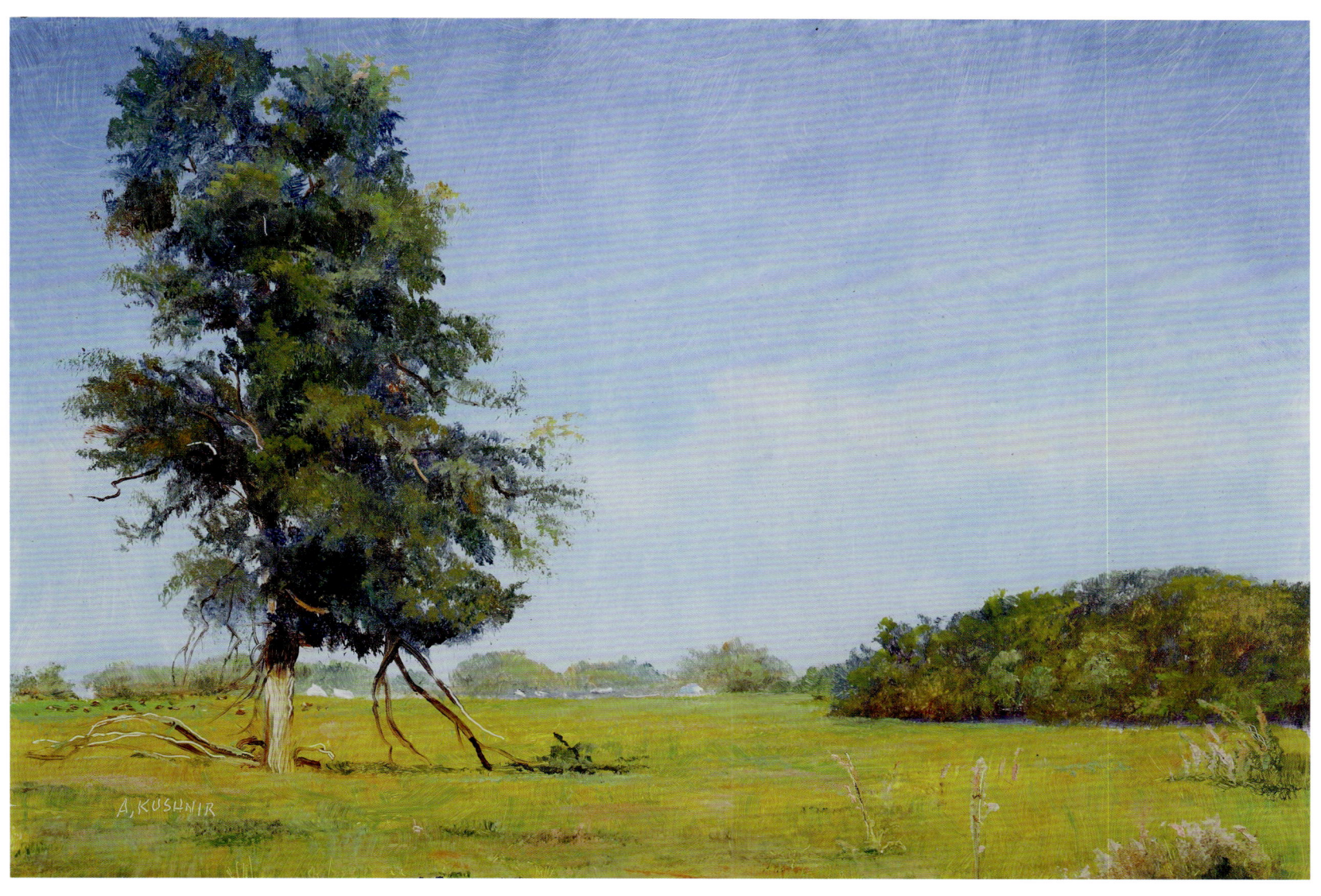

Landscape along I–81 near Exit 5, Inwood, West Virginia, oil on panel, 8" x 12," September 8, 2020.

Note: Hereafter, all locations on I-81 South are in Virginia.

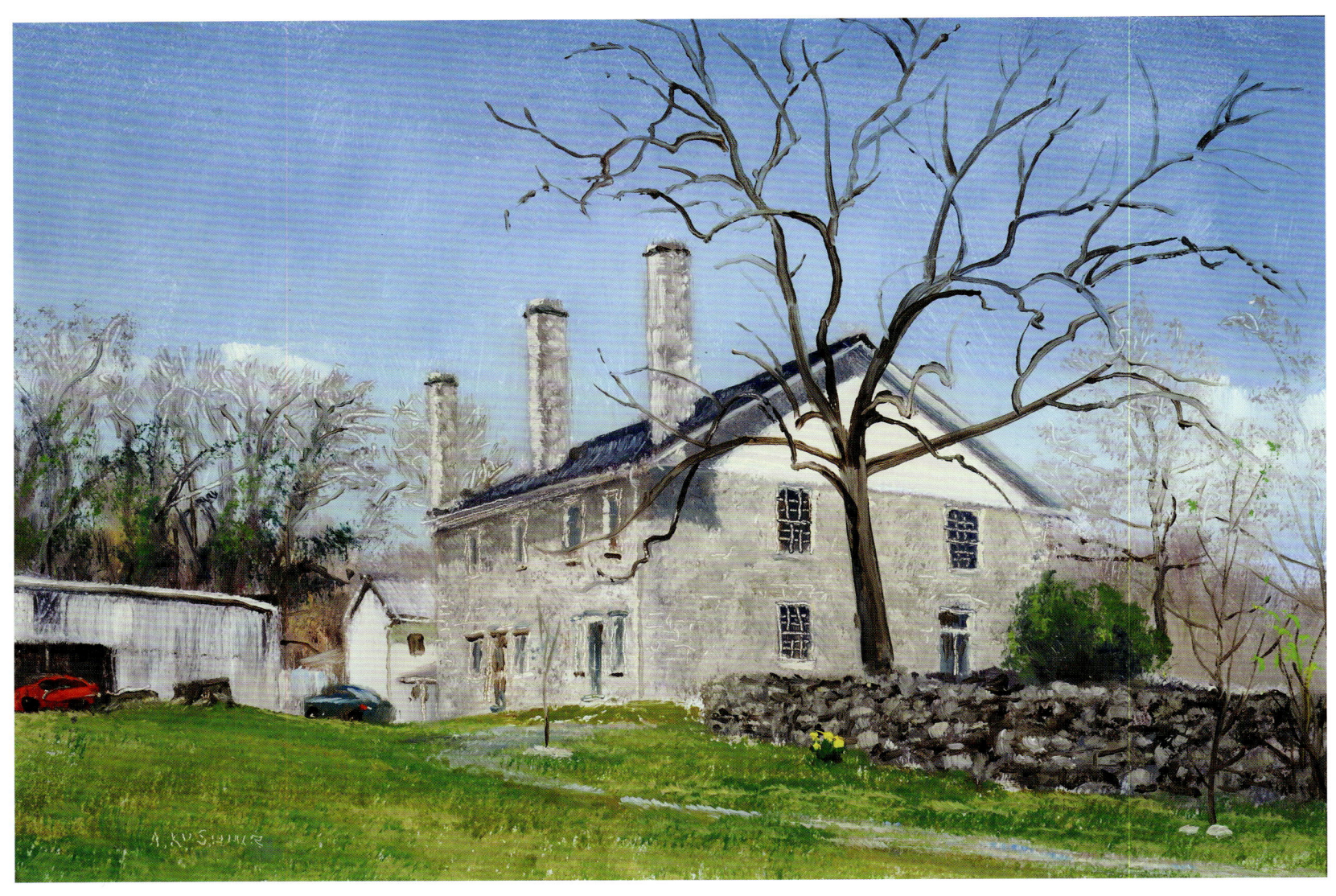

Hopewell Friends Meeting (built in 1759–1761 and expanded in 1788–1794) just west of Exit 321 on I-81,
Clear Brook, Virginia, oil on panel, 8" x 12," April 3, 2011.

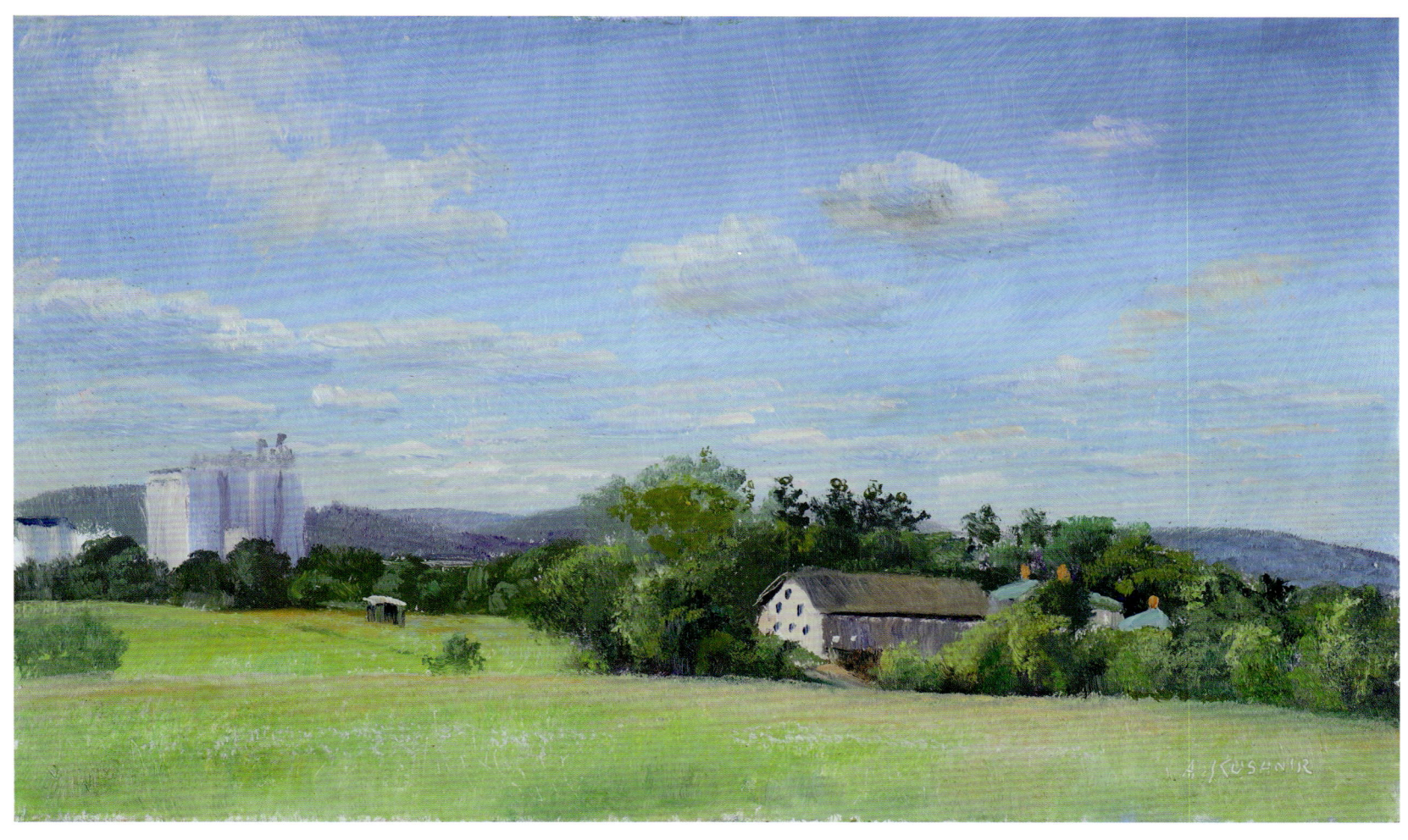

Hackwood House, Barns, and Environs, south of Exit 317 on I-81, near Stephenson, oil on panel, 7" x 12," June 14, 2019.

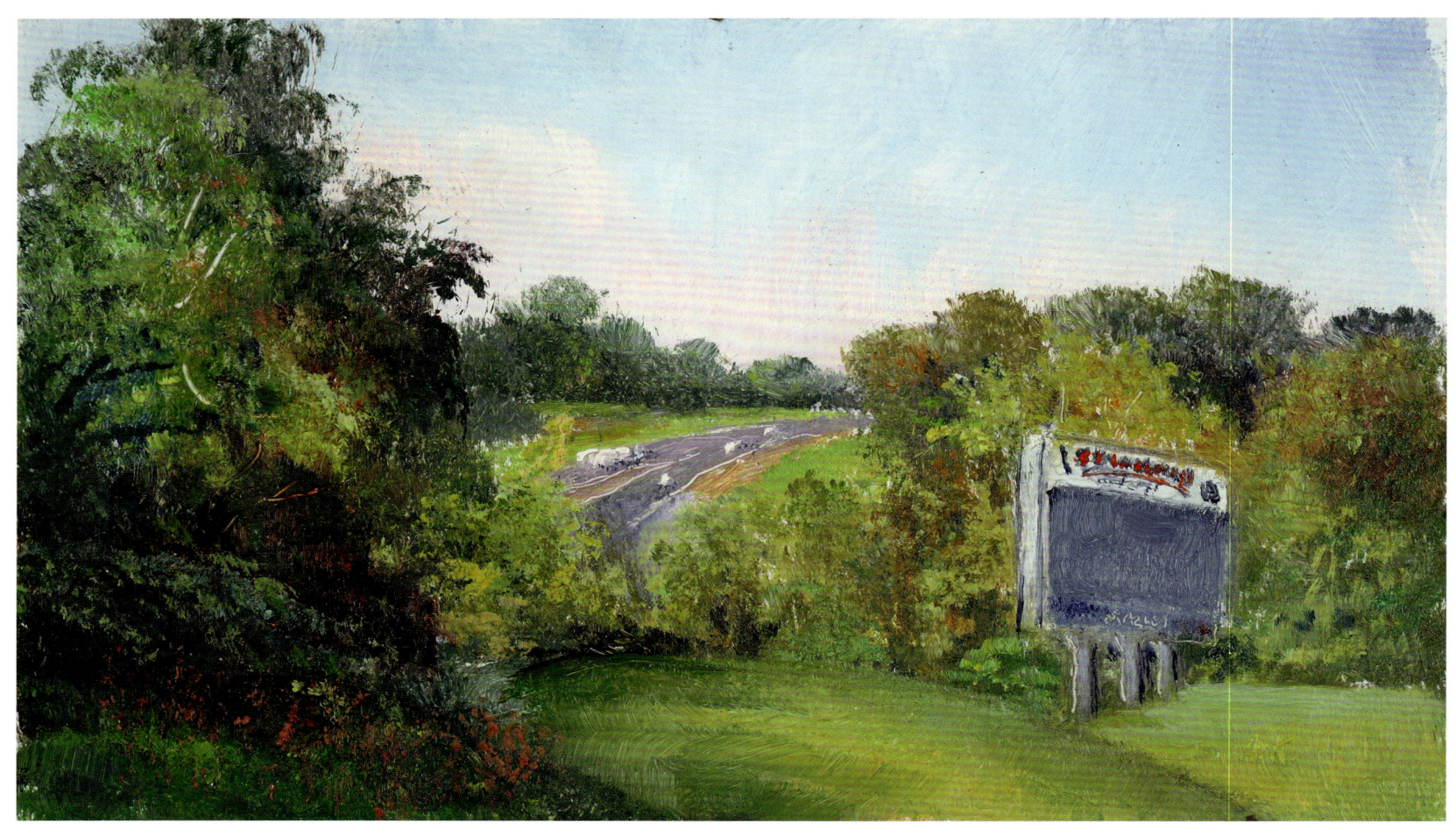

The Events and Athletic Center at Shenandoah University I, Exit 313 on I-81, Winchester, looking north, oil on panel, 4" x 7," September 7, 2020.

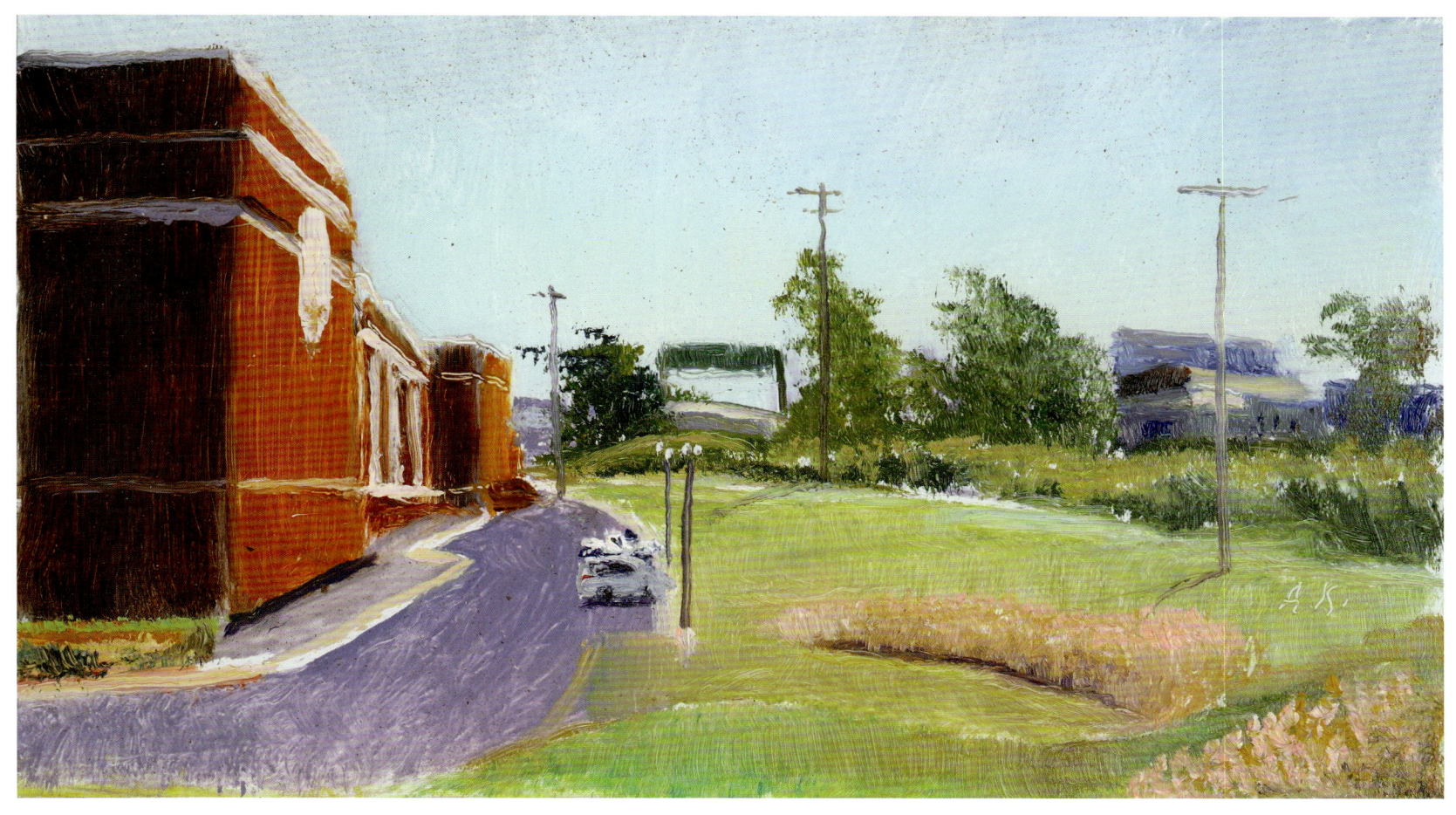

The Events and Athletic Center at Shenandoah University II, Exit 313 on I-81, Winchester, looking south, oil on panel, 4" x 7," September 7, 2020.

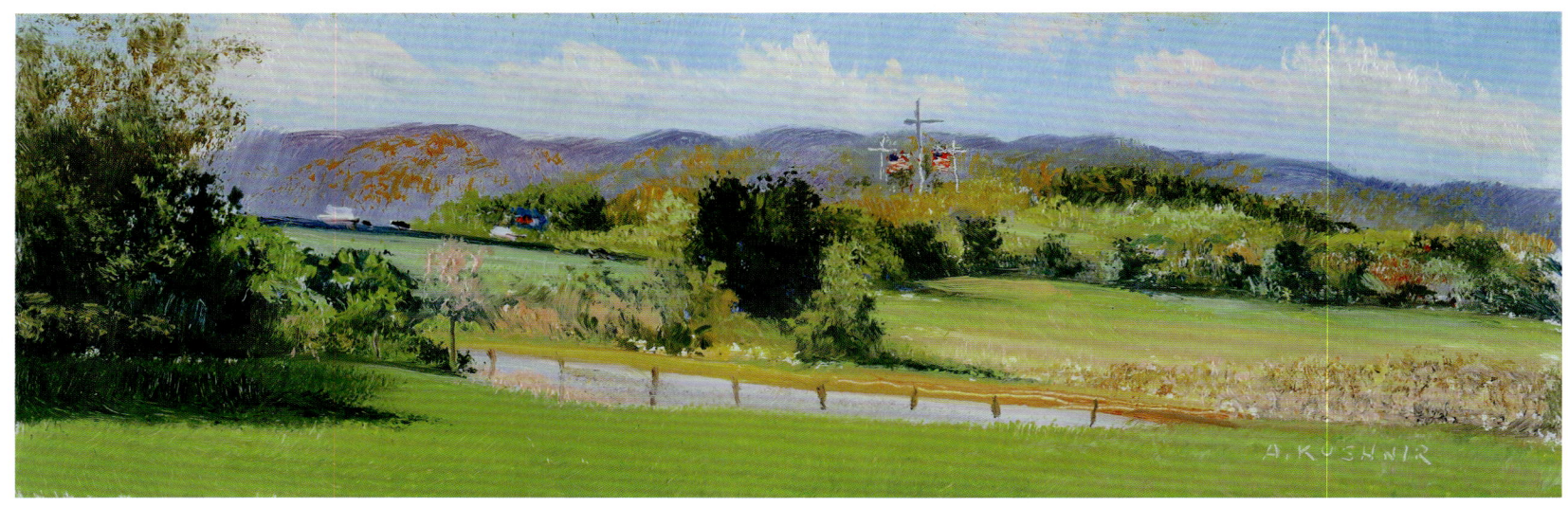

Three Crosses, looking west at I-81 from VA 630 near Exit 296, Strasburg, oil on panel, 3" x 9," October 27, 2019.

Note: I-81 and I-66 (from/toward Dulles International Airport and Washington, D.C.) intersect just north of here.

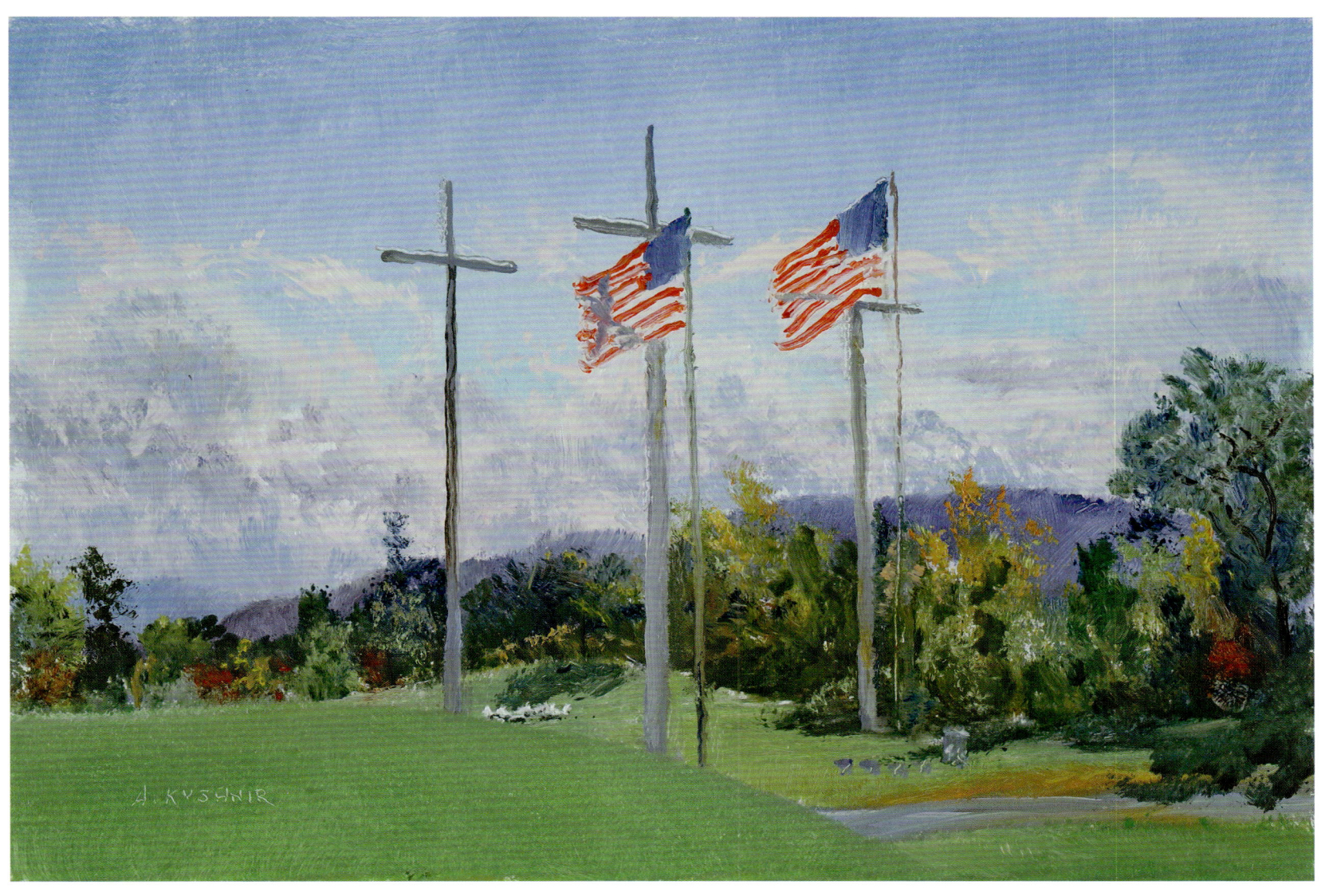

Church and State at Restoration Fellowship Church, MM 296.8 on I-81, Strasburg, oil on panel, 6" x 9," October 27, 2019.

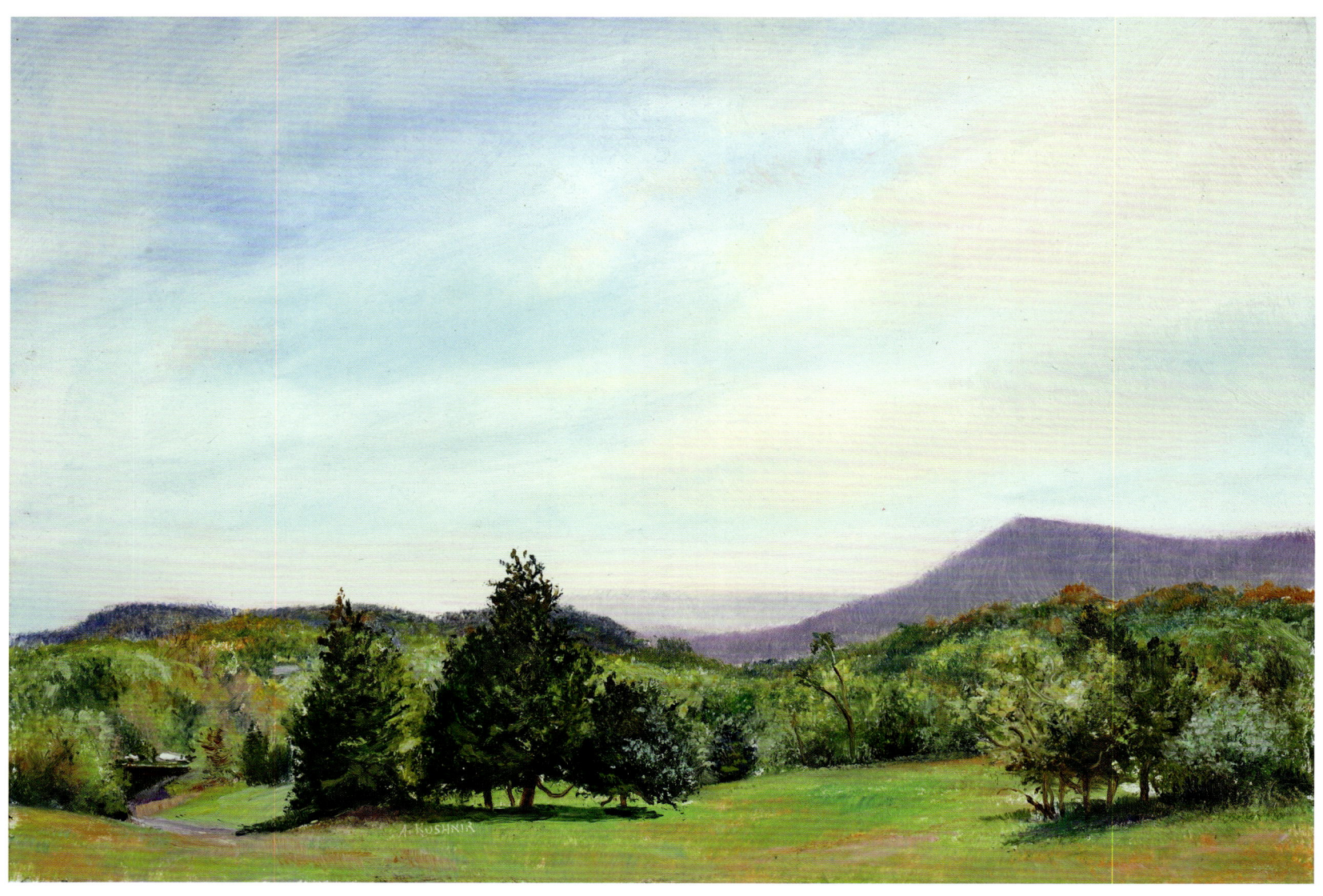

View from Fishers Hill Battlefield, near MM 293.3 on I-81, south of Strasburg, highlighting Signal Knob, the northernmost peak of Massanutten Mountain, a synclinal ridge that bisects the Shenandoah Valley from Front Royal to Harrisonburg, oil on panel, 8" x 12," October 20, 2020.

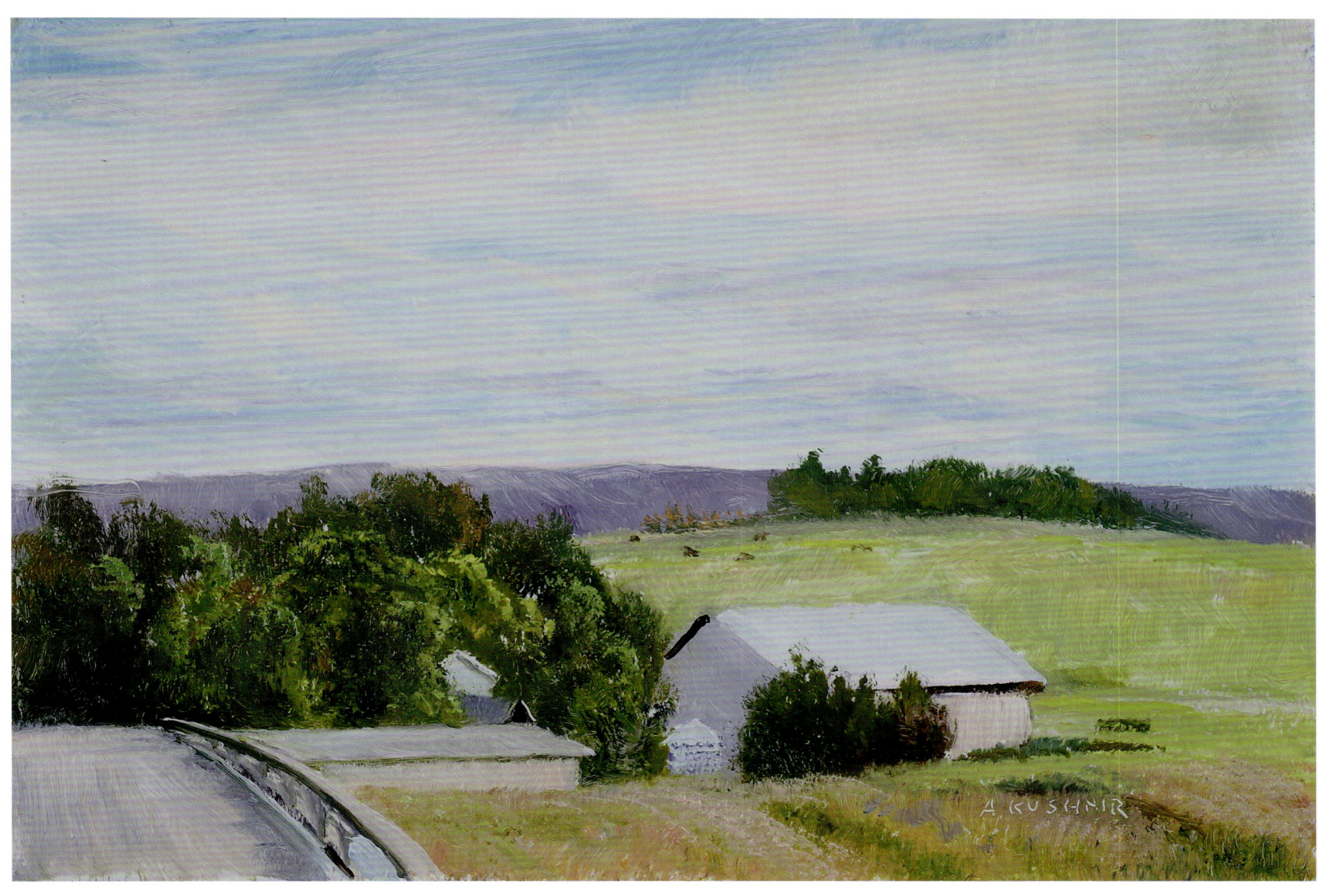

Classic Farmstead, from the VA 653 bridge at I-81, south of Toms Brook, oil on panel, 6" x 9," October 21, 2019.

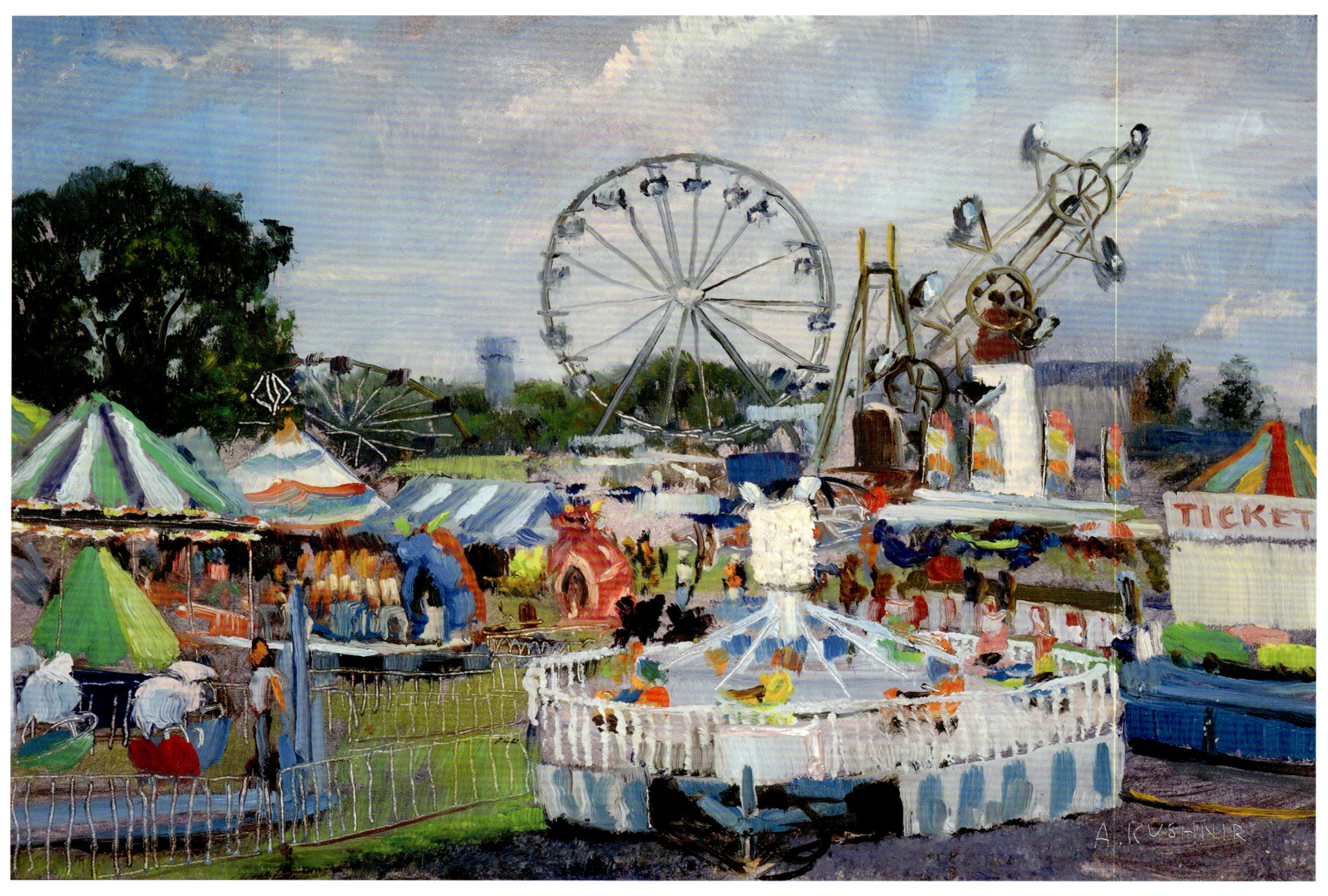

Shenandoah County Fair (Carnival Rides), Exit 283 on I-81, Woodstock, oil on canvas, 8" x 12," September 1, 2011.

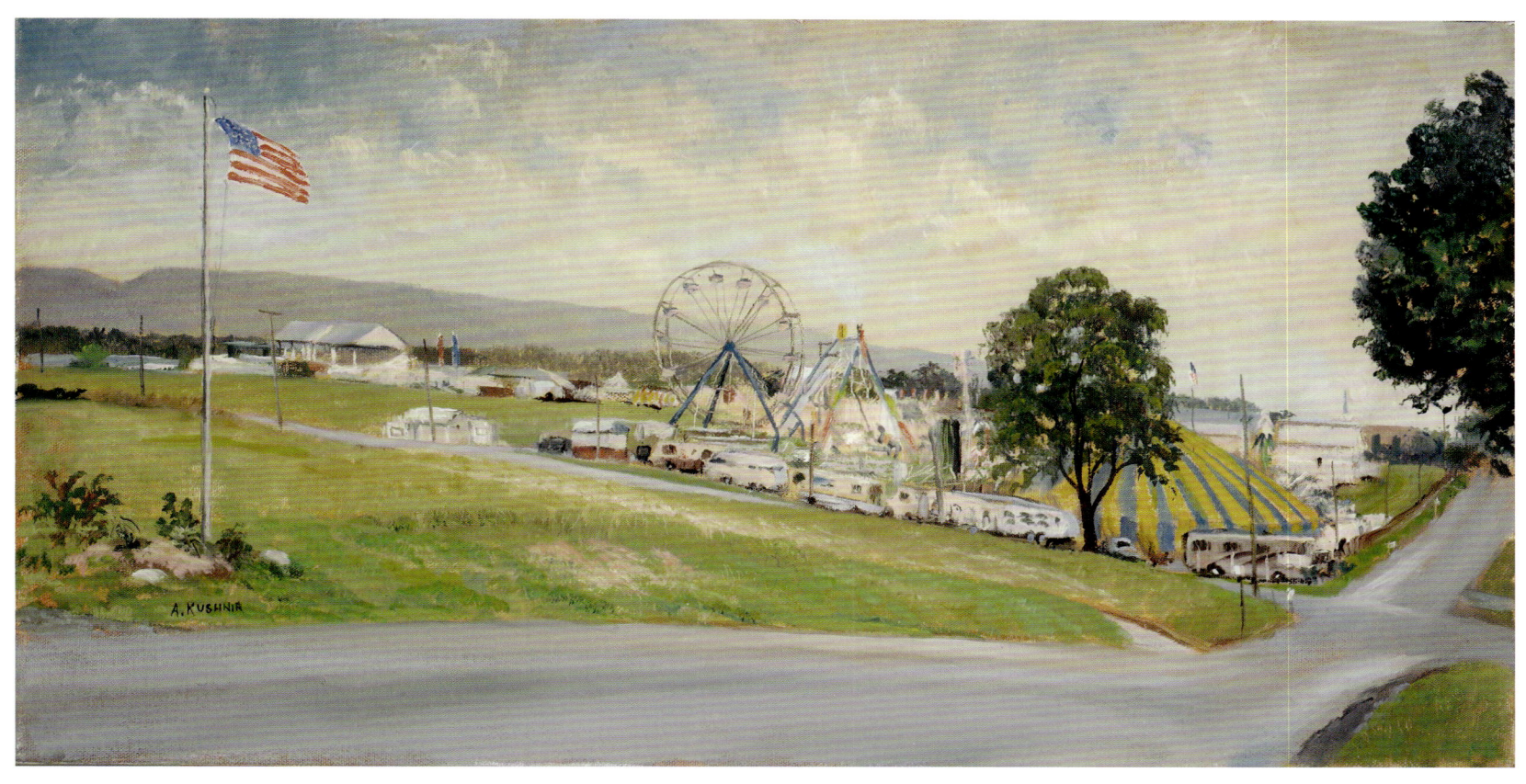

Shenandoah County Fair, Woodstock, Exit 283 on I-81, oil on canvas, 12" x 24," September 1, 2011.

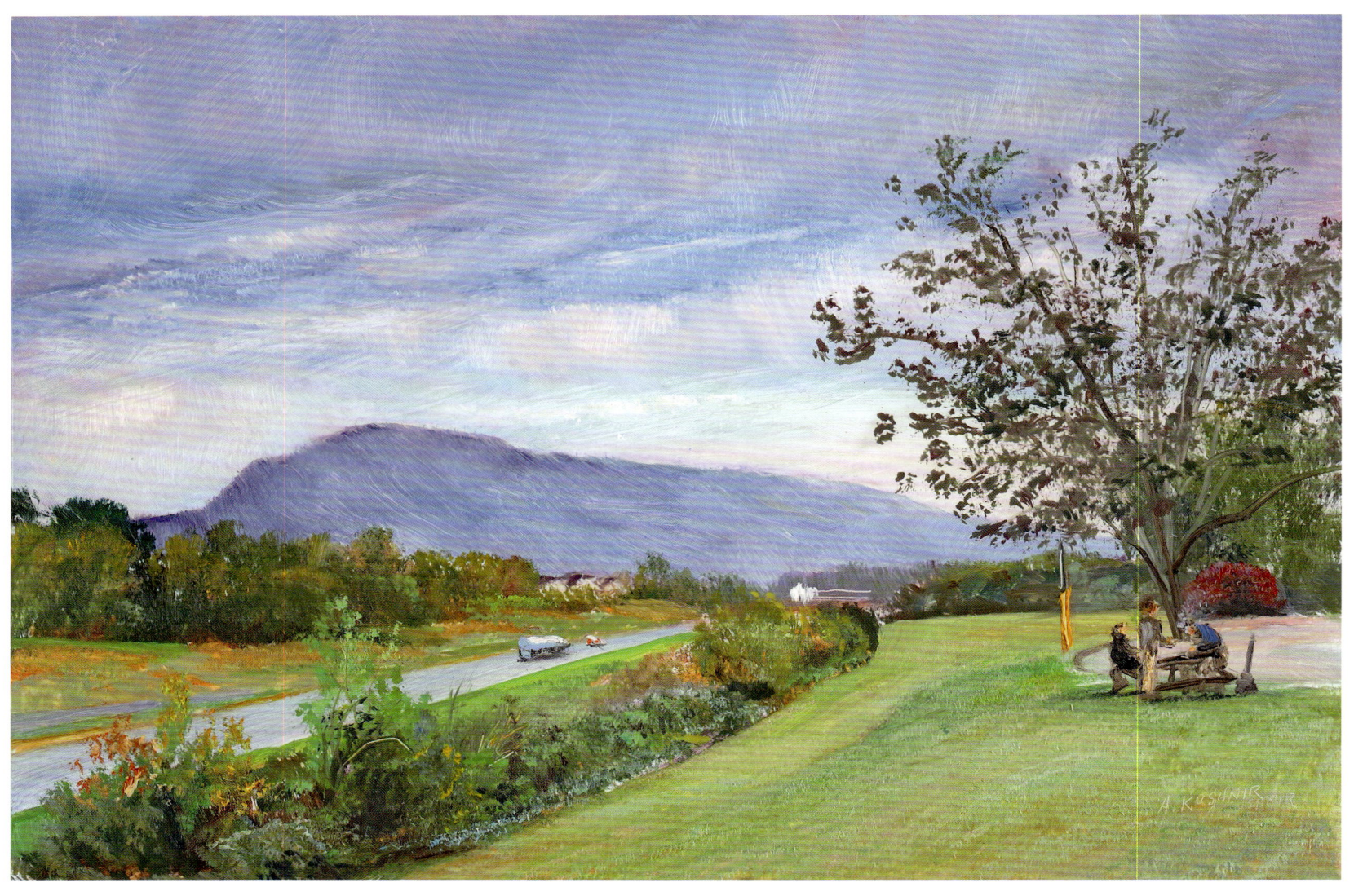

Break Time, view south of Massanutten Mountain, from the Walmart at Exit 283 on I-81, Woodstock, oil on panel, 8" x 12," November 1, 2017.

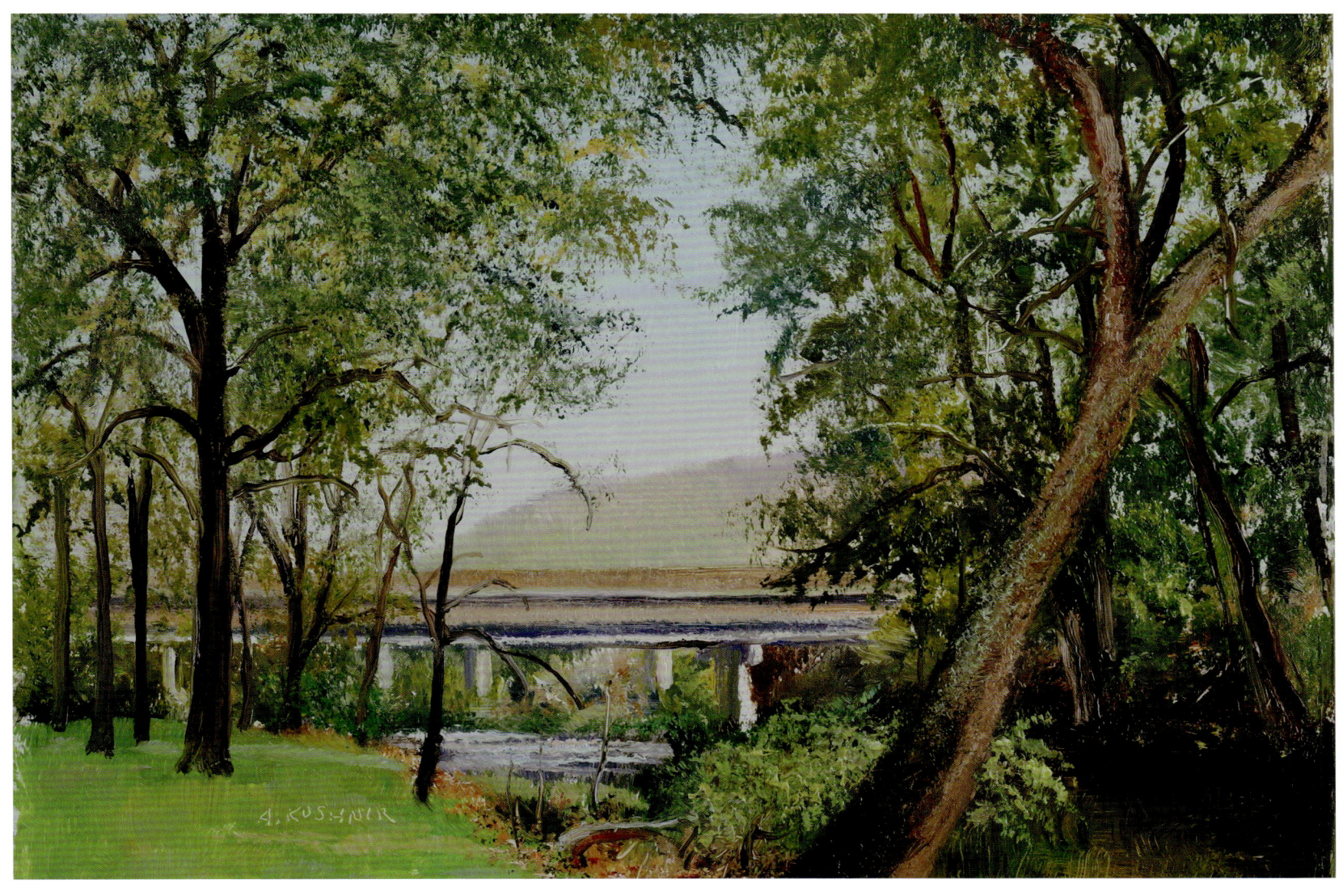

At Stoney Creek, looking east at I-81 and Massanutten Mountain at Exit 279, Edinburg, oil on panel, 6" x 9," October 21, 2019.

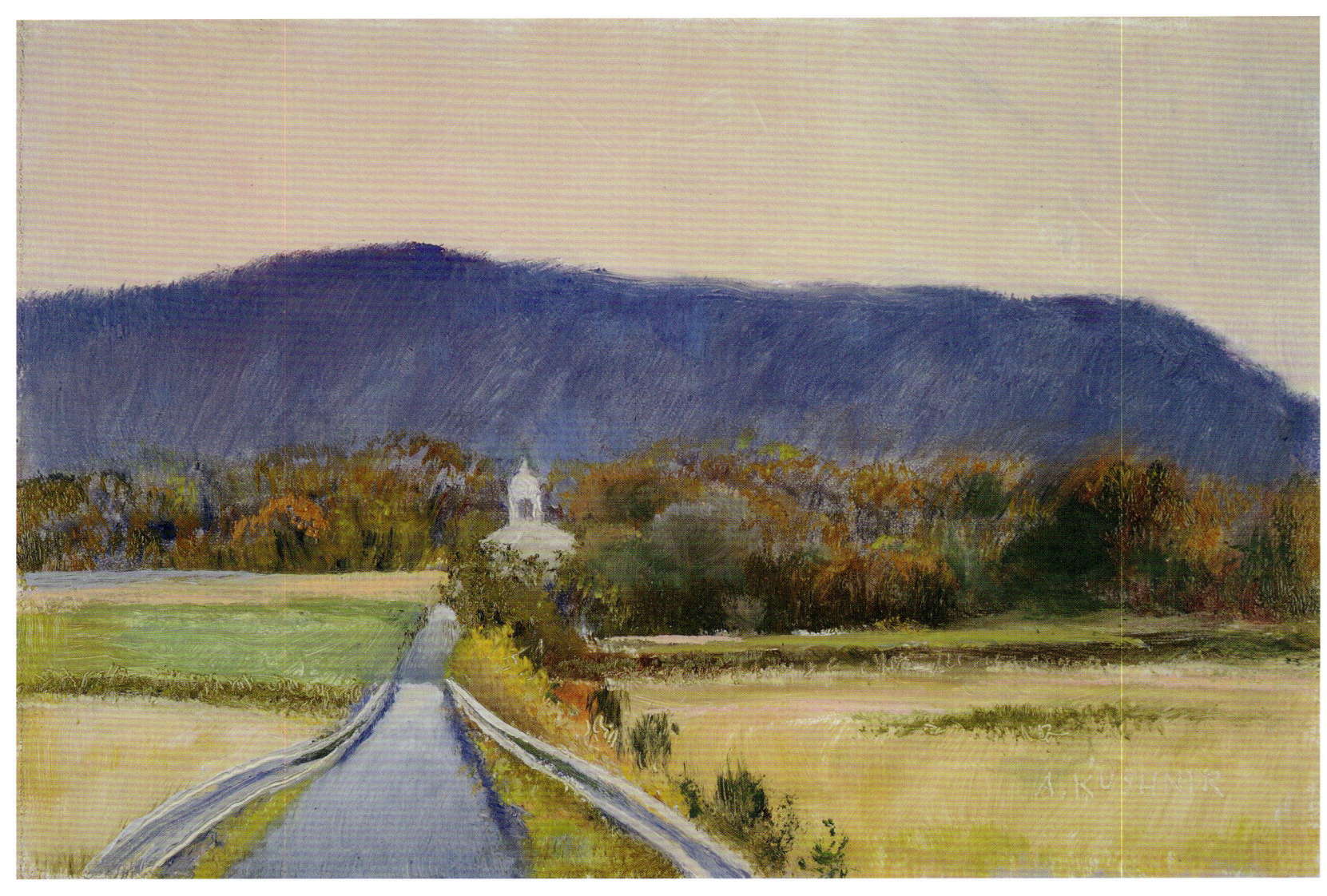

Church at Mount Jackson, view east from I-81 toward Massanutten Mountain and Hawkingstown United Methodist Church on VA 796, MM 274.5, north of Mount Jackson, oil on panel, 6" x 9," January 16, 2020.

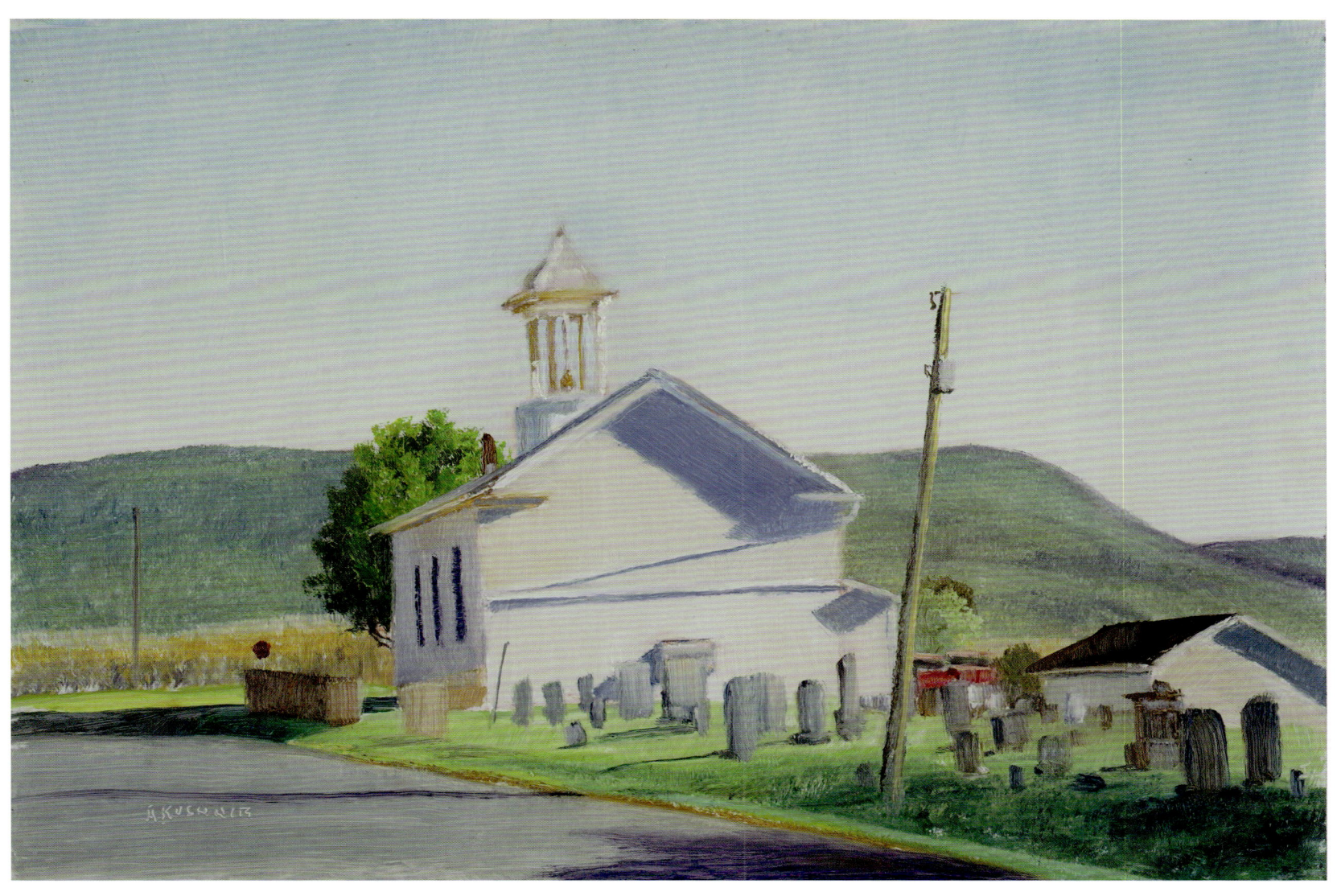

Hawkingstown United Methodist Church and Cemetery at U.S. 11 and VA 796, oil on panel, 8" x 12," October 22, 2019.

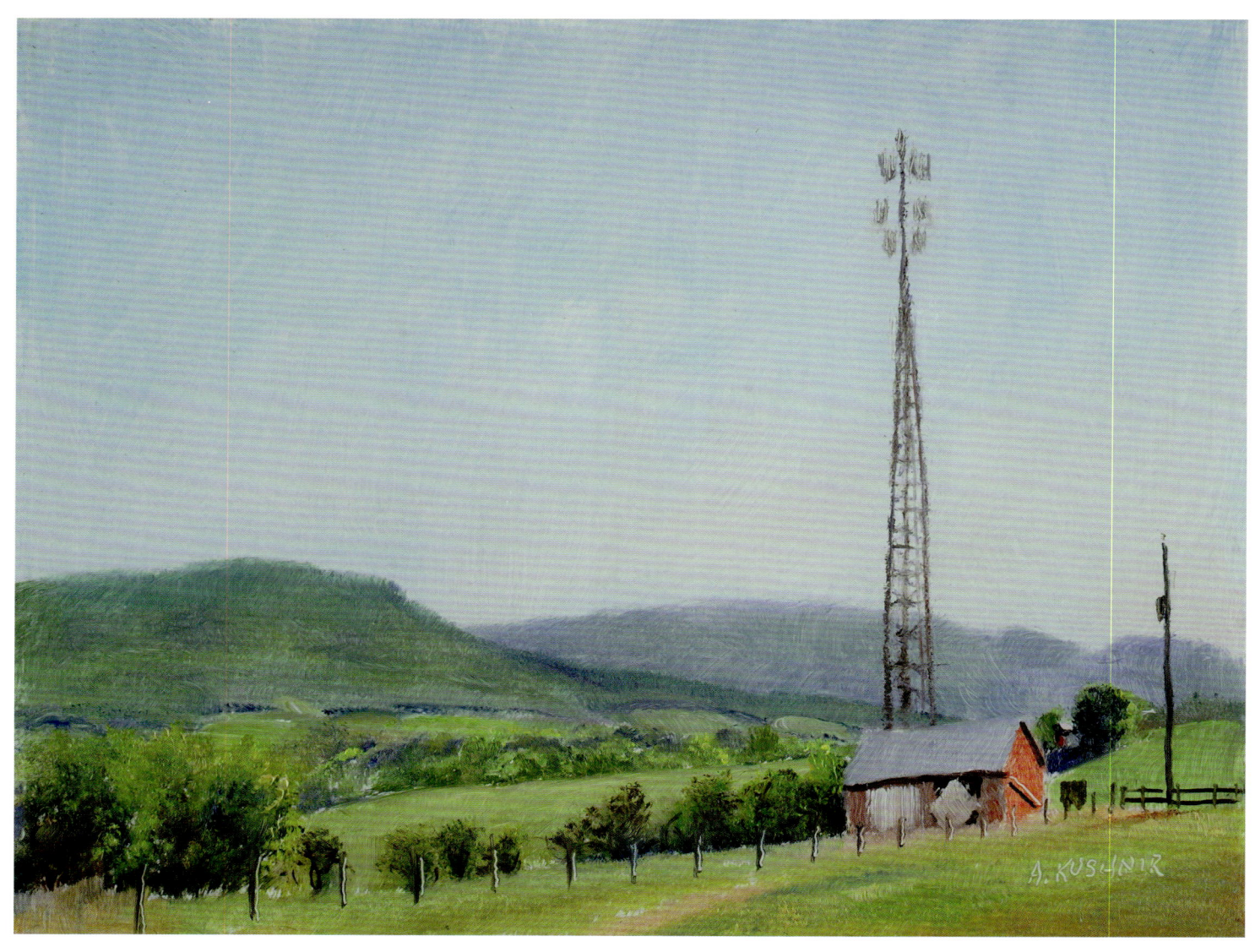

Cellphone Tower, view of the Knob at Moreland Gap and Massanutten Mountain at MM 274.2 on I-81 north of Mount Jackson, oil on panel, 6" x 8," October 22, 2019.

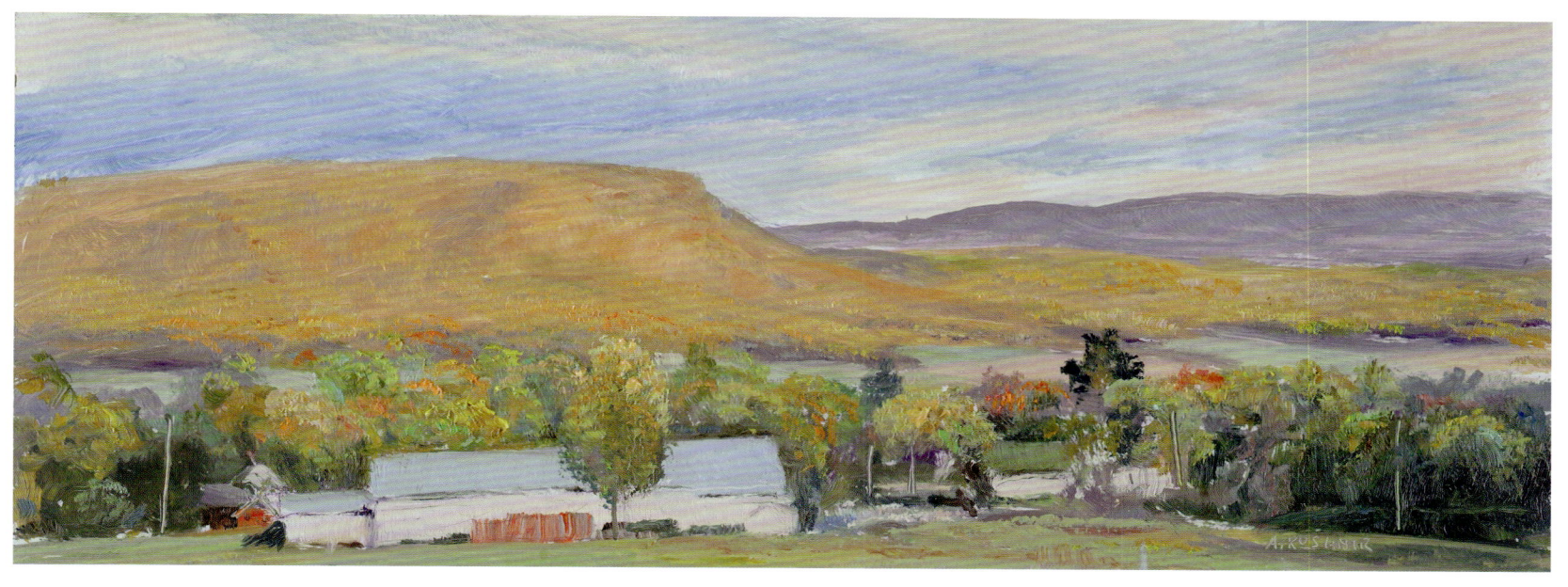

At Mt. Jackson, view east the Knob at Moreland Gap and Massanutten Mountain from I-81 near MM 273.2, 4½" x 12," oil on panel, November 1, 2017.

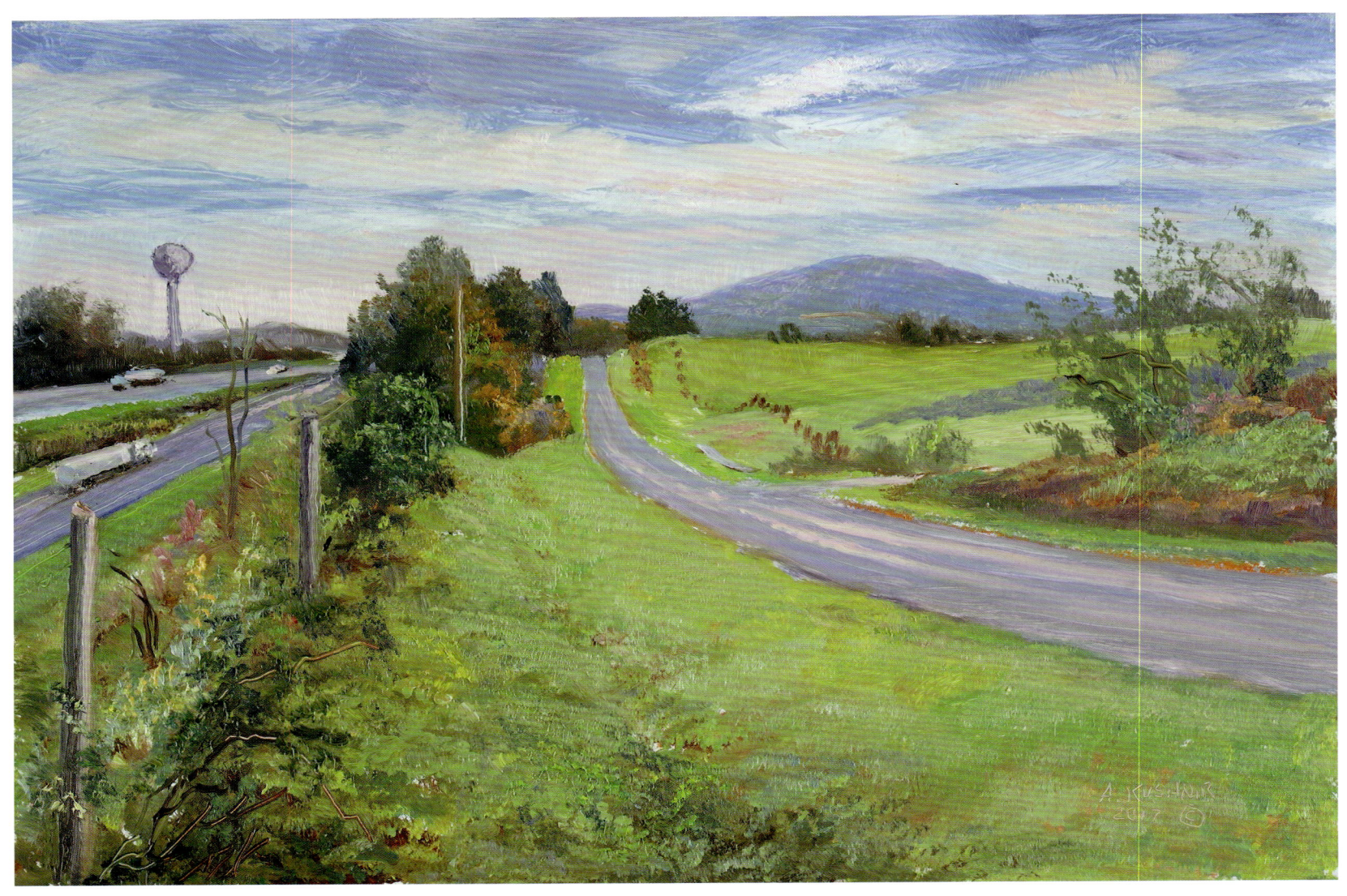

Country Roads, view south of I-81 at Mount Jackson near Exit 273, oil on panel, 8" x 12," November 1, 2017.

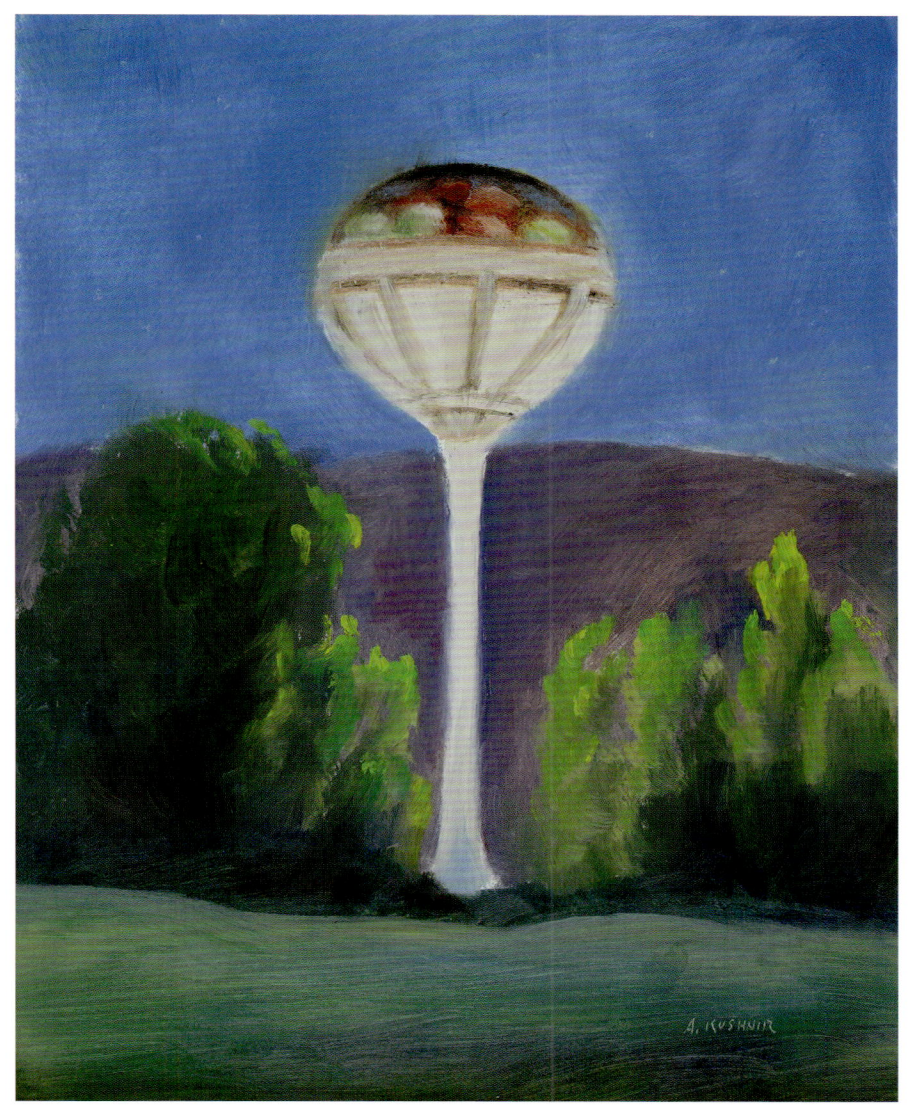

Night View, Mount Jackson's Apple Basket Water Tower, MM 272.8 on I-81,
oil on panel, 10" x 8," November 1, 2017.

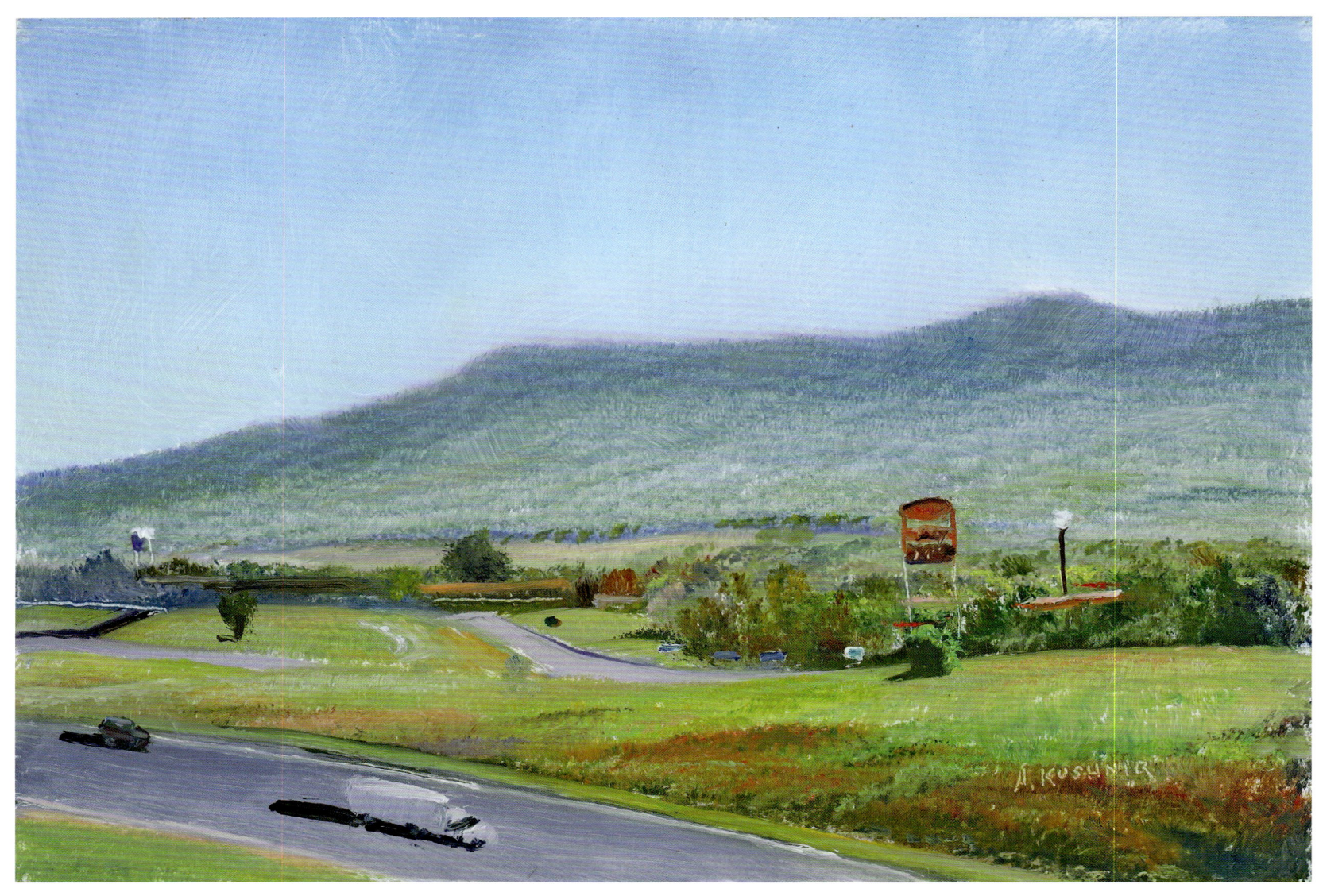

I-81 and Mount Jackson at Exit 273, looking northeast toward Massanutten Mountain, 6" x 9," oil on panel, October 11, 2019.

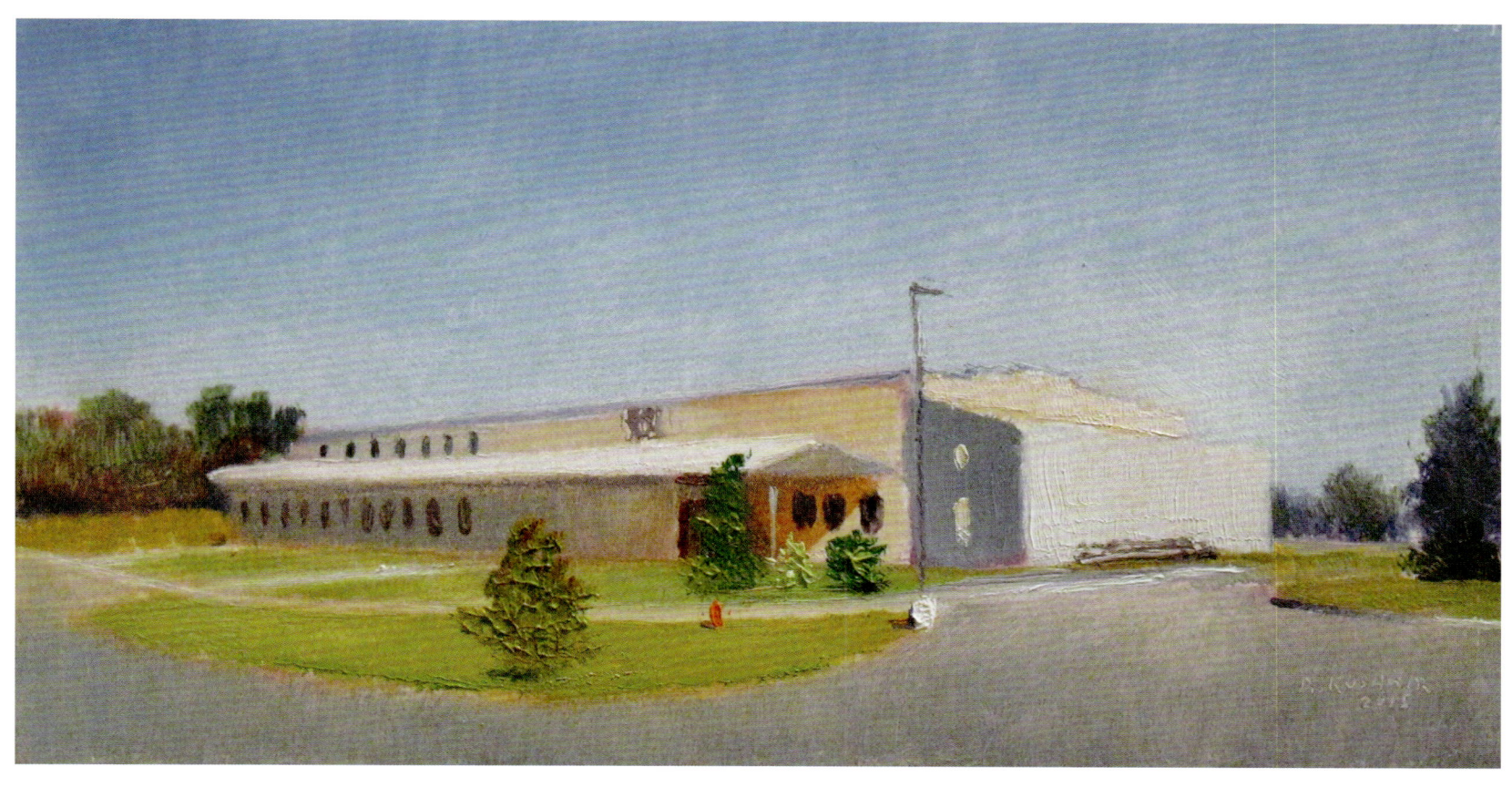

Route 11 Potato Chip Factory, MM 269 on I-81, south of Mount Jackson, 4" x 8," oil on panel, September 7, 2015.

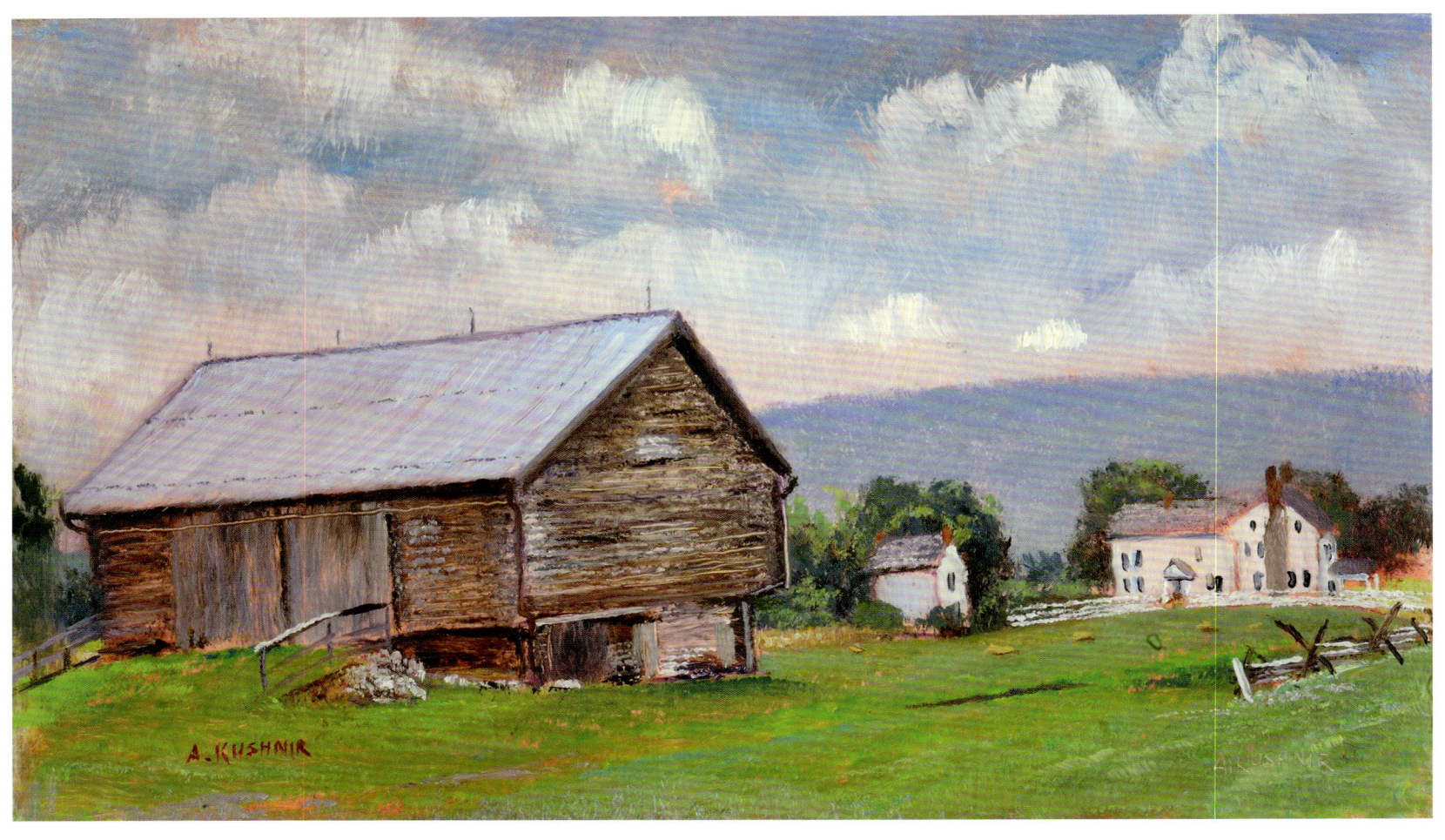

Pennsylvania Bank Barn, Bushong Farm, New Market Battlefield State Historical Park, Exit 264 on I-81, oil on panel, 7"x 12," July 9, 2015.

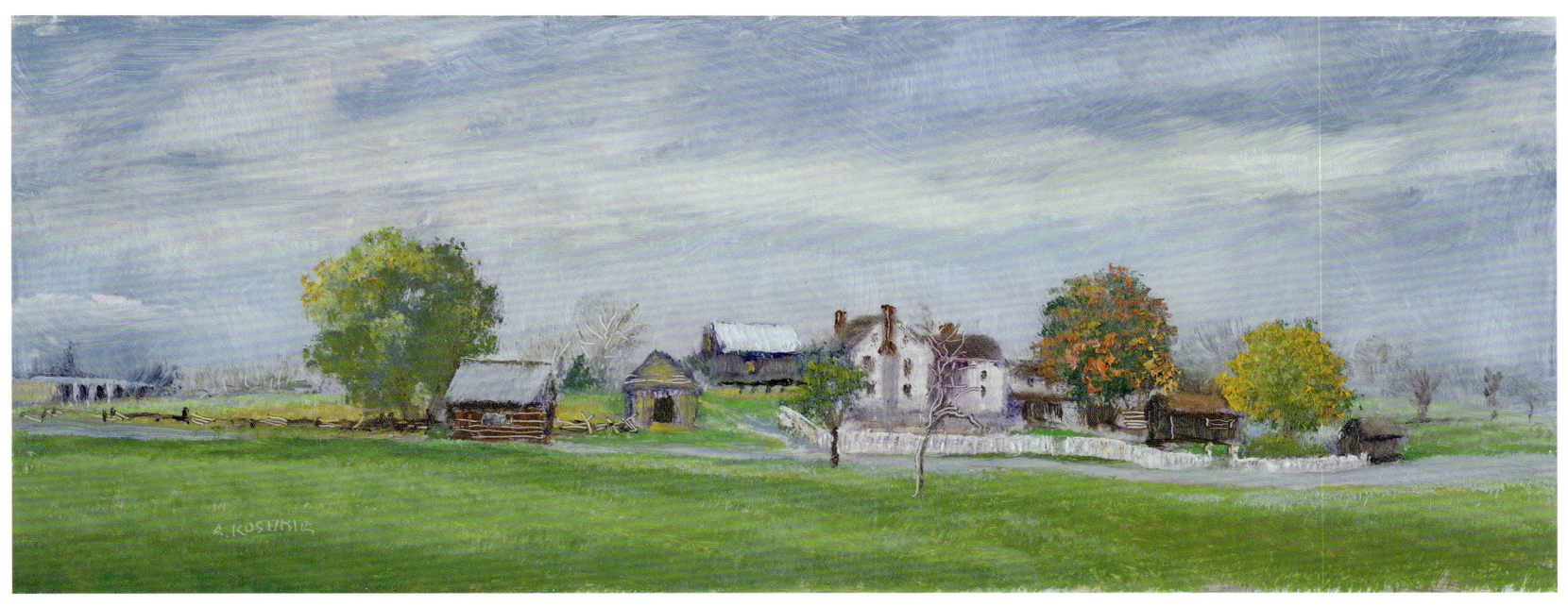

The Historic Bushong Farm (established in 1818) on the New Market Battlefield State Historical Park, view from I-81, MM 266, oil on panel, 4½" x 12," November 1, 2017.

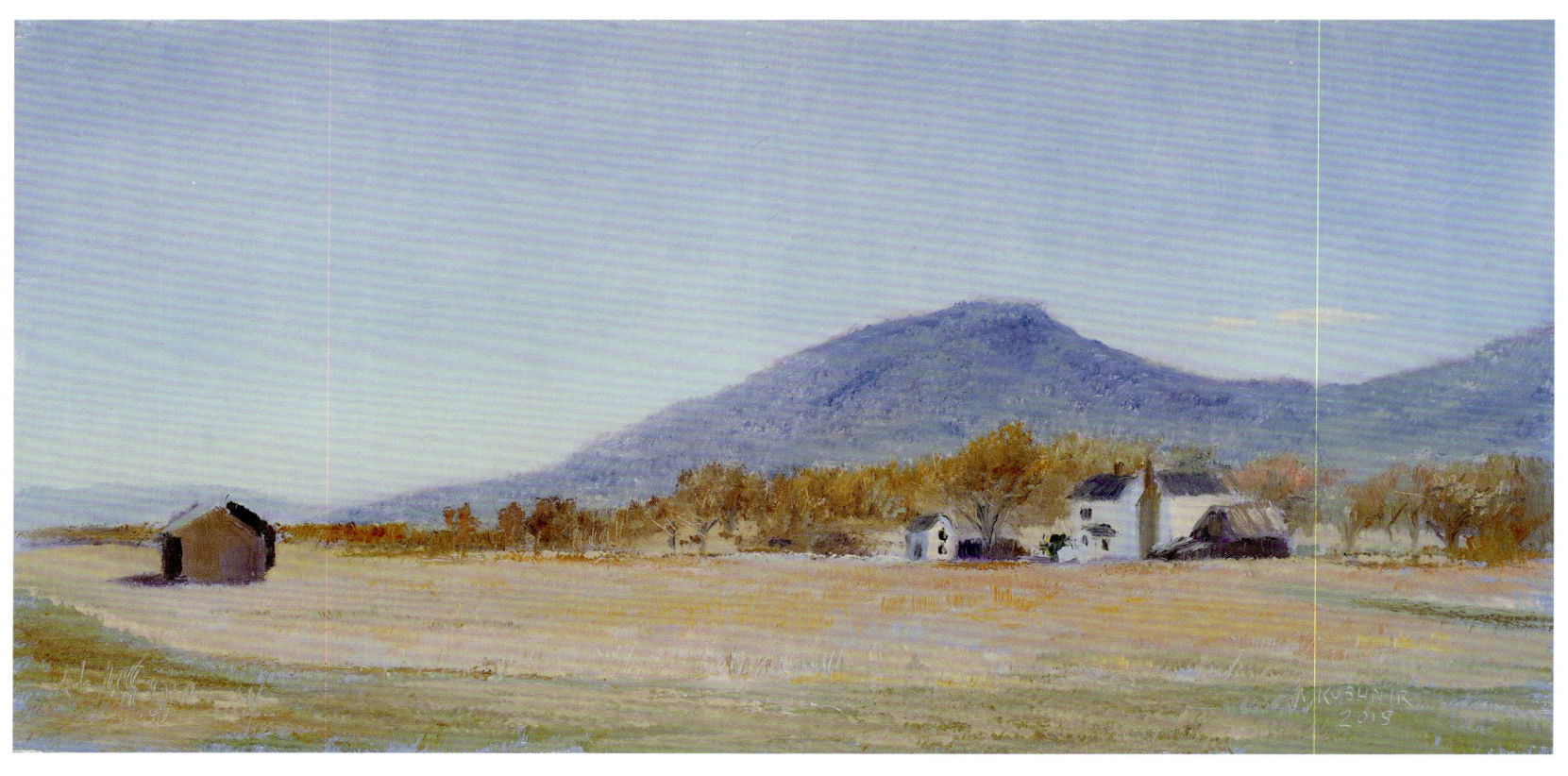

New Market Battlefield State Historical Park, view of the Knob at Moreland Gap, Exit 266 on I-81, New Market, 6" x 12½," oil on panel, March 23, 2015.

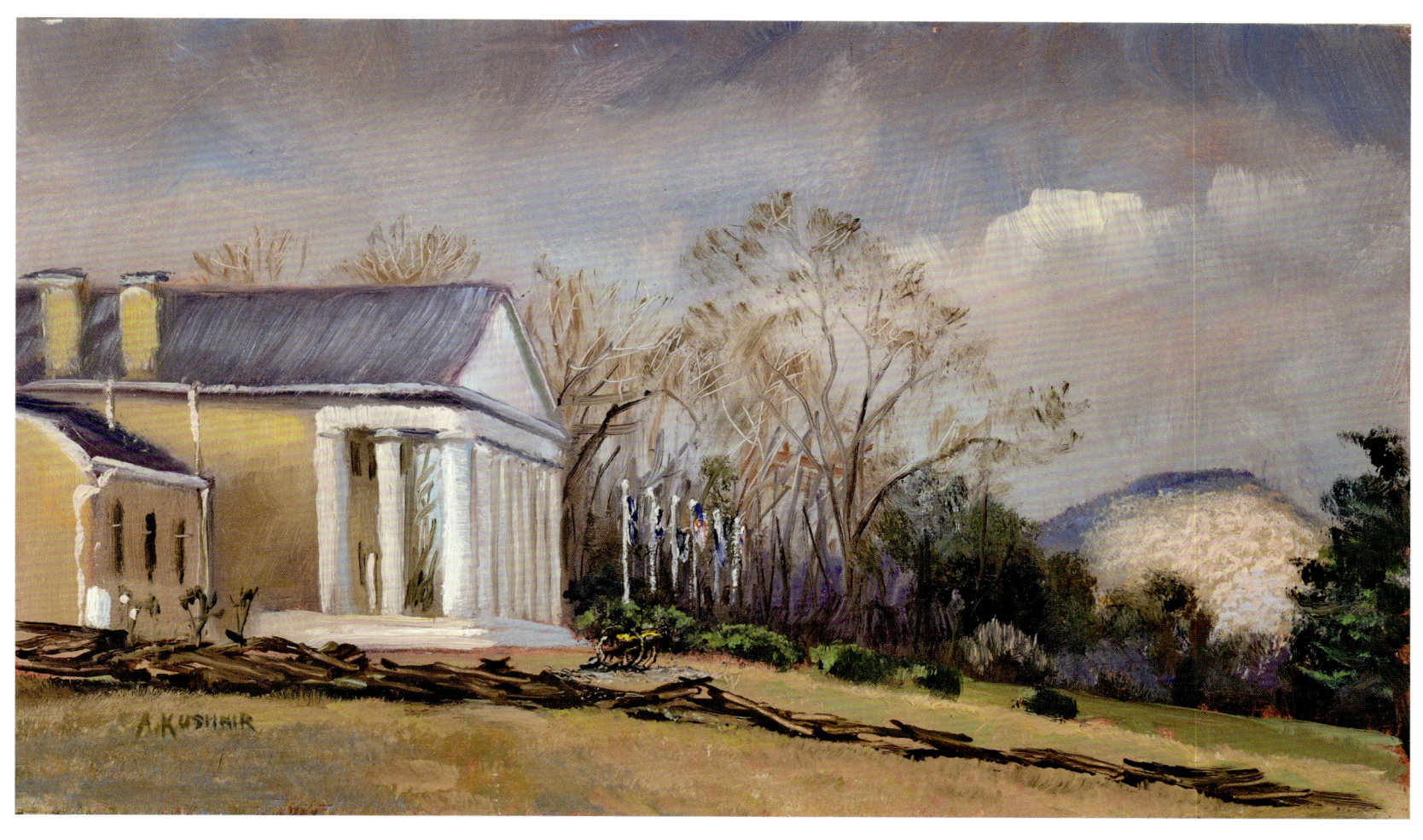

New Market Battlefield Military Museum, Exit 266 on I-81, New Market, 6" x 10½," oil on panel, March 22, 2015.

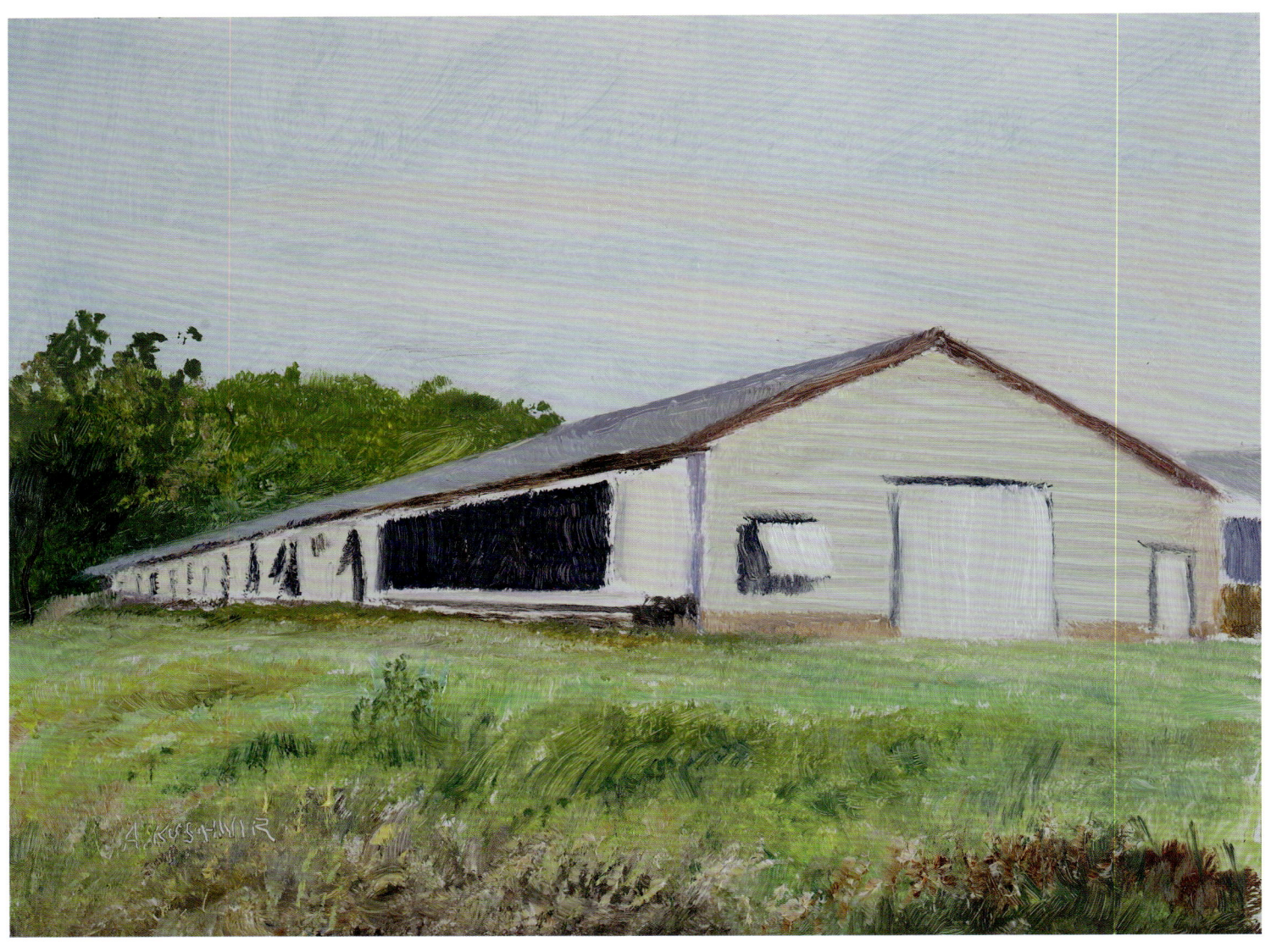

Turkey Brooding House at MM 263.6 on I-81, south of New Market, oil on panel, 6" x 8," October 22, 2019.

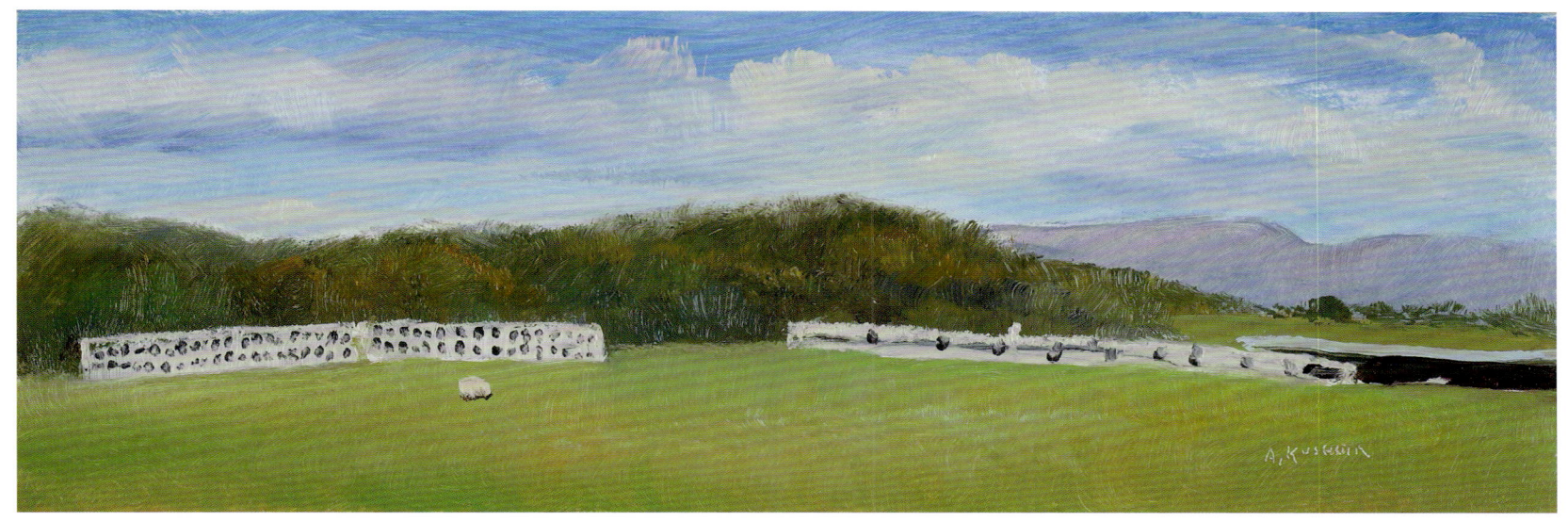

Turkey Brooding Houses and Supin Lick Mountain (distant right), looking west from MM 263.6 on I-81, south of New Market, oil on panel, 3" x 9," October 27, 2019.

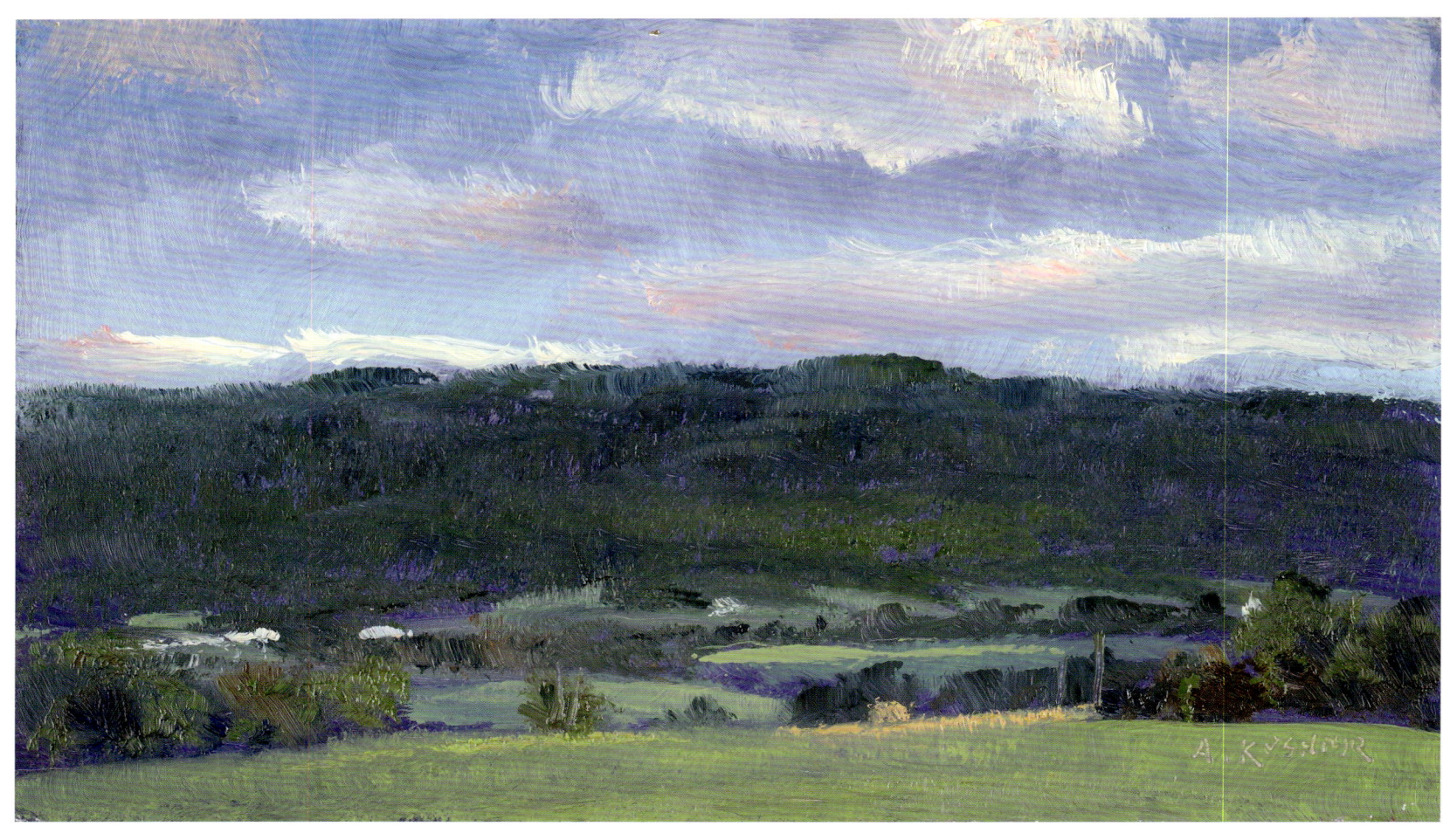

View East from Rest Stop at Exit 262 on I-81, south of New Market, oil on panel, 4" x 7," August 23, 2017.

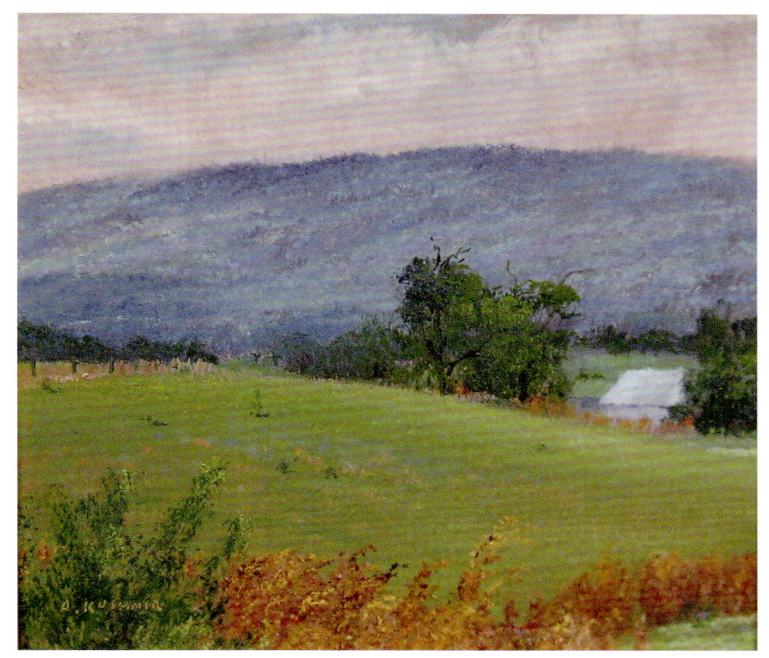 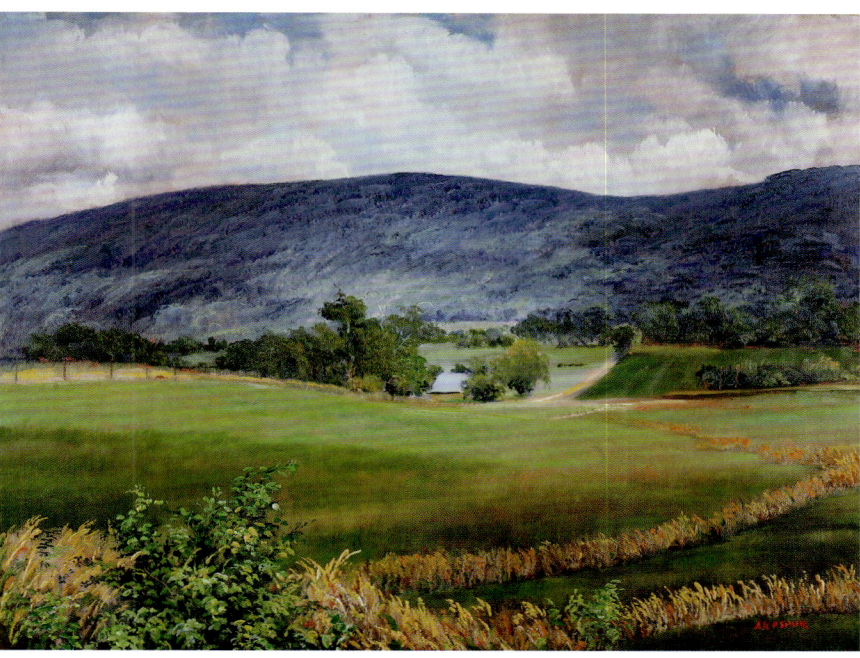

(Left) Morning View East from Rest Stop at Exit 262 on I-81, south of New Market, oil on panel, 7" x 8," August 23, 2017.

(Right) Afternoon View East from Rest Stop at Exit 262 on I-81, oil on canvas, 18" x 24," August 23, 2017.

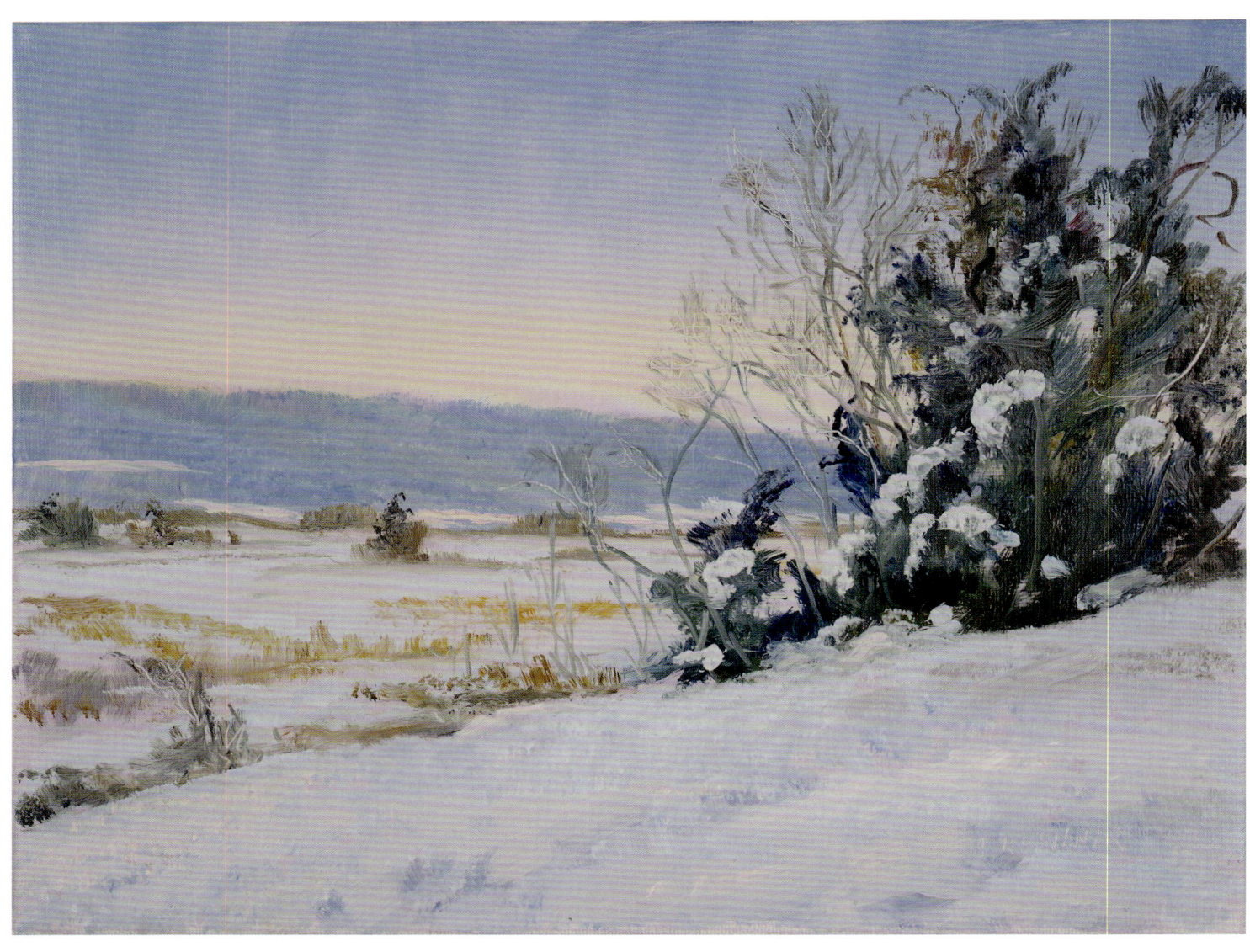

Winter in the Valley, Rest Stop at Exit 262 on I-81, south of New Market, oil on canvas, 9" x 12," January 7, 2022.

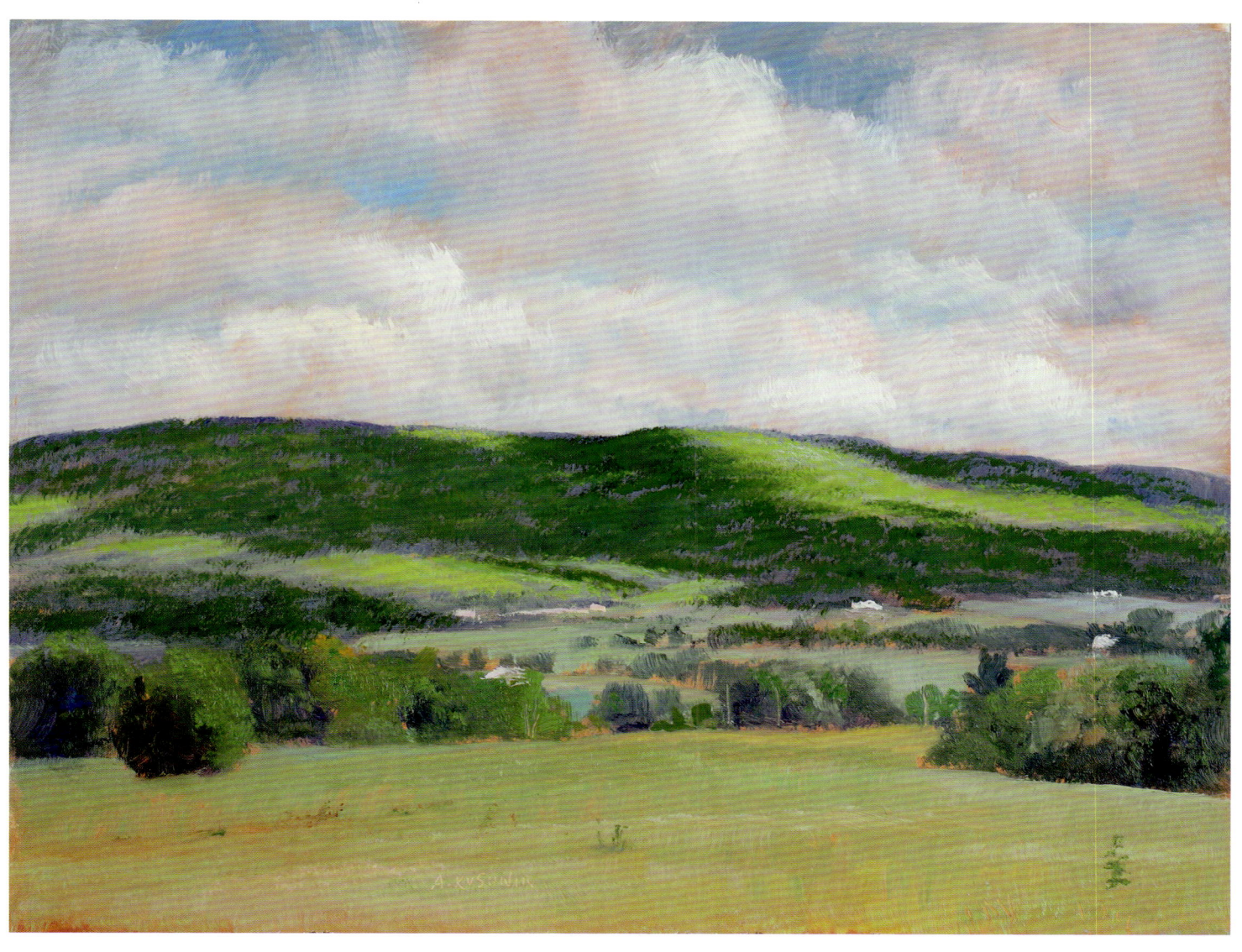

Sunlight and Shadow, looking east from I-81 near MM 262, south of New Market, oil on panel, 9" x 12," August 23, 2019.

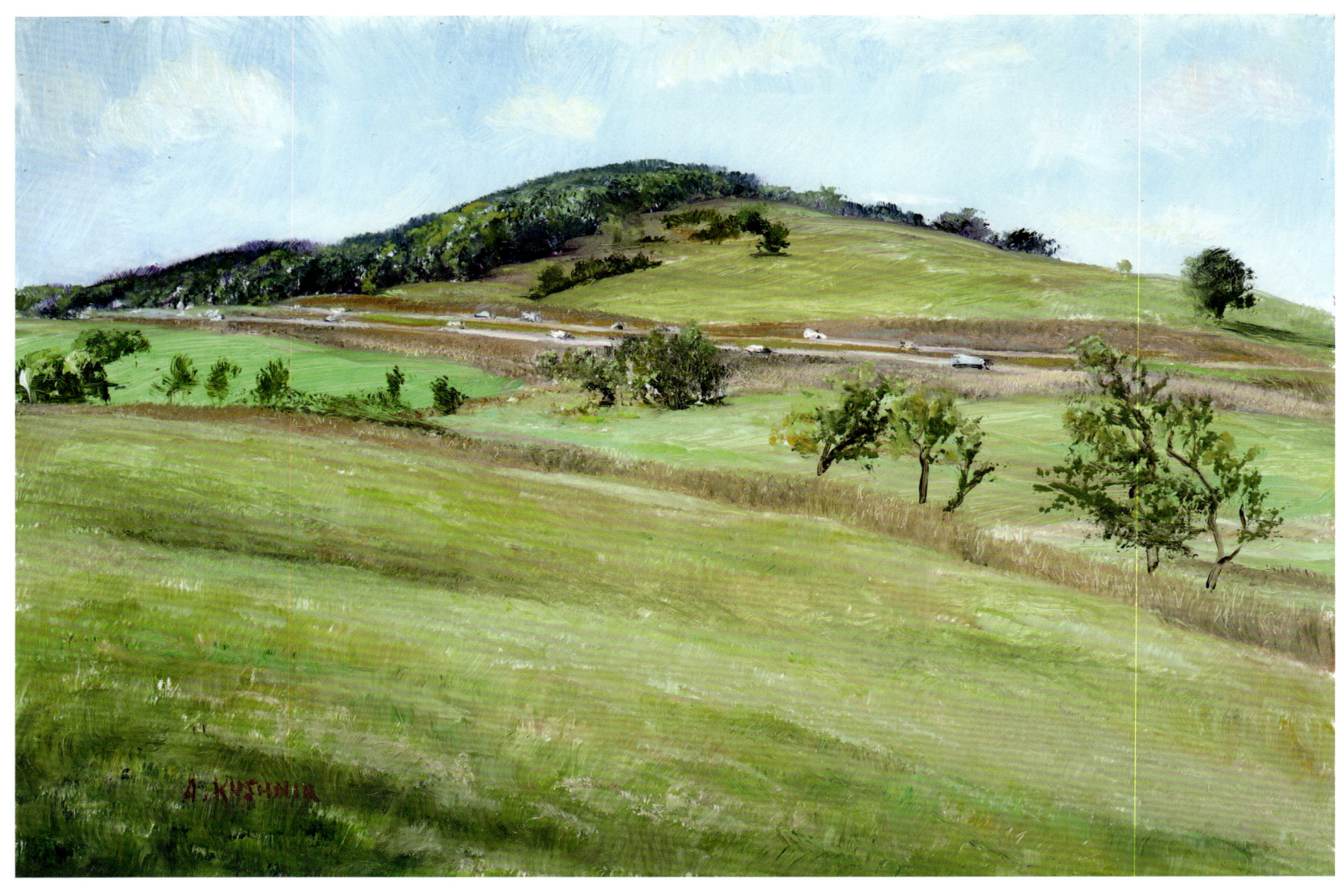

Interstate and Landscape, looking west at I-81 from VA 795 near the Fairview Church of the Brethren, south of New Market, oil on panel, 8" x 12," October 22, 2019.

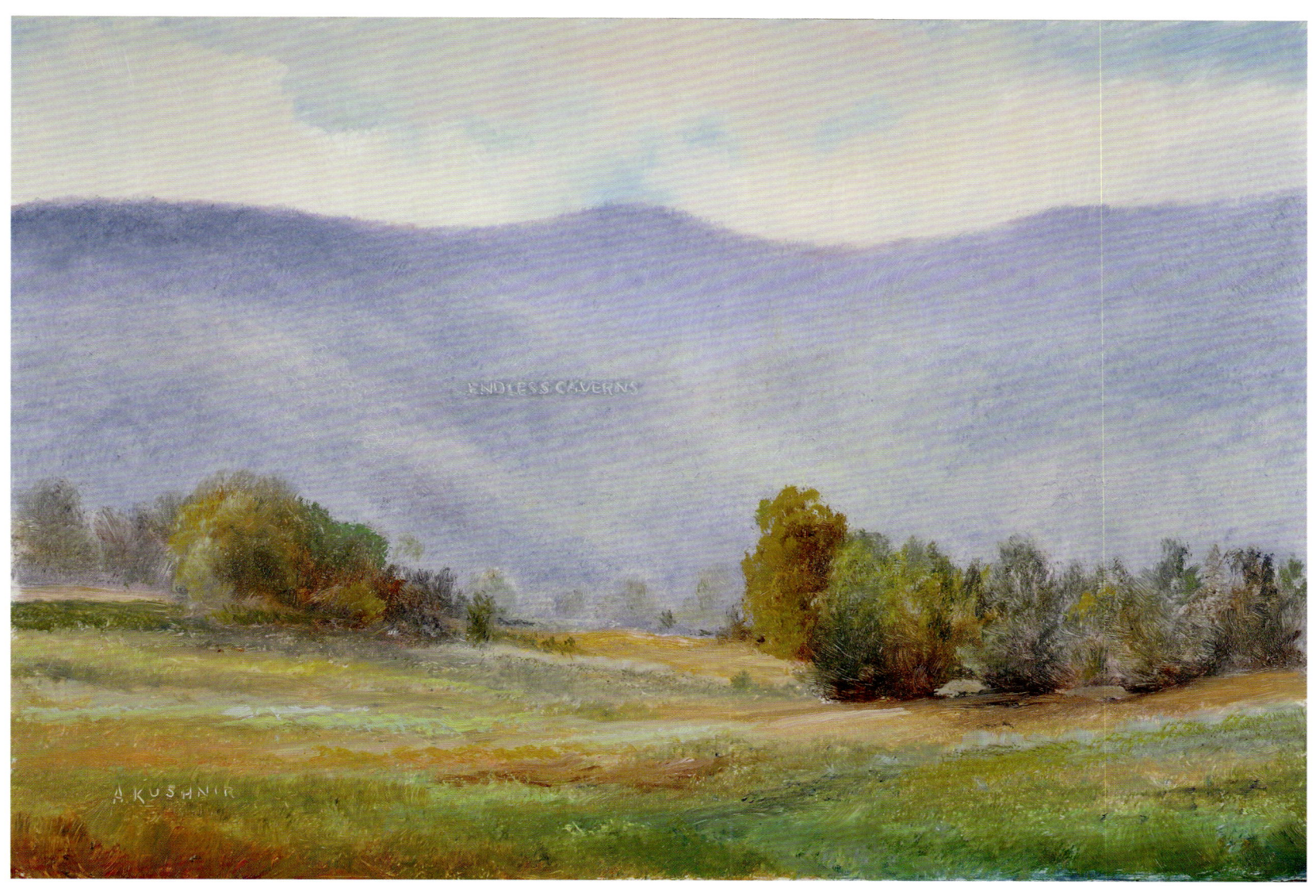

Endless Caverns Sign and First Mountain, looking east from I-81 and VA 793, south of New Market, oil on panel, 8" x 12," March 30, 2020.

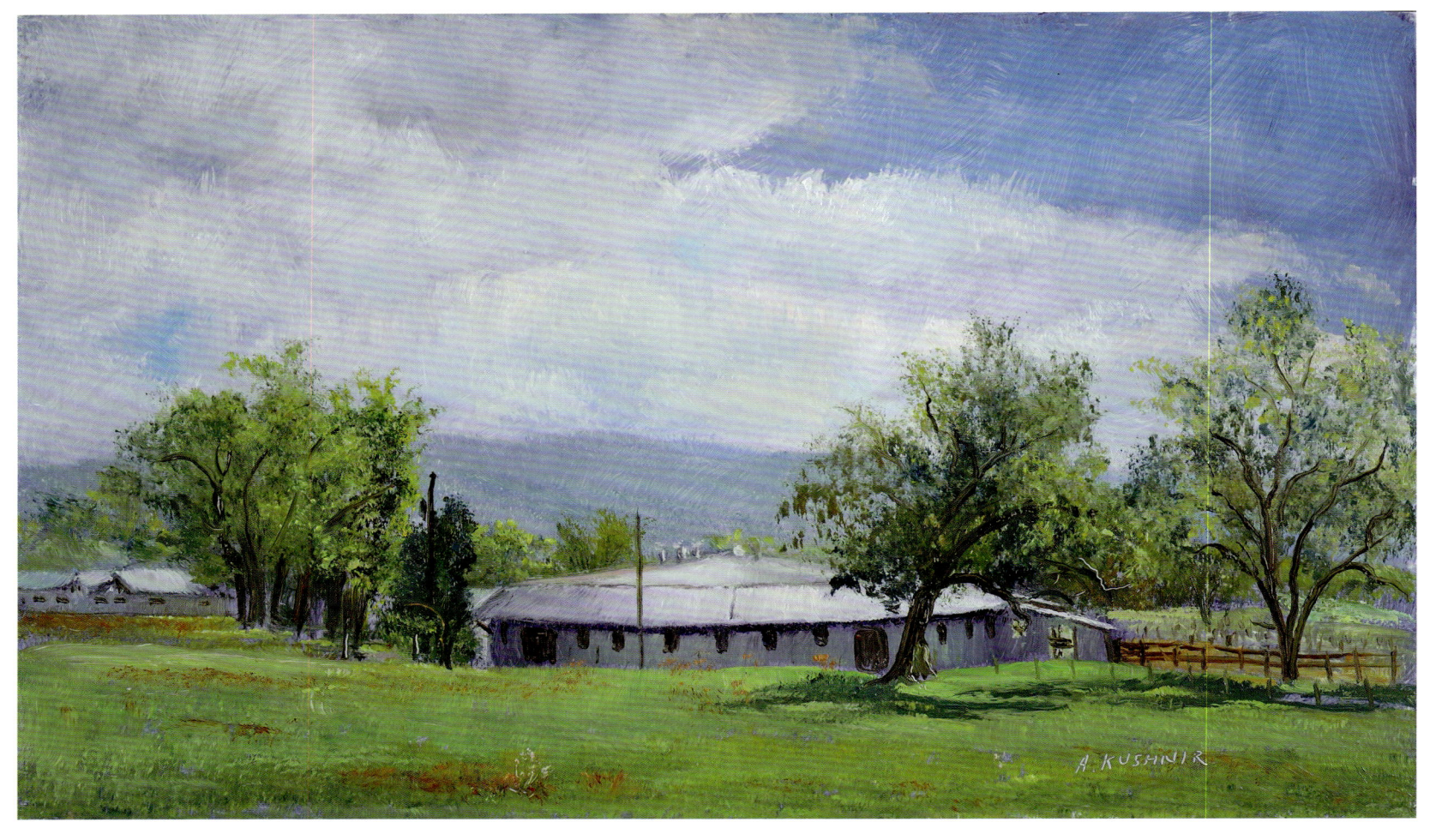

Old Zoo, looking east at the grounds of ZOORAMA (ca. late 1950s/early 1960s) and Massanutten Mountain at MM 261 on I-81, south of New Market, oil on panel, 7" x 12," October 22, 2019.

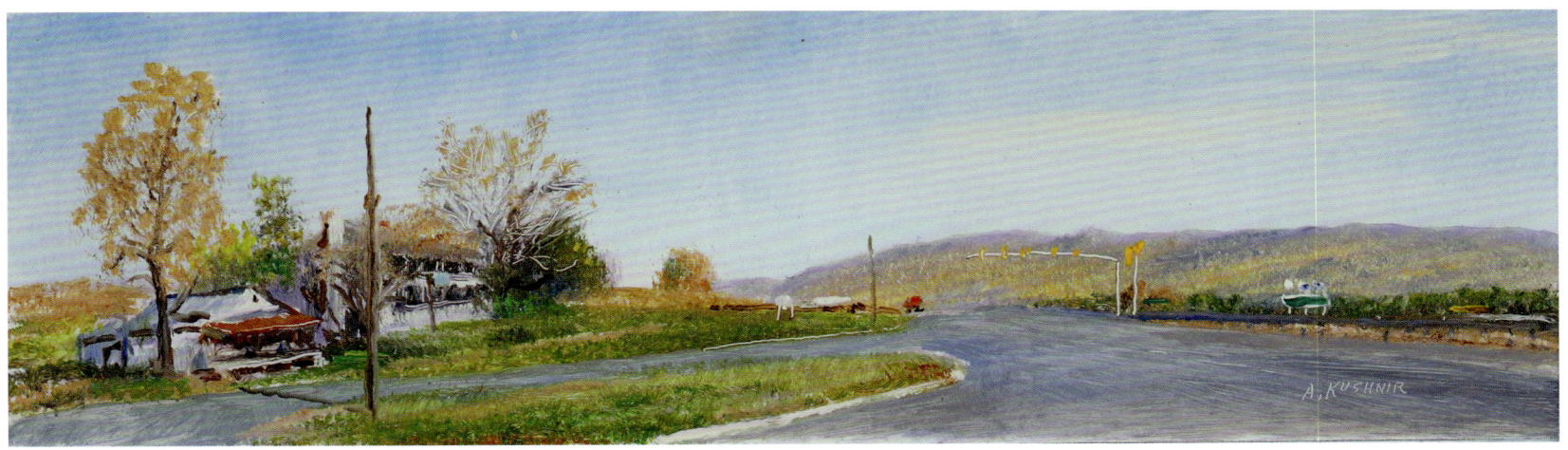

The Shoppes at Mauzy at Exit 257 on I-81, oil on panel, 3½" x 12," November 10, 2021. To the lament of many, these historic early nineteenth-century buildings, long associated as a tavern and stagecoach inn on the Old Valley Road/Pike (U.S. 11), were demolished during the fall of 2022 to make room for a large Dollar General Store. The property also included an old schoolhouse and jail in the back.

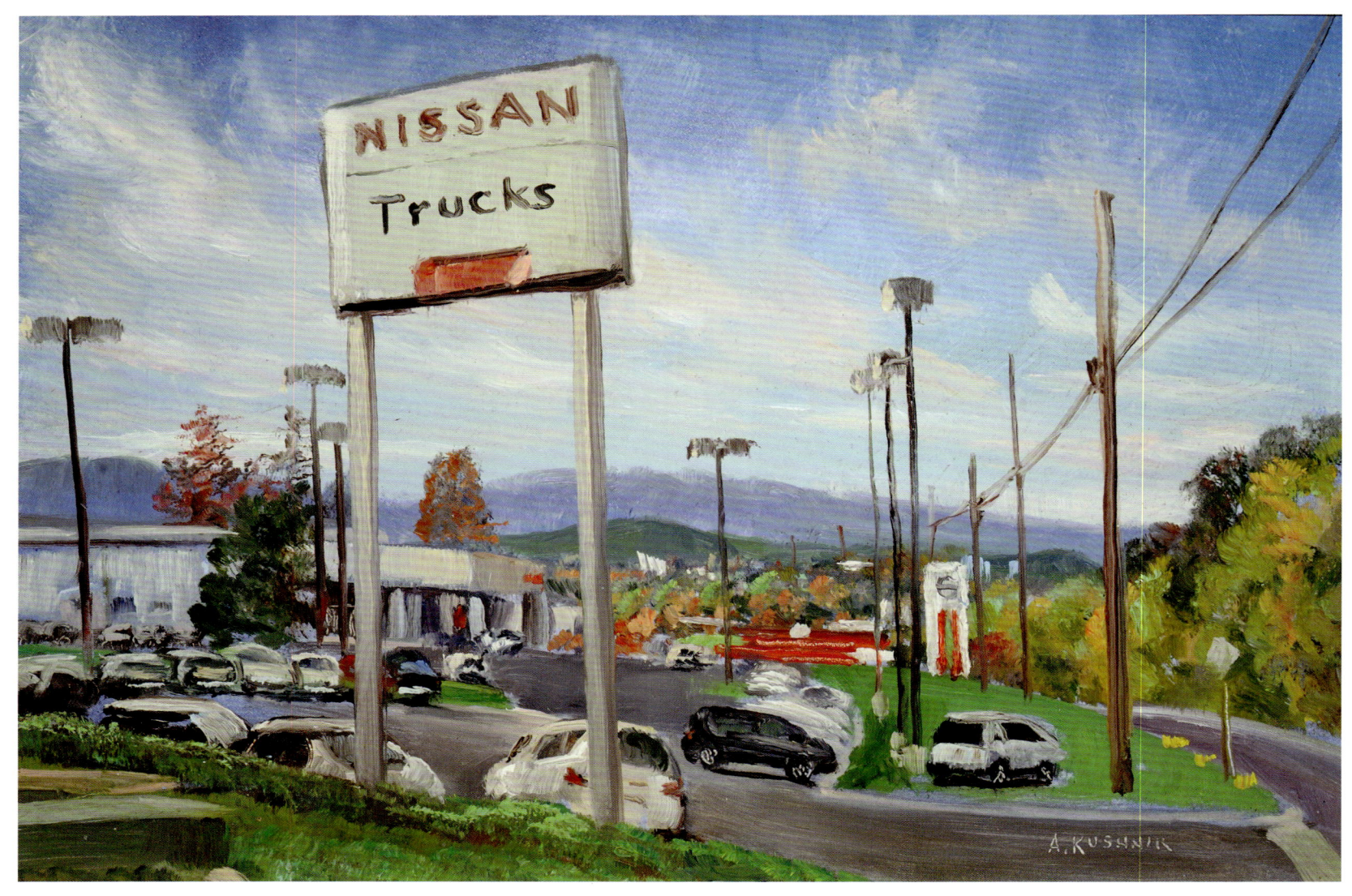

U.S. 33 at Harrisonburg, looking toward Massanutten Mountain, just east of Exit 247A on I-81, oil on panel, 8" x 12," October 23, 2011.

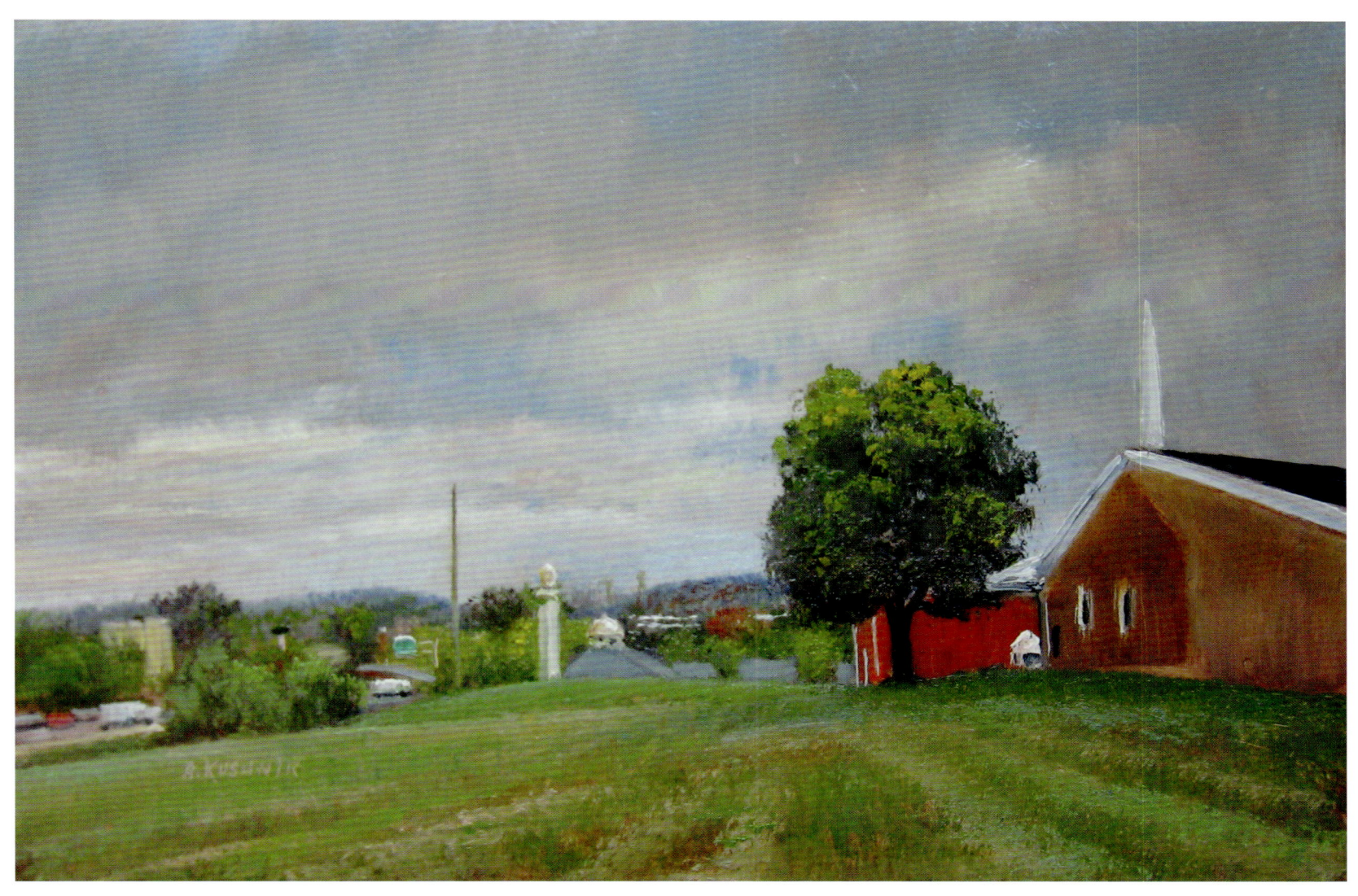

Islamic Association of the Shenandoah Valley Mosque from the Grounds of Victory Baptist Church, Exit 247B on I-81, Harrisonburg, looking south, oil on panel, 8" x 12," October 16, 2022.

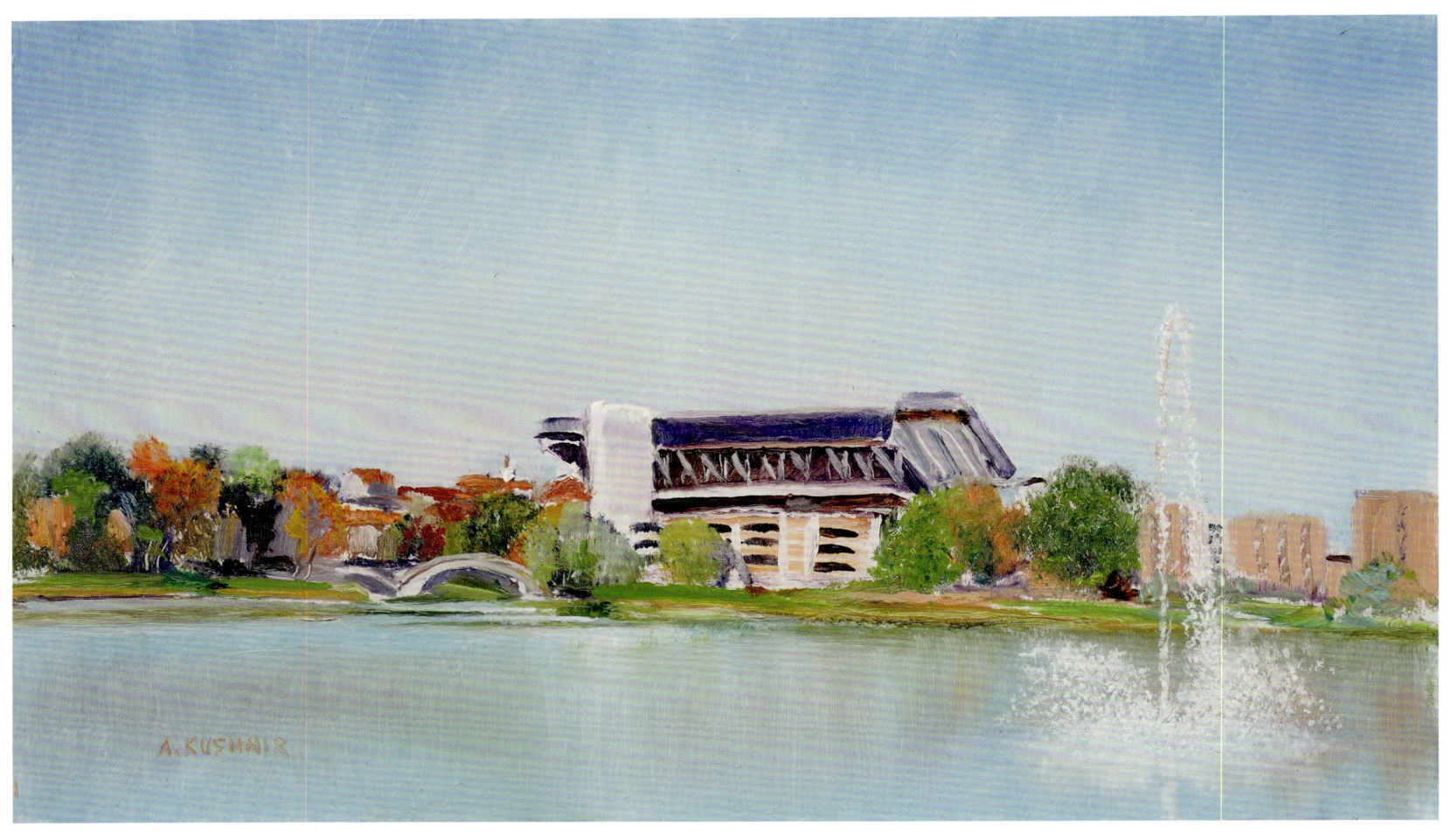

Newman Lake and Bridgeforth Stadium at James Madison University, **Exit 245 on I-81, Harrisonburg, oil on panel, 7" x 12," November 10, 2021.**

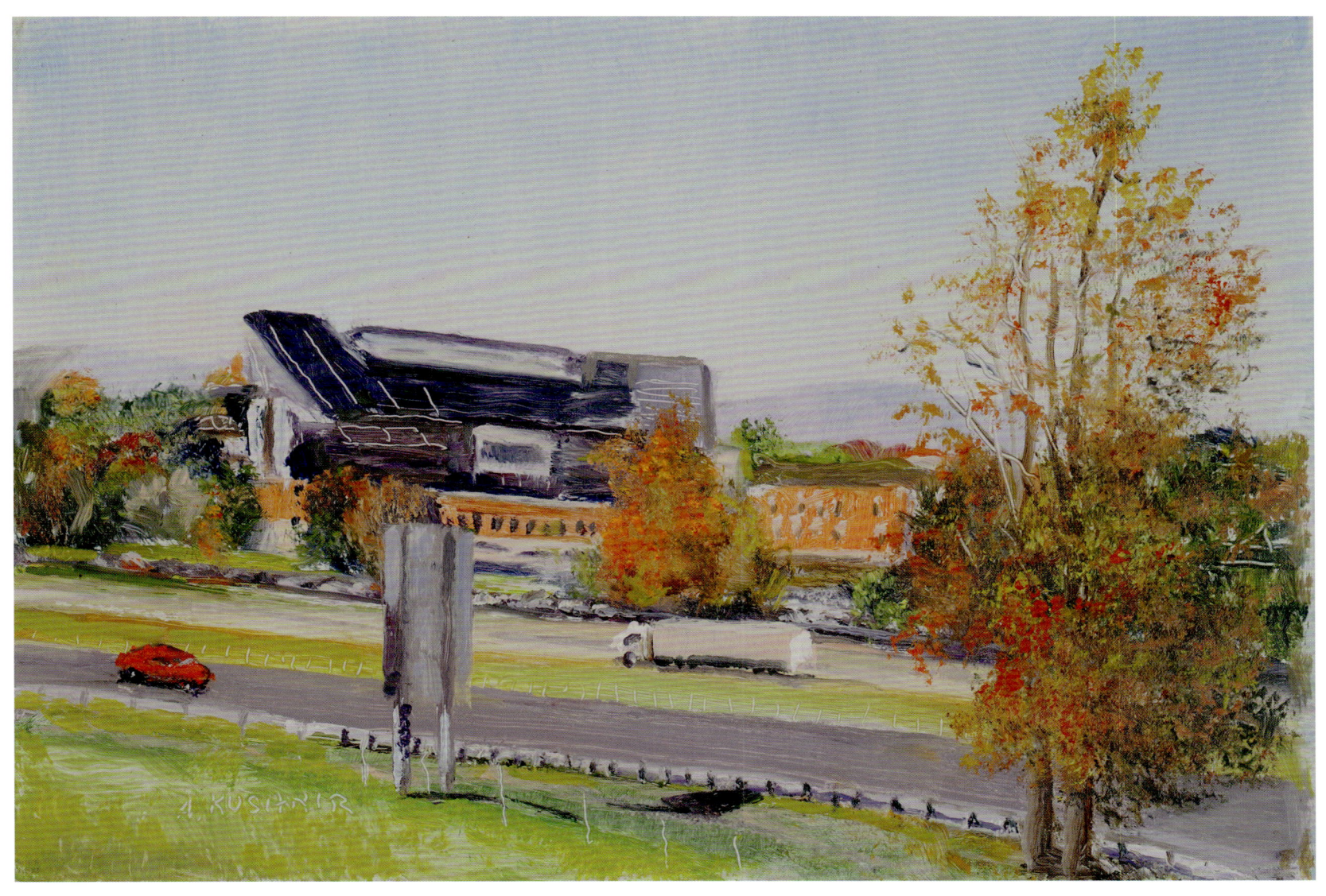

Bridgeforth Stadium at James Madison University, Exit 245 on I-81, Harrisonburg, looking west with Reddish Knob (elevation 4,397 feet/1,340 meters) in the distant background, oil on panel, 6" x 9," November 10, 2021.

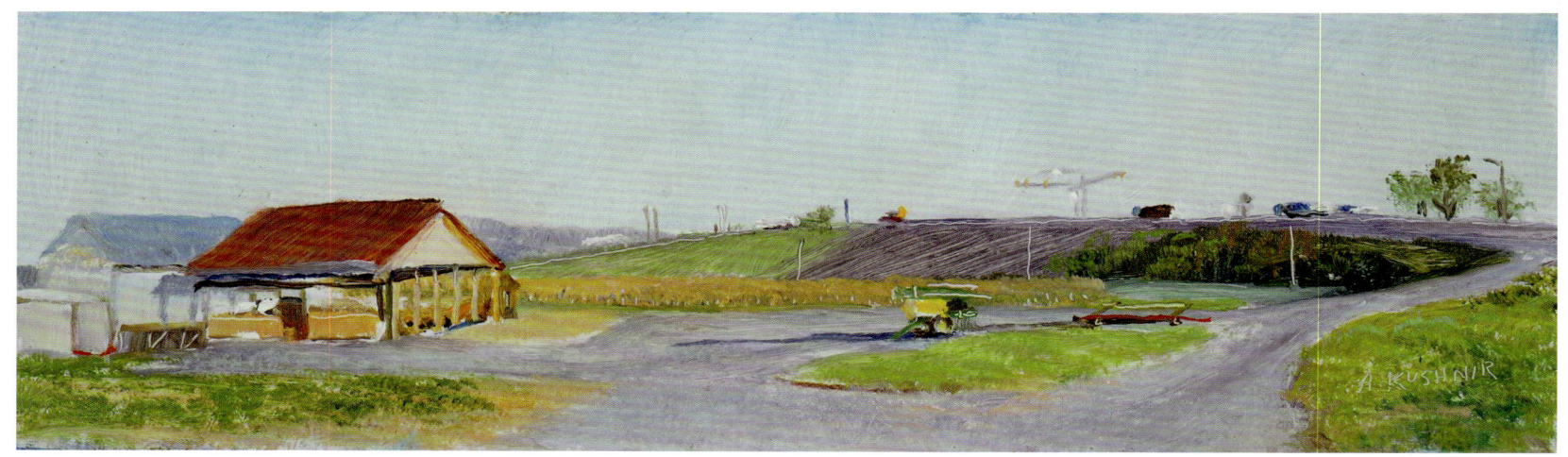

Overlook Produce, a Mennonite Market (moved to this interstate location in 2016), looking east, at Exit 240 on I-81, near Mount Crawford, oil on panel, 3½" x 12," November 10, 2021.

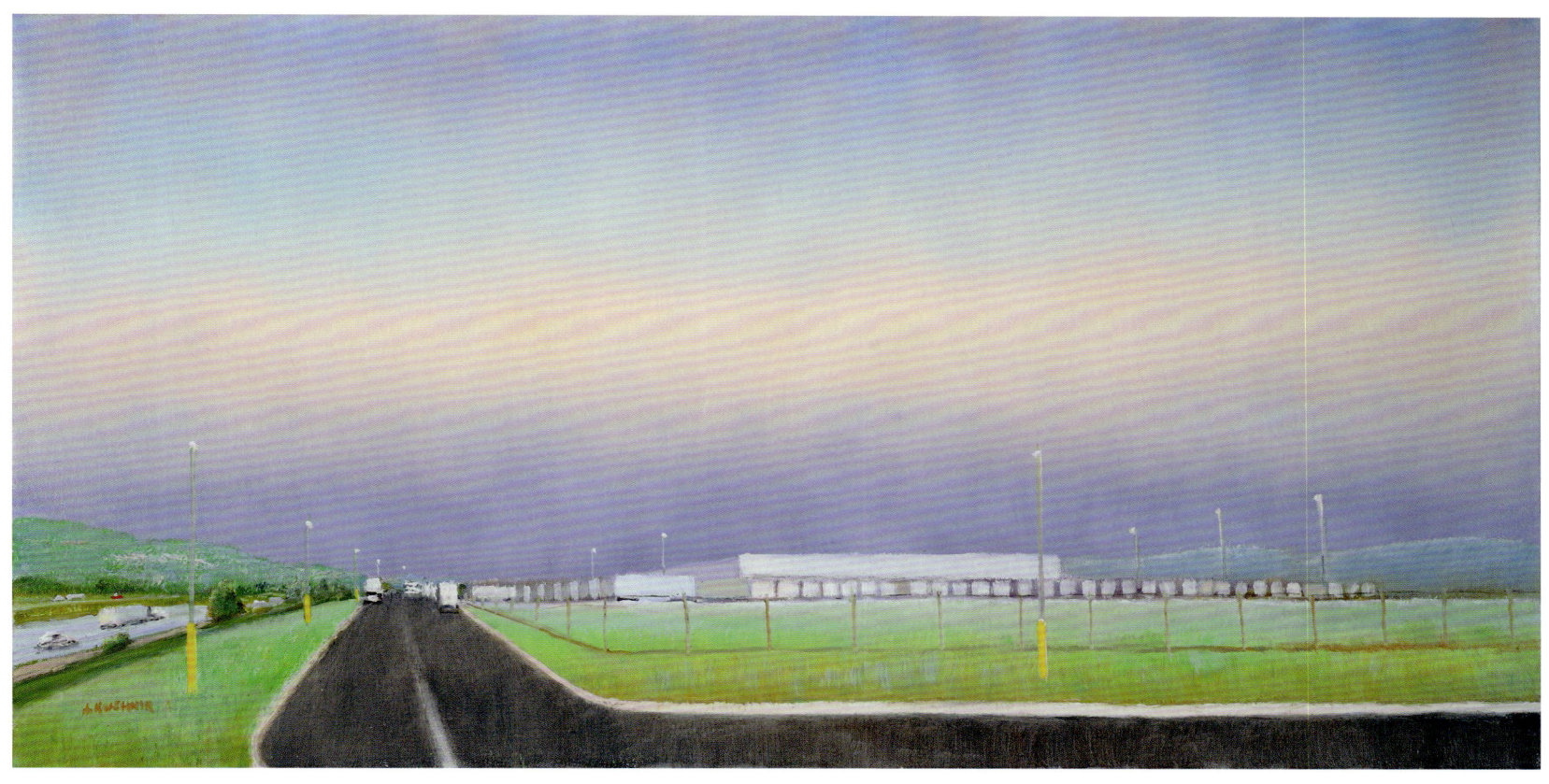

Walmart Distribution Center #7045, looking north from Walton Way (off VA 682) at Exit 240 on I-81, near Mount Crawford, oil on canvas, 10" x 20," February 2, 2022.

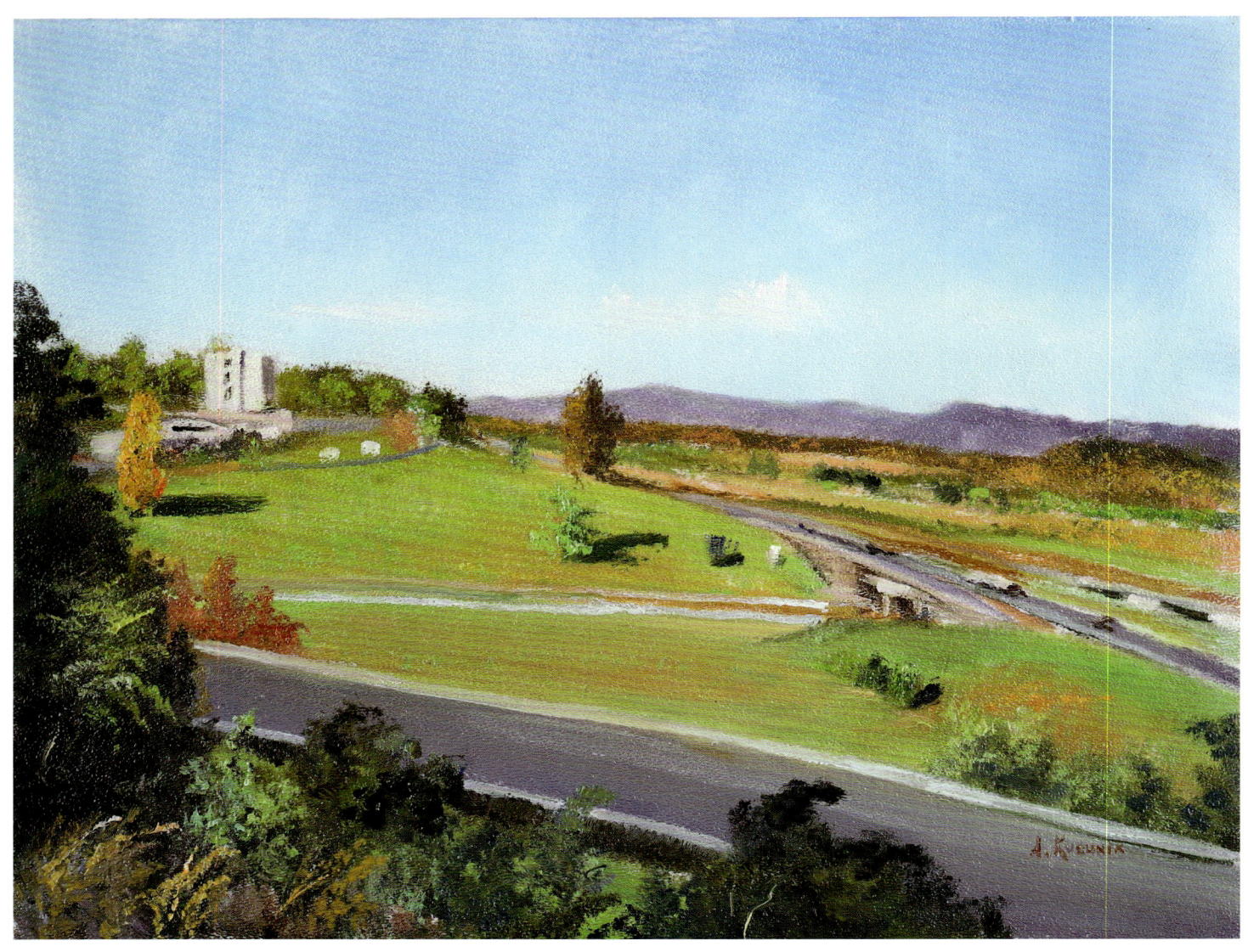

I-81 and Holiday Inn from the Travelers Inn, looking north at Exit 225, north of Staunton, oil on panel, 9" x 12," October 27, 2019.
This Travelers Inn was formerly a Days Inn and later became a Red Roof Inn & Suites.

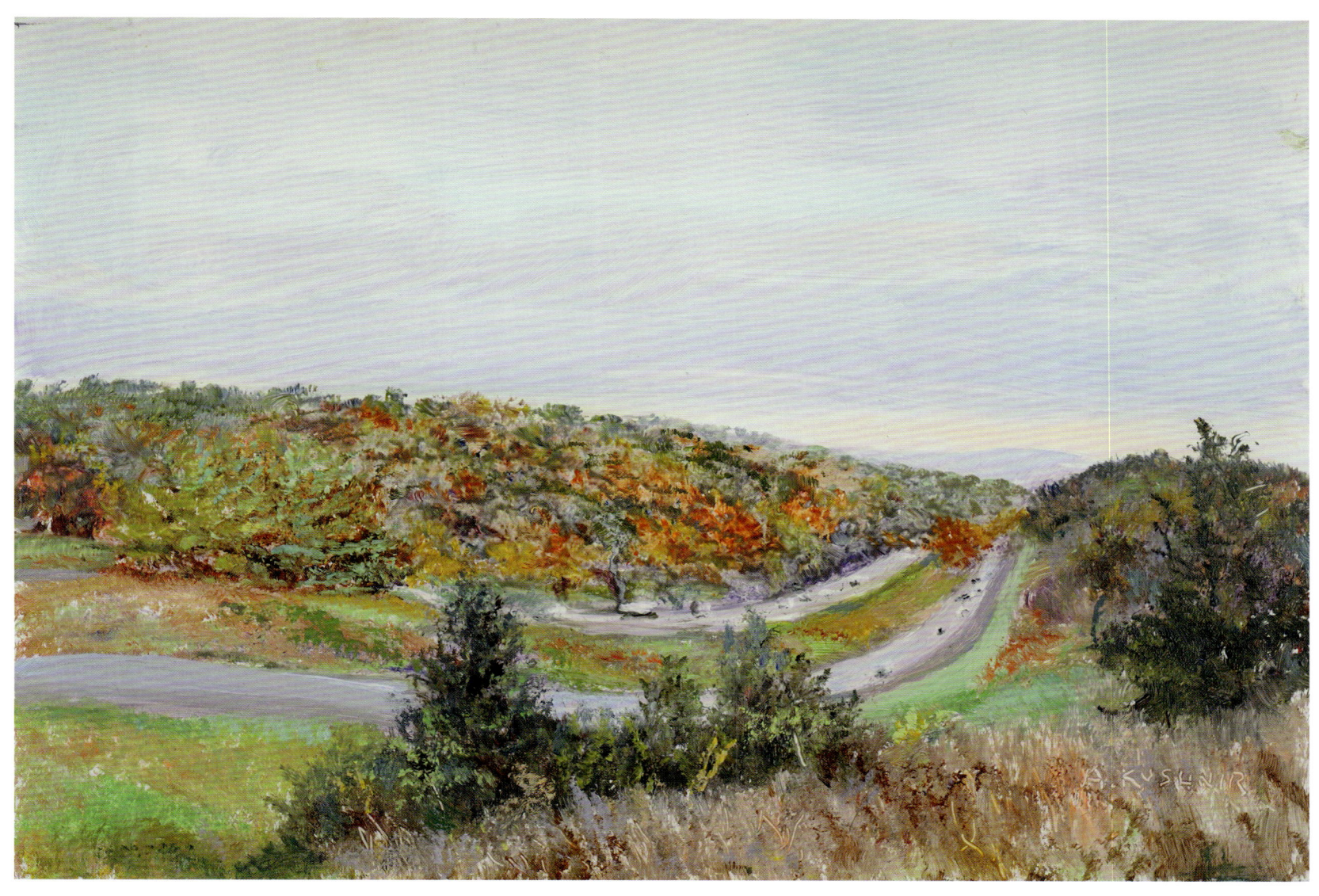

I-81 from the Travelers Inn, looking south at Exit 225, north of Staunton, oil on panel, 6" x 8," October 29, 2019.

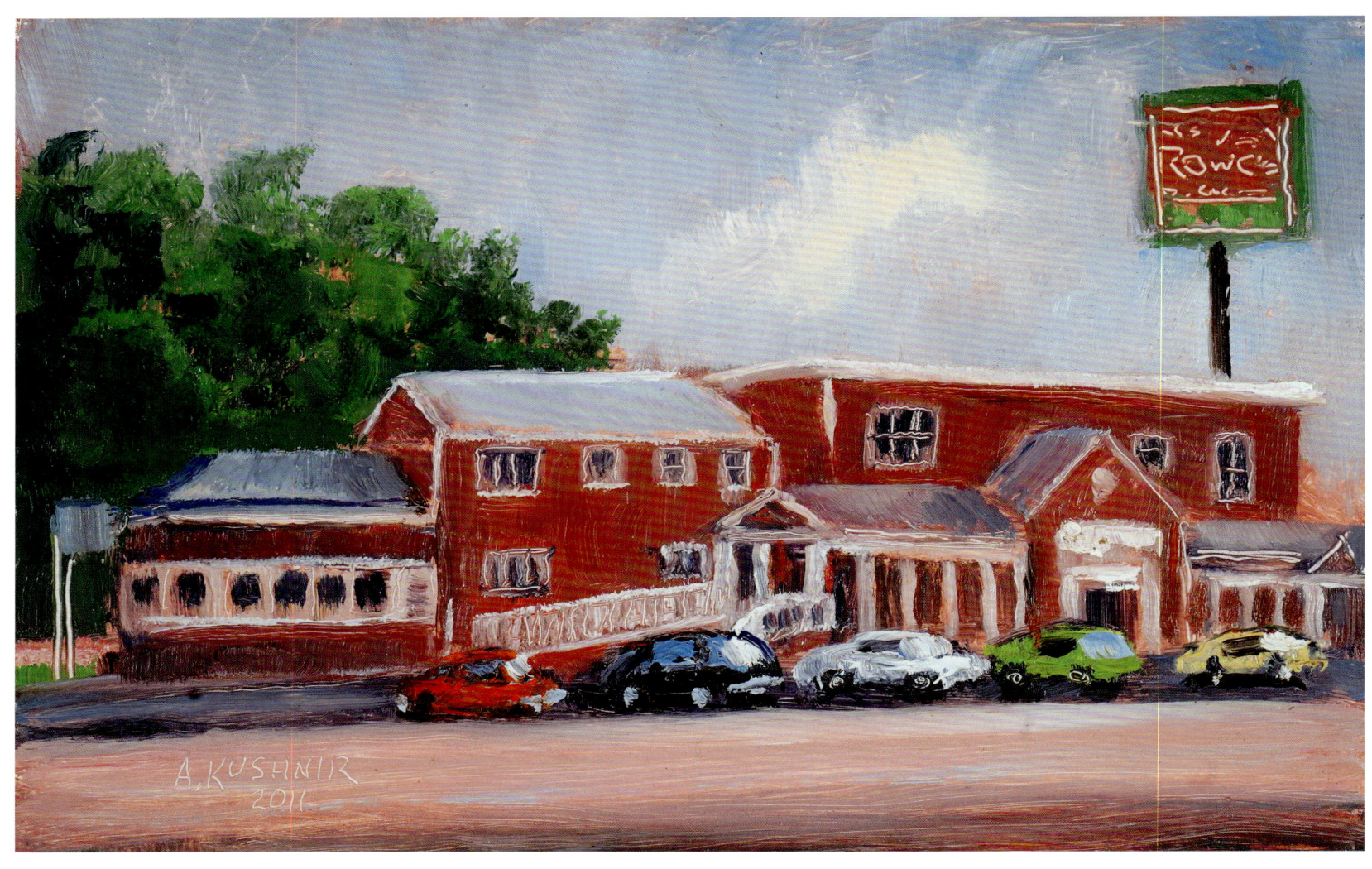

Mrs. Rowe's Restaurant (opened in 1947), at Exit 222 on I-81, Staunton, oil on panel, 5" x 8," July 11, 2011.

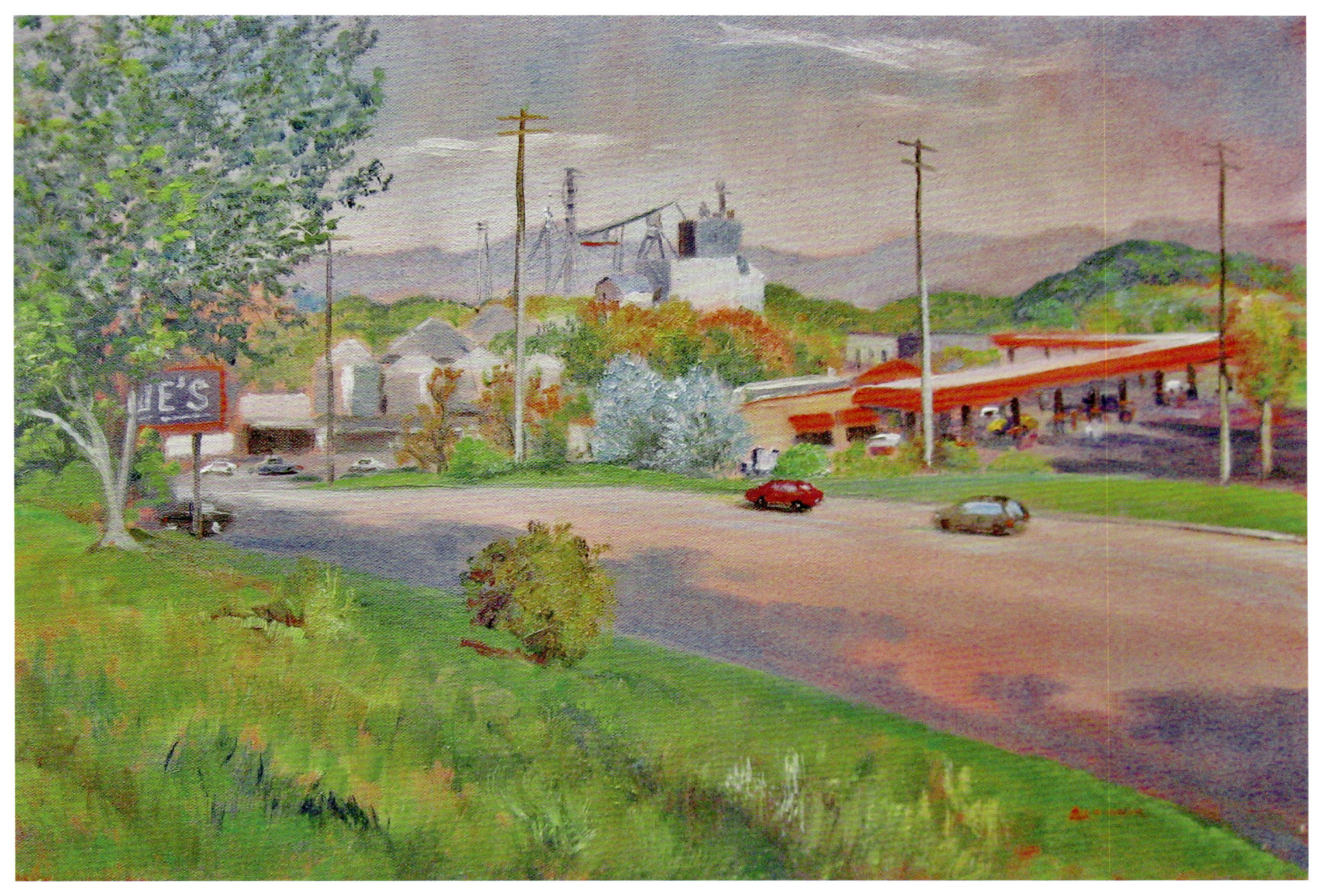

New Development and the Augusta Farm Co-op (established in 1929 as the Augusta Cooperative Farm Bureau),
Exit 222 on I-81, Staunton, oil on canvas, 16" x 24," November 9, 2021.

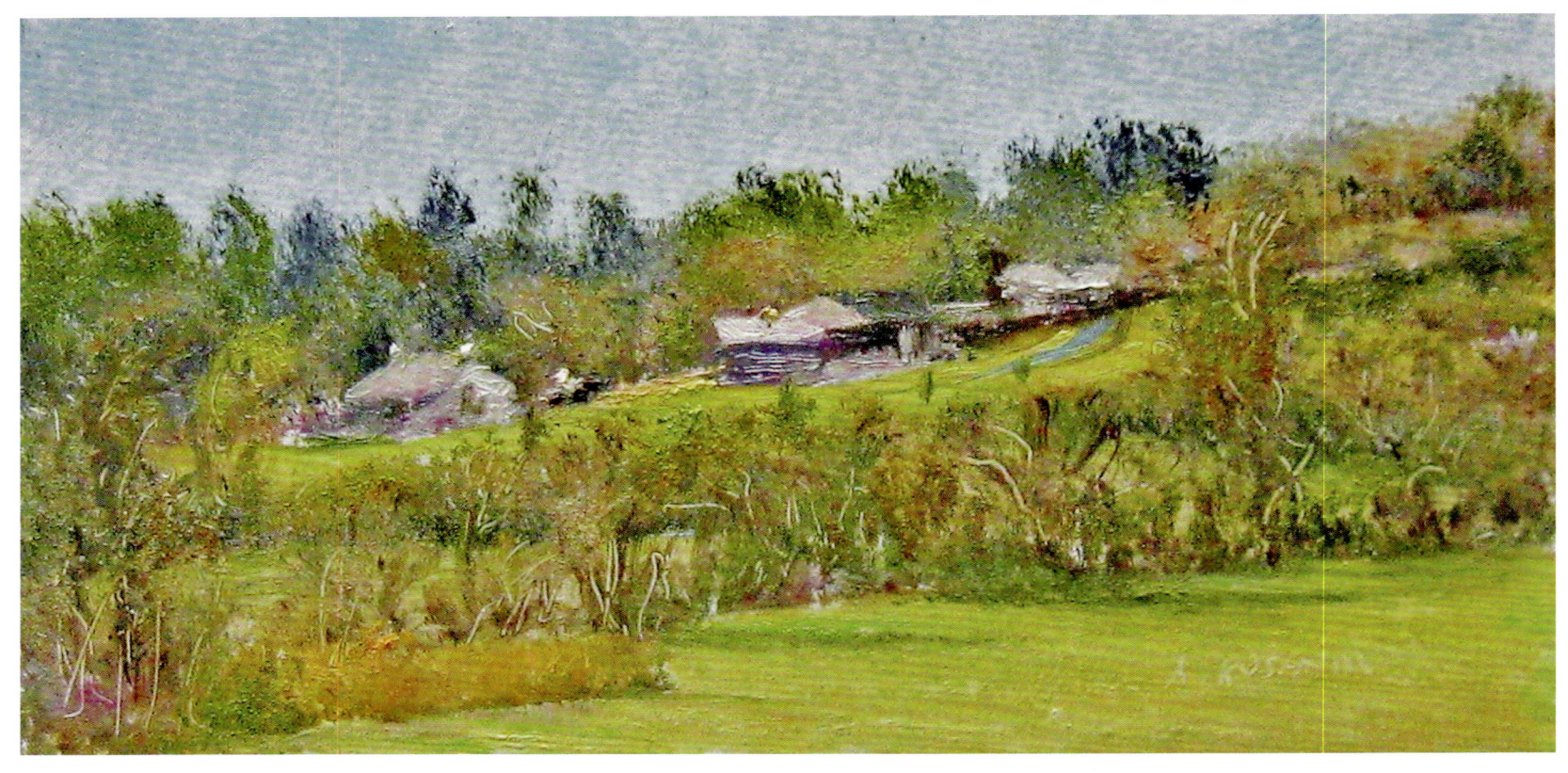

Historic Buildings, Frontier Culture Museum, Exit 222 on I-81, Staunton, oil on panel, 4" x 8," January 16, 2020.

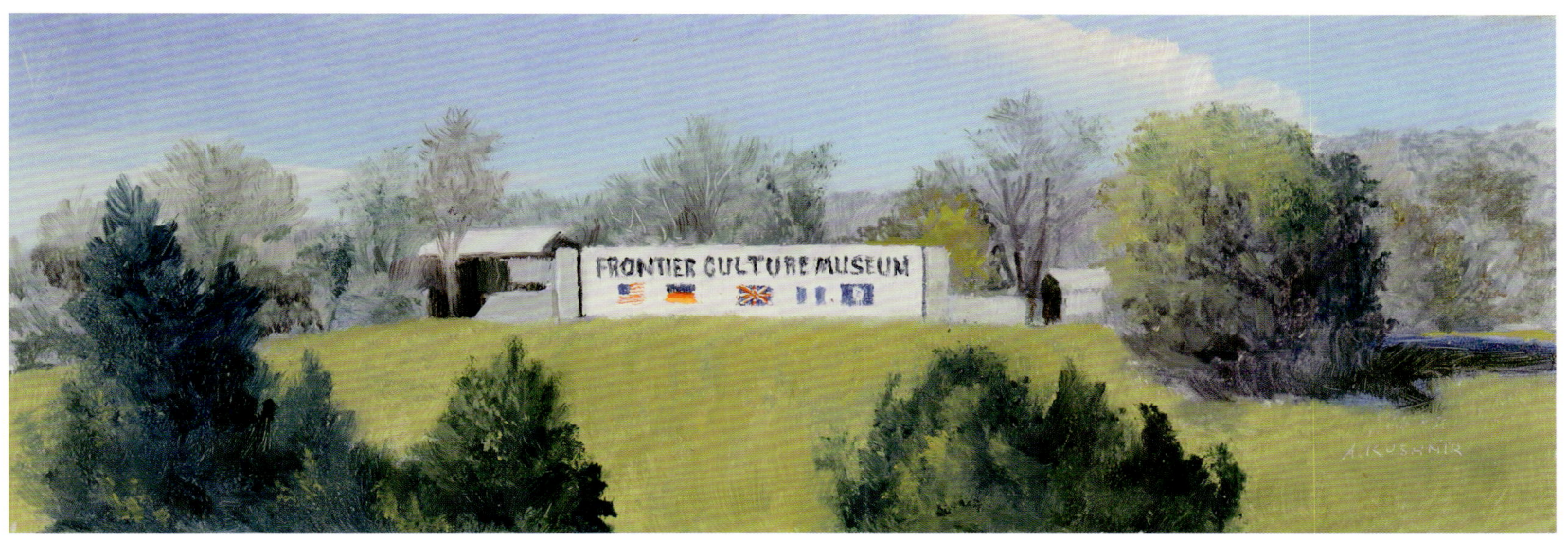

Frontier Culture Museum (opened in 1975) on I-81 at Exit 222 on I-81, Staunton, oil on panel, 4¼" x 12," March 2020.

Note: I-81 and I-64 (from/toward Charlottesville and Richmond) intersect at this location.

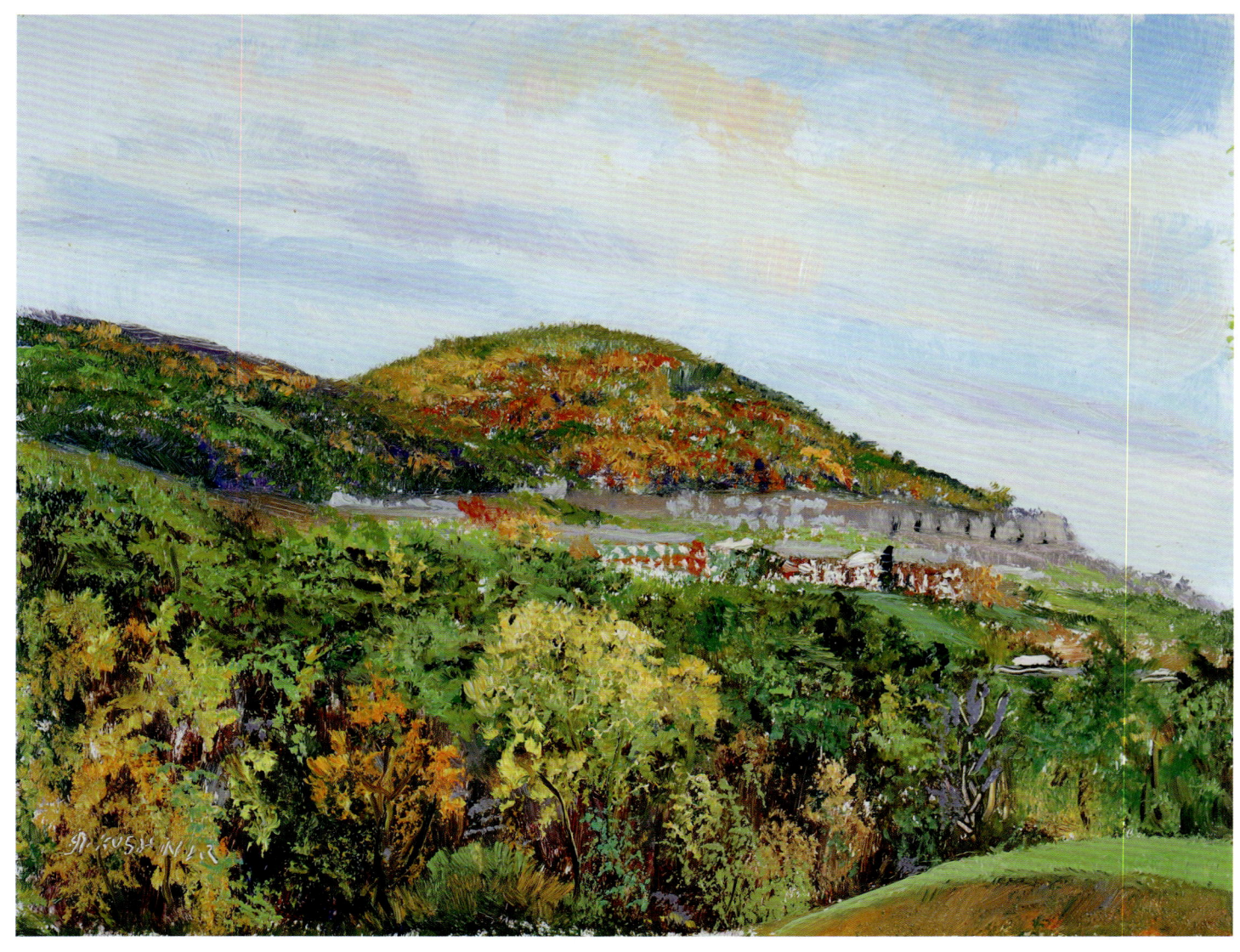

View West of the DeJarnette Center (1932–1975), Blue Sky Apartment Homes, and Betsy Bell Mountain,
Exit 222 on I-81, Staunton, oil on panel, 6" x 8," October 29, 2019.

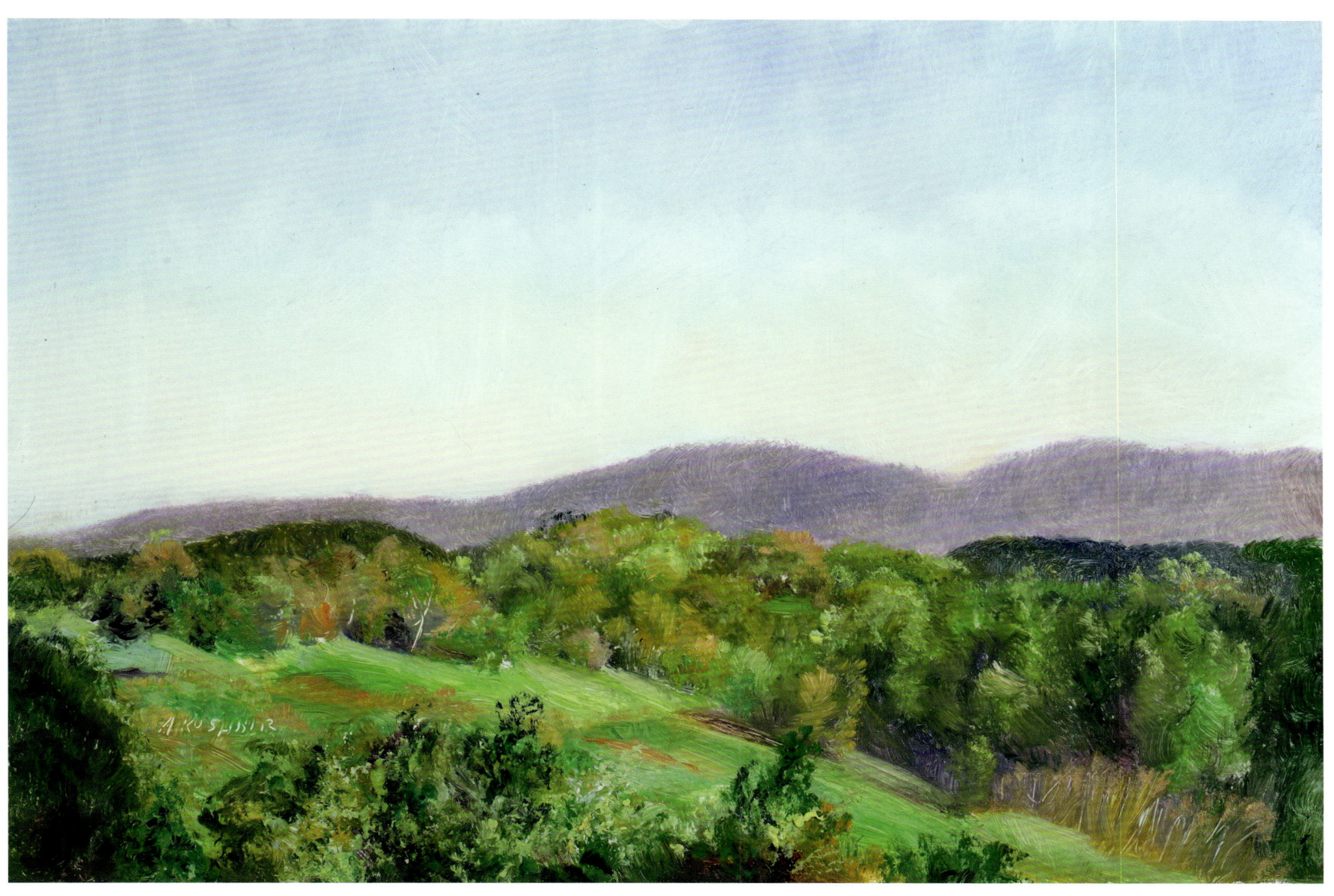

View East from the Days Inn at Exit 217 on I-81, Mint Springs, oil on panel, 8" x 12," September 20, 2020.

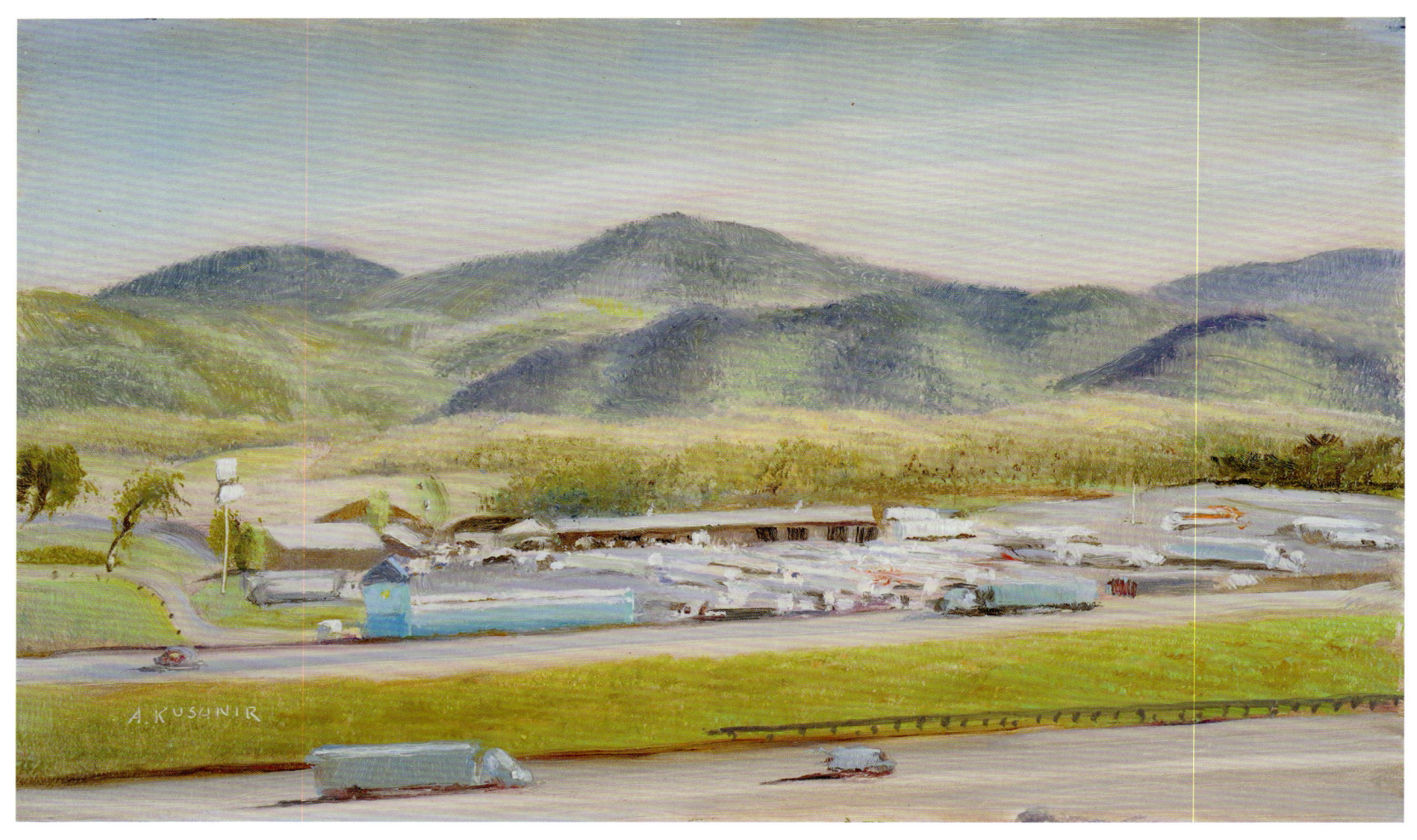

I–81 and the Pilot Truck Stop at Raphine, looking east toward St. Mary's Wilderness and the Blue Ridge Mountains from Exit 205, oil on panel, 7" x 12," January 16, 2020.

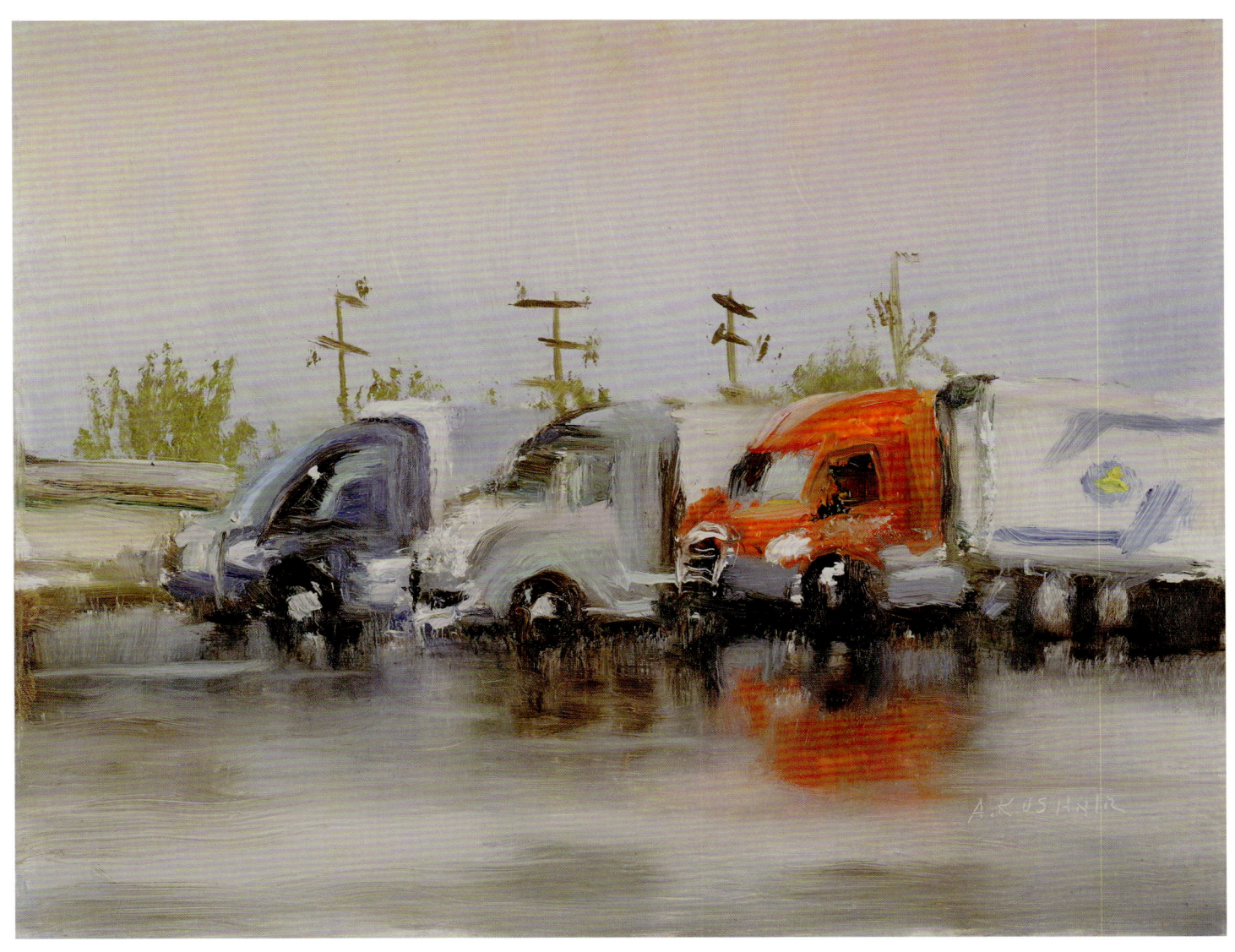

Sunshine Truck Stop at Exit 205 on I-81, Raphine, oil on panel, 6" x 8," March 2, 2020.

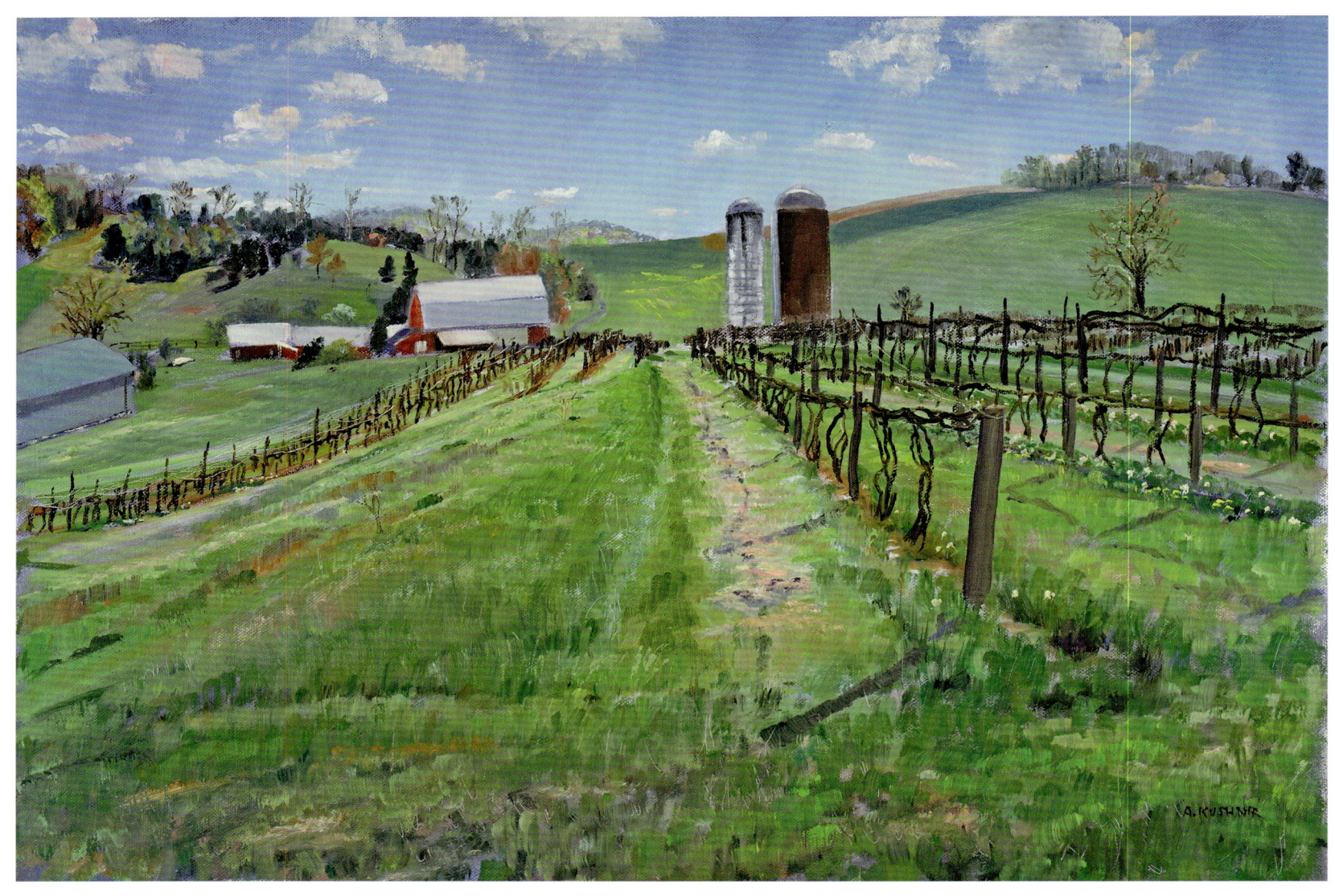

Rockbridge Vineyard, just west of Exit 205 on I-81, near Raphine, oil on canvas, 16" x 24," April 28, 2015.

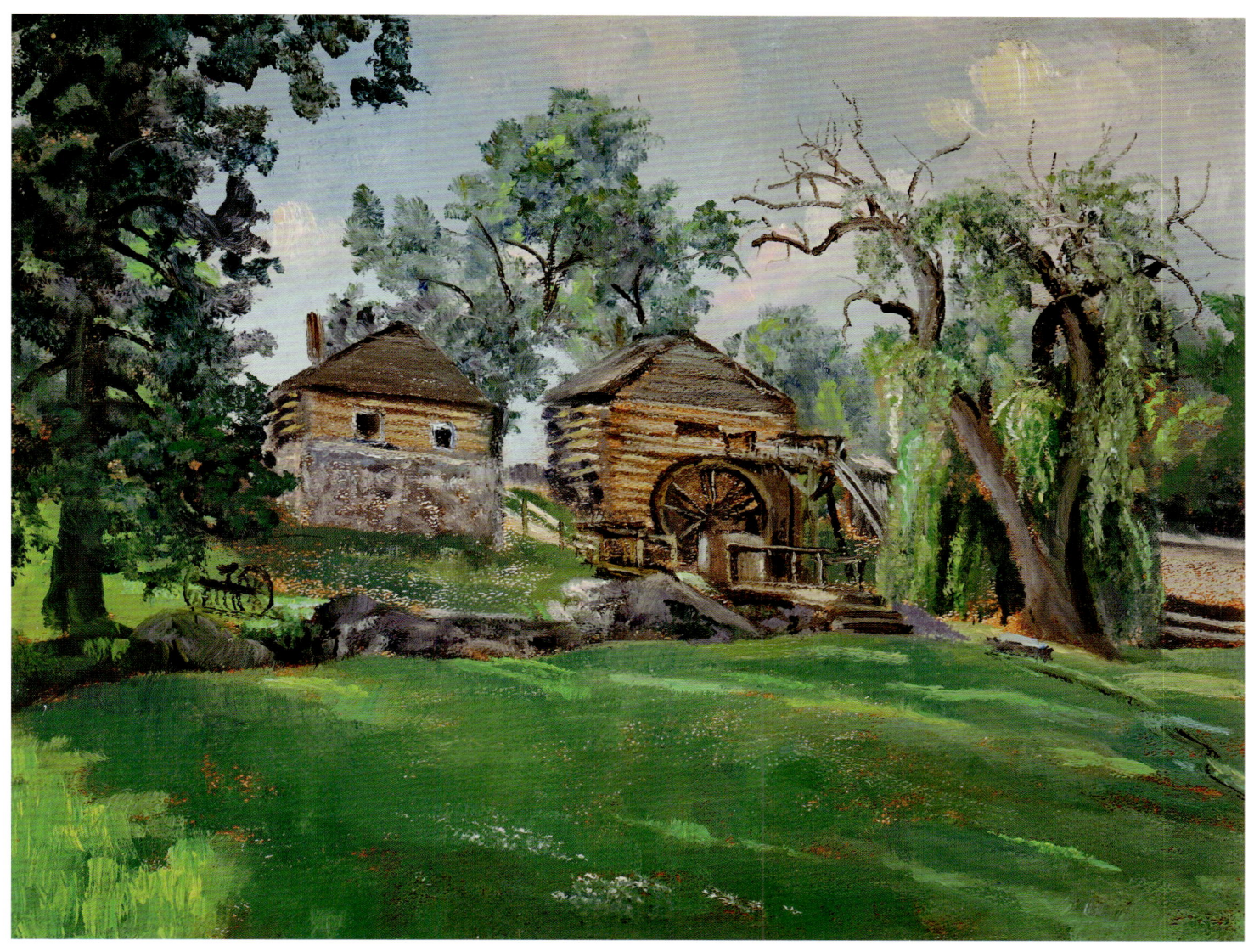

Cyrus McCormick Farm (Walnut Grove), just east of Exit 205 on I-81, Steeles Tavern, oil on panel, 9" x 12," July 10, 2011.

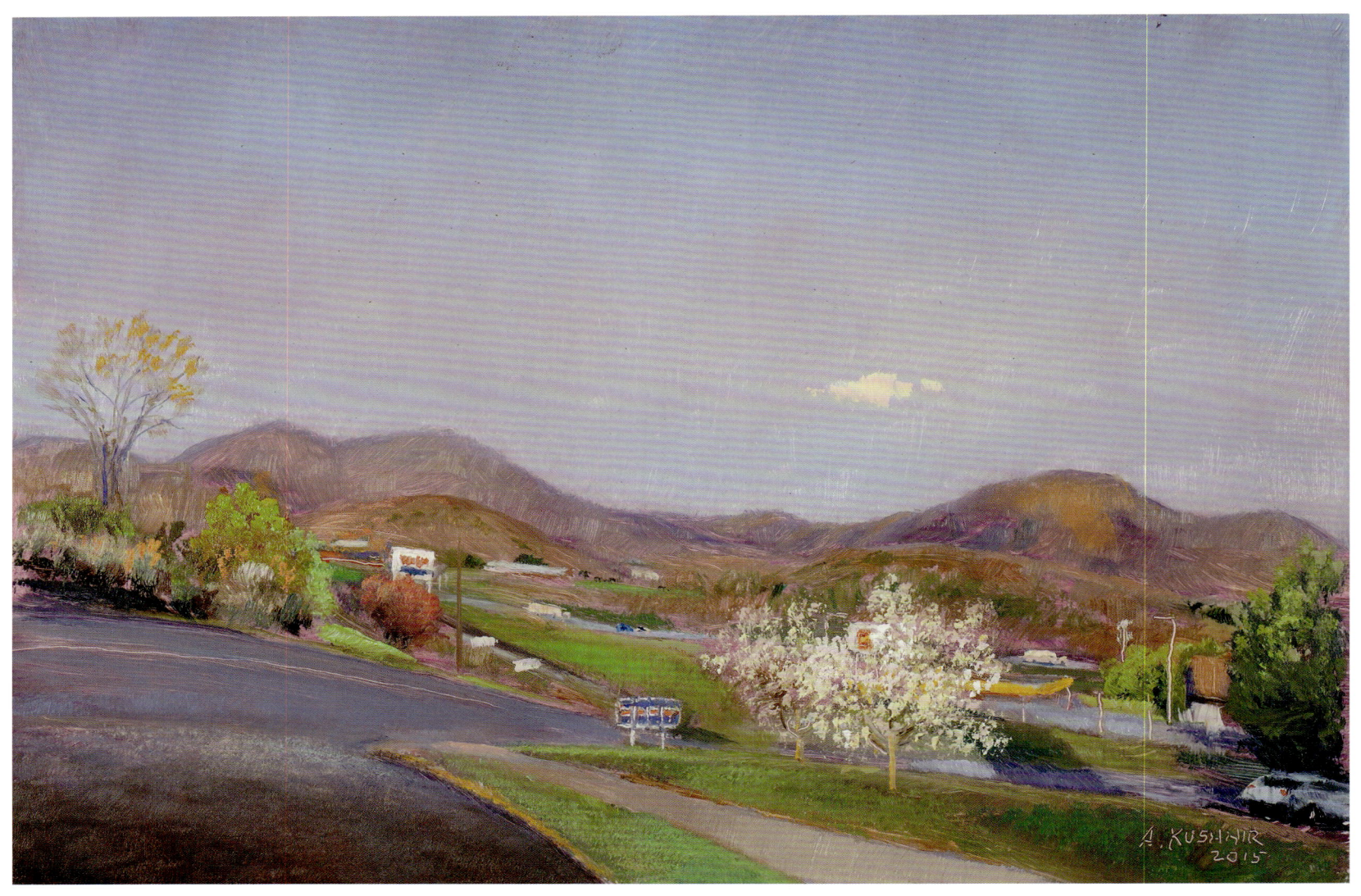

Truck Stop and Exxon, looking northeast at Exit 200 on I-81, Fairfield, oil on panel, 8" x 12," April 28, 2015.

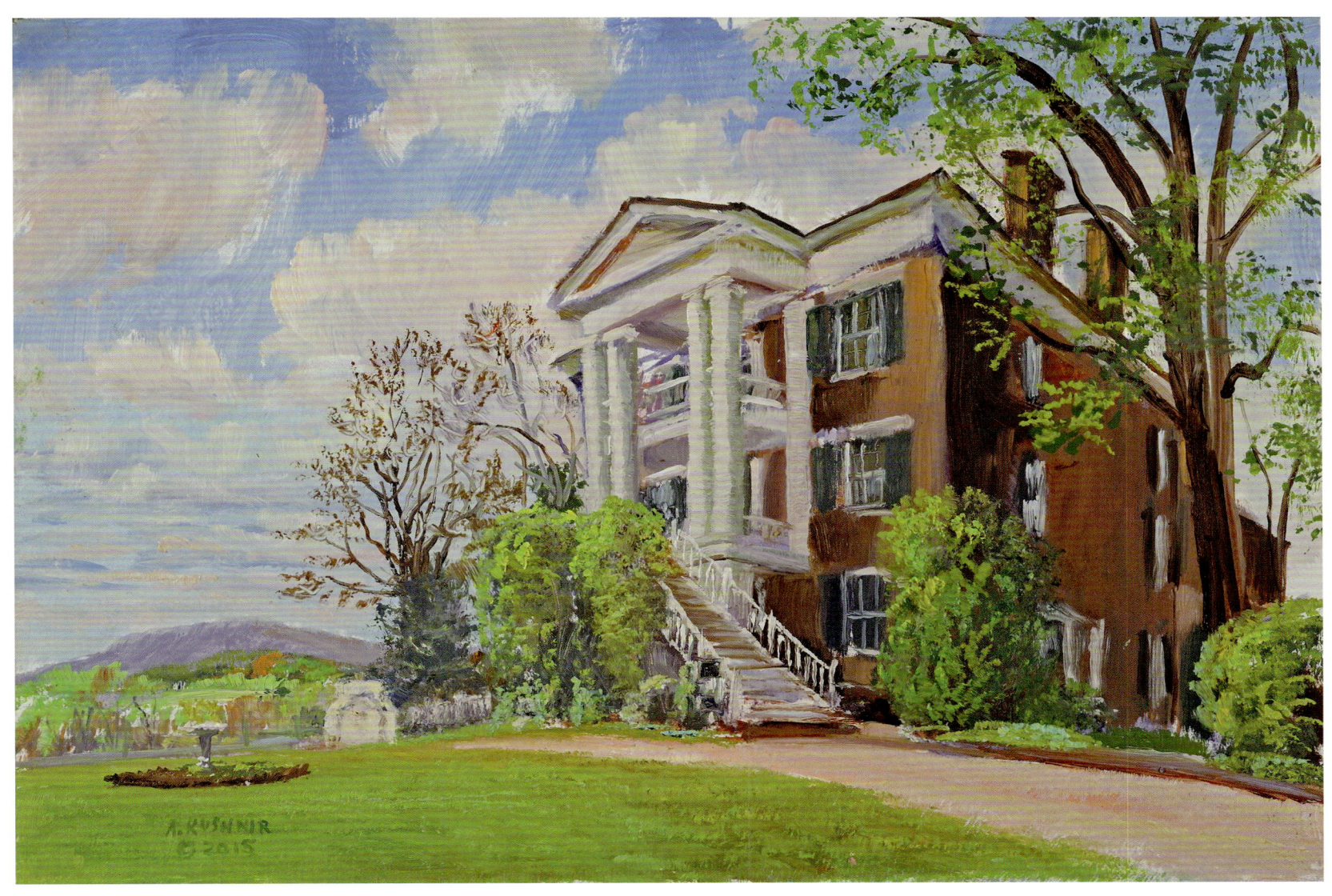

Historic Maple Hall Inn (established in 1855) at Exit 195 on I-81, north of Lexington, oil on panel, 8" x 12," April 27, 2015.

Note: I-81 and I-64 (from/toward West Virginia and Kentucky) intersect 3.5 miles/5.6 kilometers south of here.

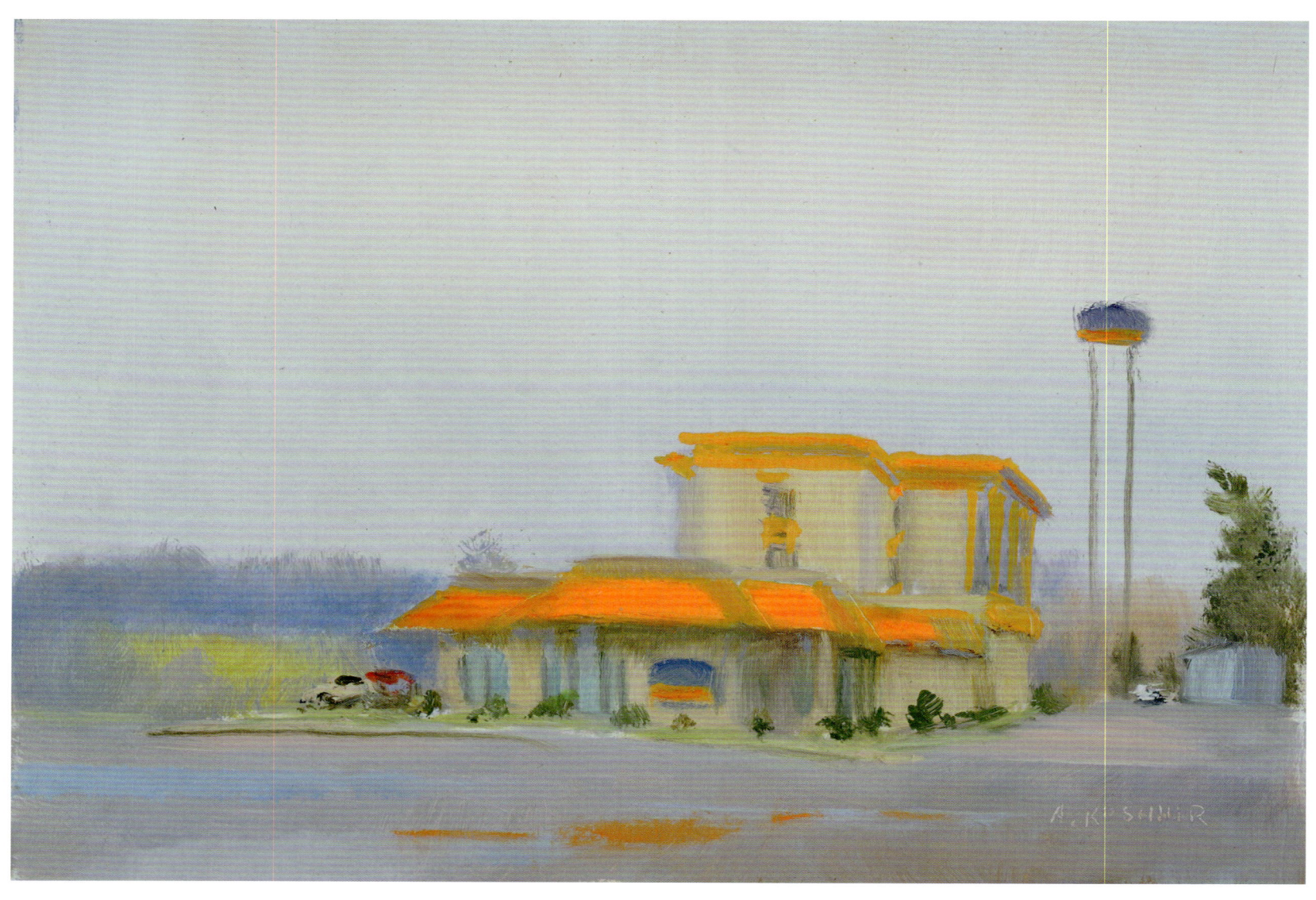

A Classic Howard Johnson Inn and Restaurant (opened in 1977) at Exit 195 on I-81, north of Lexington, oil on panel, 6" x 8," March 2, 2020.
Note: I-81 and I-64 intersect 3.5 miles/5.6 kilometers south of here.

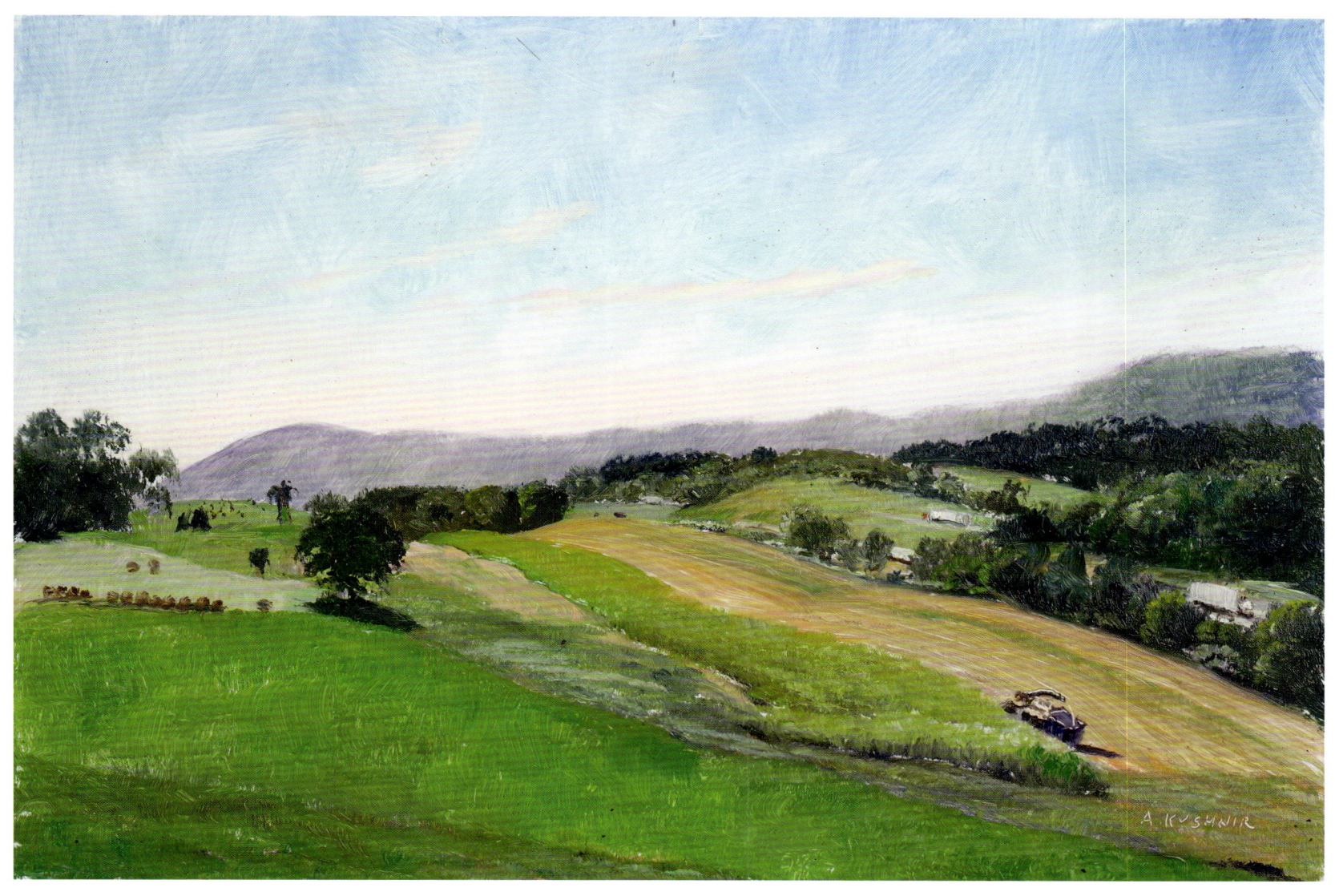

Harvesting along I-81 at Exit 180, from an old gas station, north of Natural Bridge, oil on panel, 8" x 12," September 22, 2020.

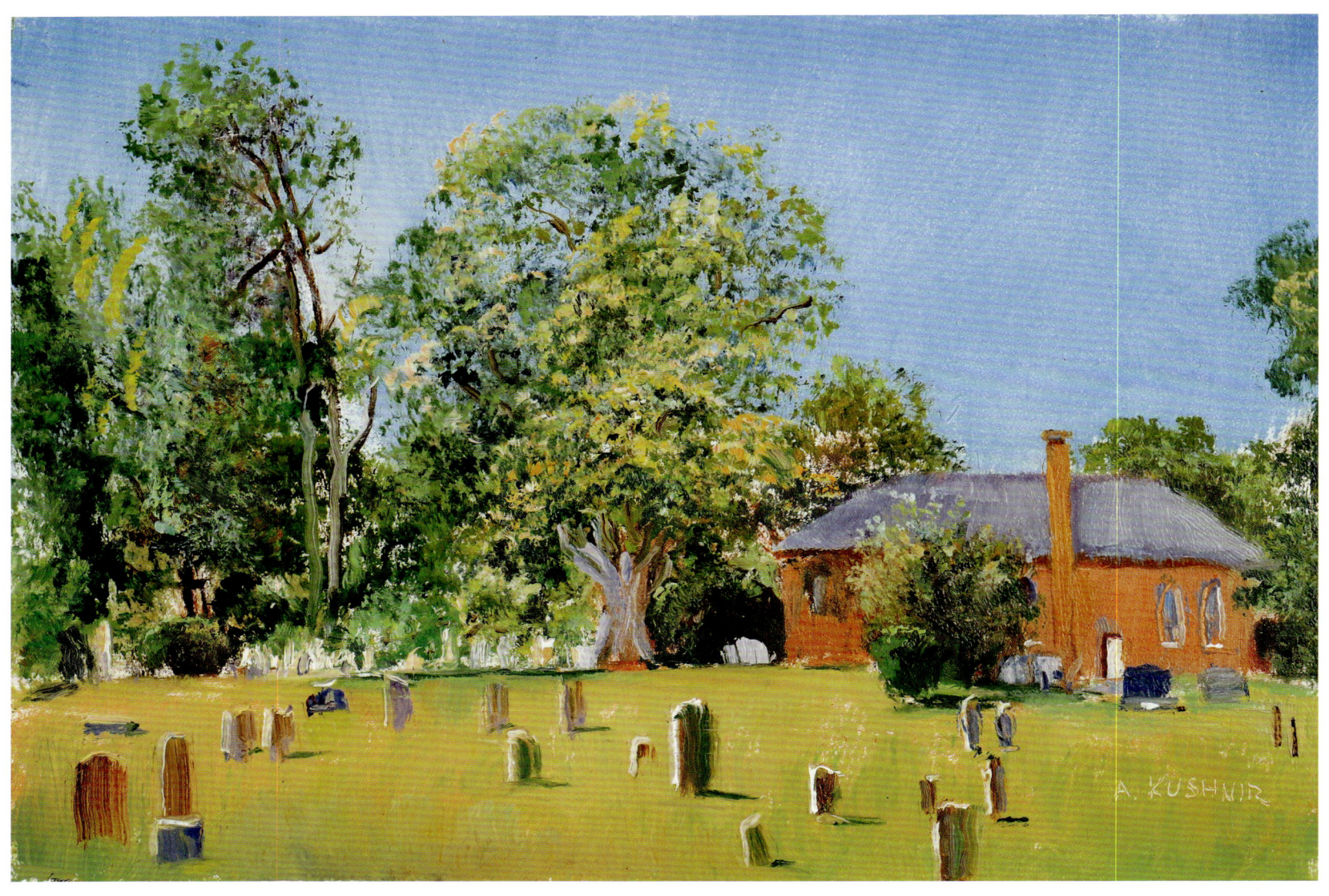

High Bridge Presbyterian Church and Cemetery (established in 1770) on VA 693 by I-81 at MM 175.3, south of Exit 175, Springfield, oil on panel, 6" x 9," September 21, 2020.

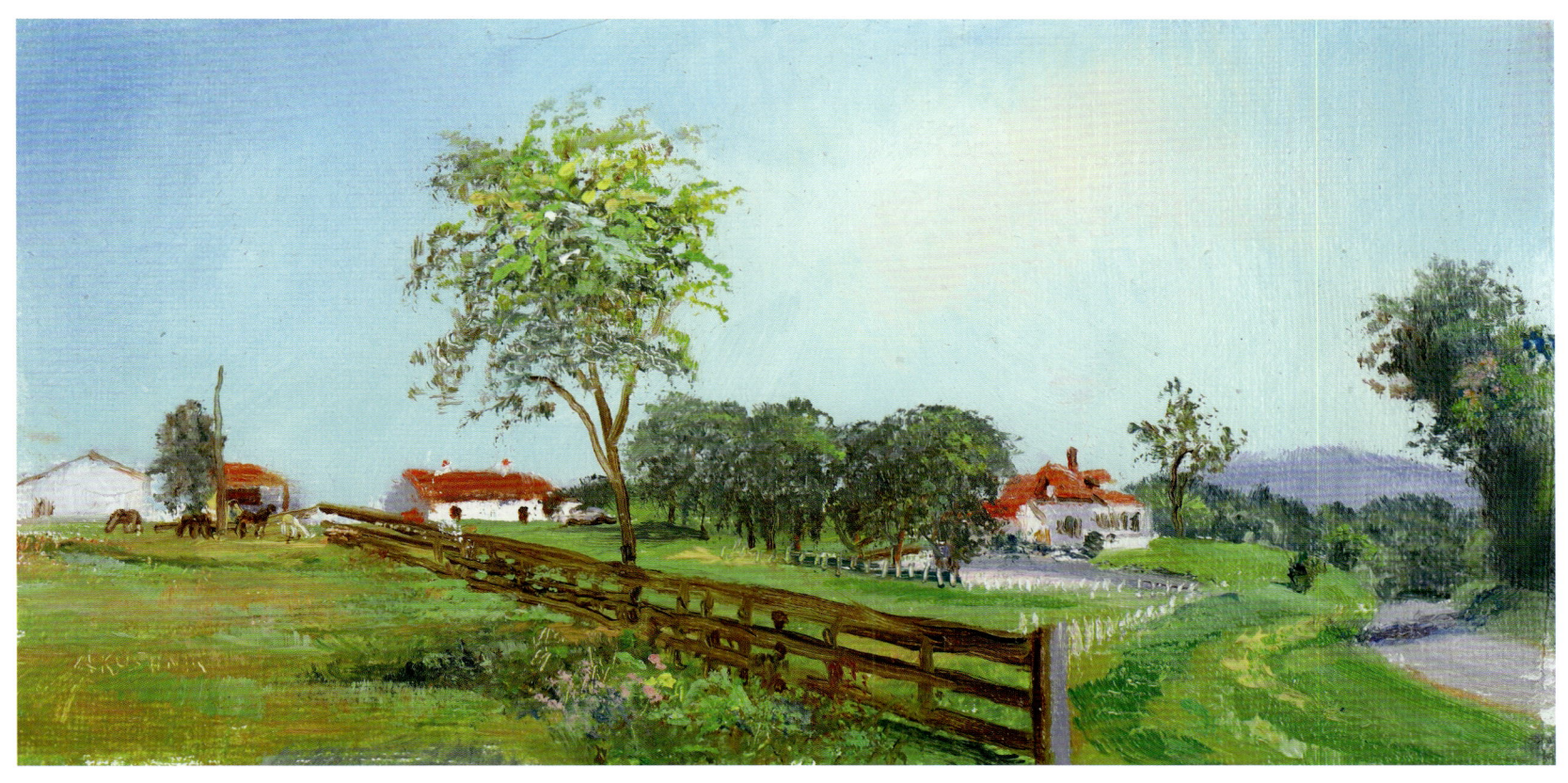

Agricultural Landscape on VA 622 along I-81 near MM 173, oil on panel, 4" x 8," September 21, 2020.

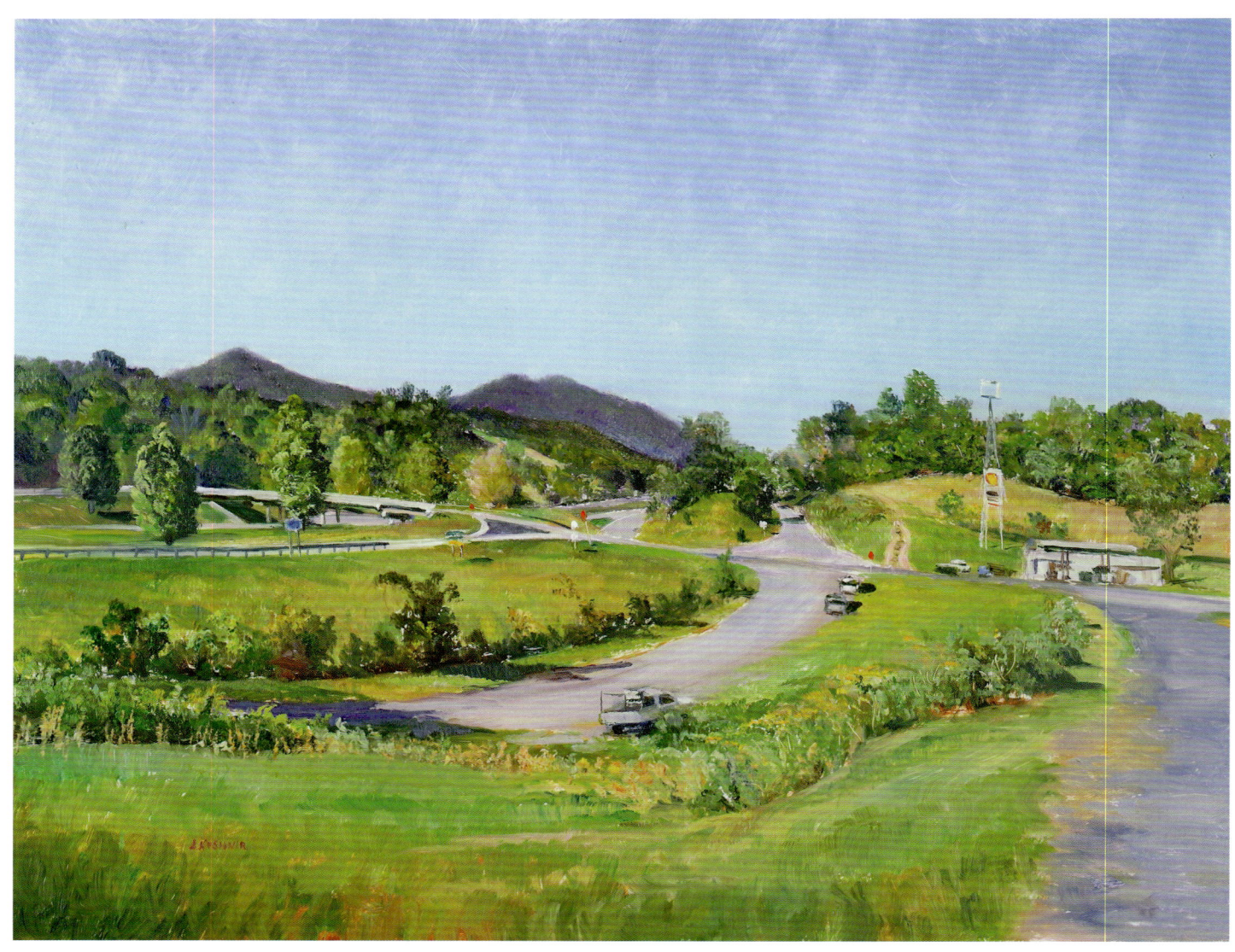

View North from the Foot of the Mountain Cafe at Exit 168, Arcadia/Buchanan, the southernmost exit on I-81 in the Shenandoah Valley, oil on panel, 18" x 24," September 22, 2020.

PORTFOLIO II: Interstate 66

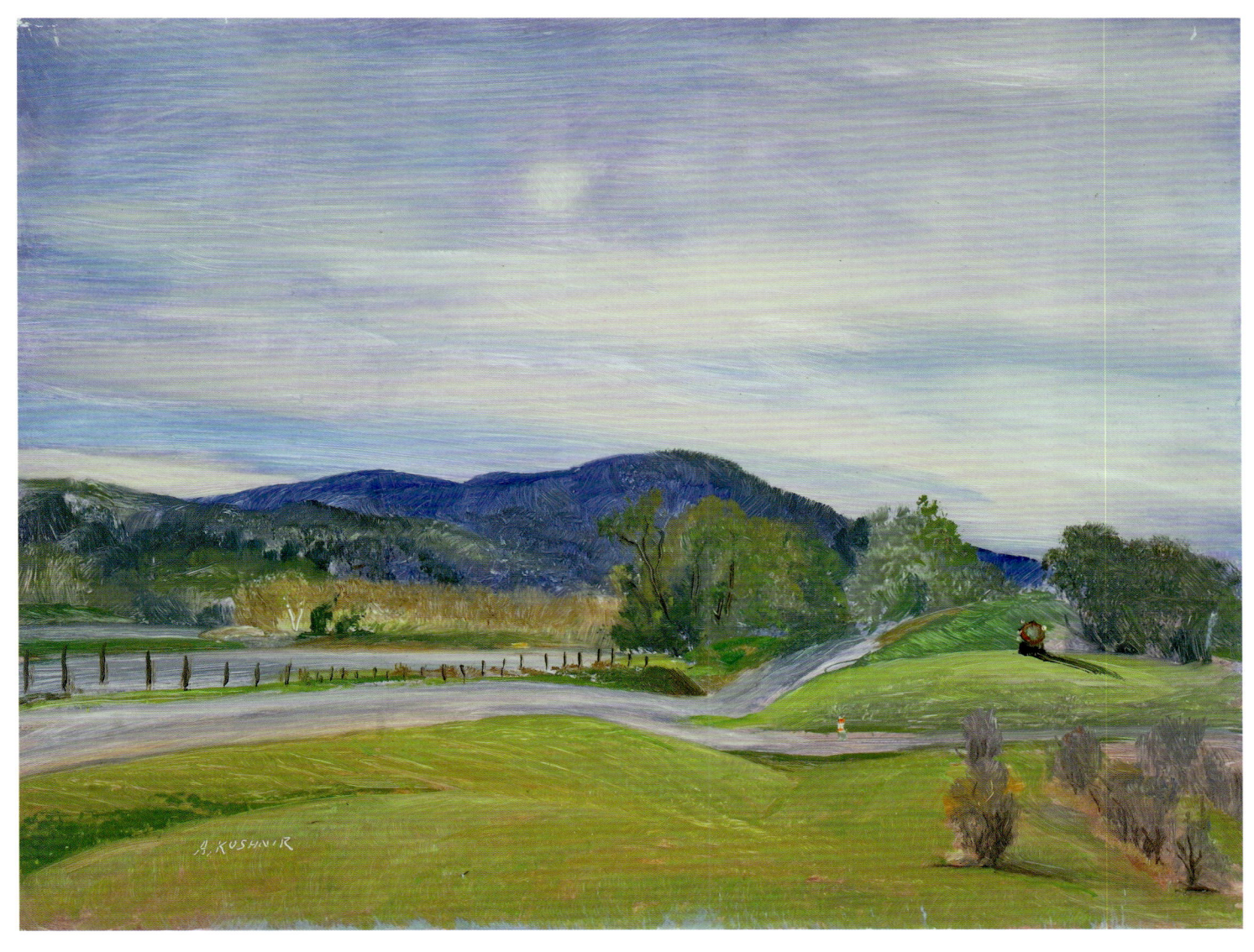

View West of Manassas Gap from Hartland Orchard near Exit 18 on I-66, Markham, oil on panel, 9" x 12," October 19, 2018.

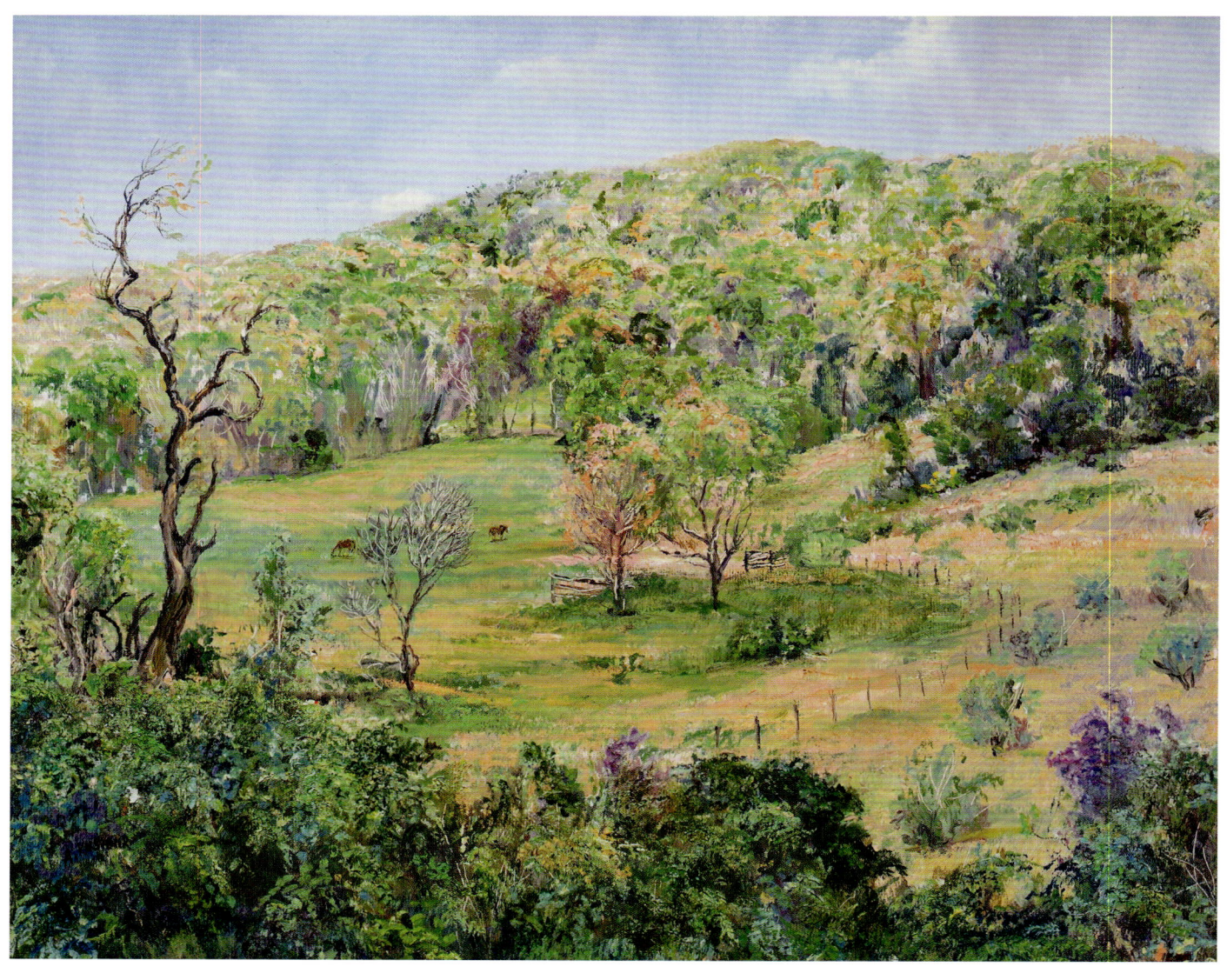

Spring Hillside near Exit 18 on I-66, Markham, oil on linen, 14" x 18," April 28, 2001.

Note: This is the first plein-air painting that Andrei Kushnir made along the Shenandoah Valley's interstates.

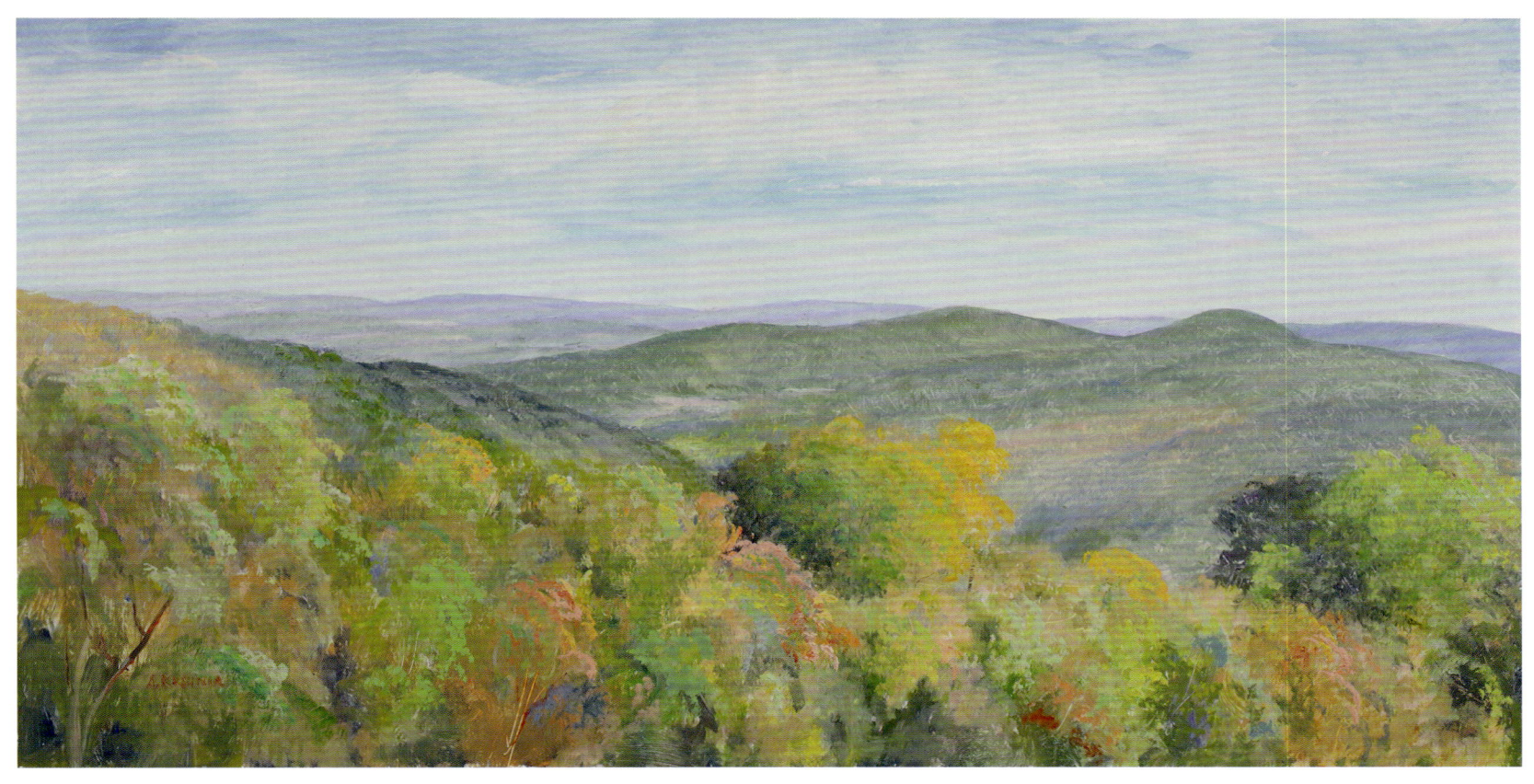

View East of Manassas Gap from St. Dominic's Monastery near Exit 13 on I-66, Linden, oil on panel, 12" x 24," October 19, 2018.

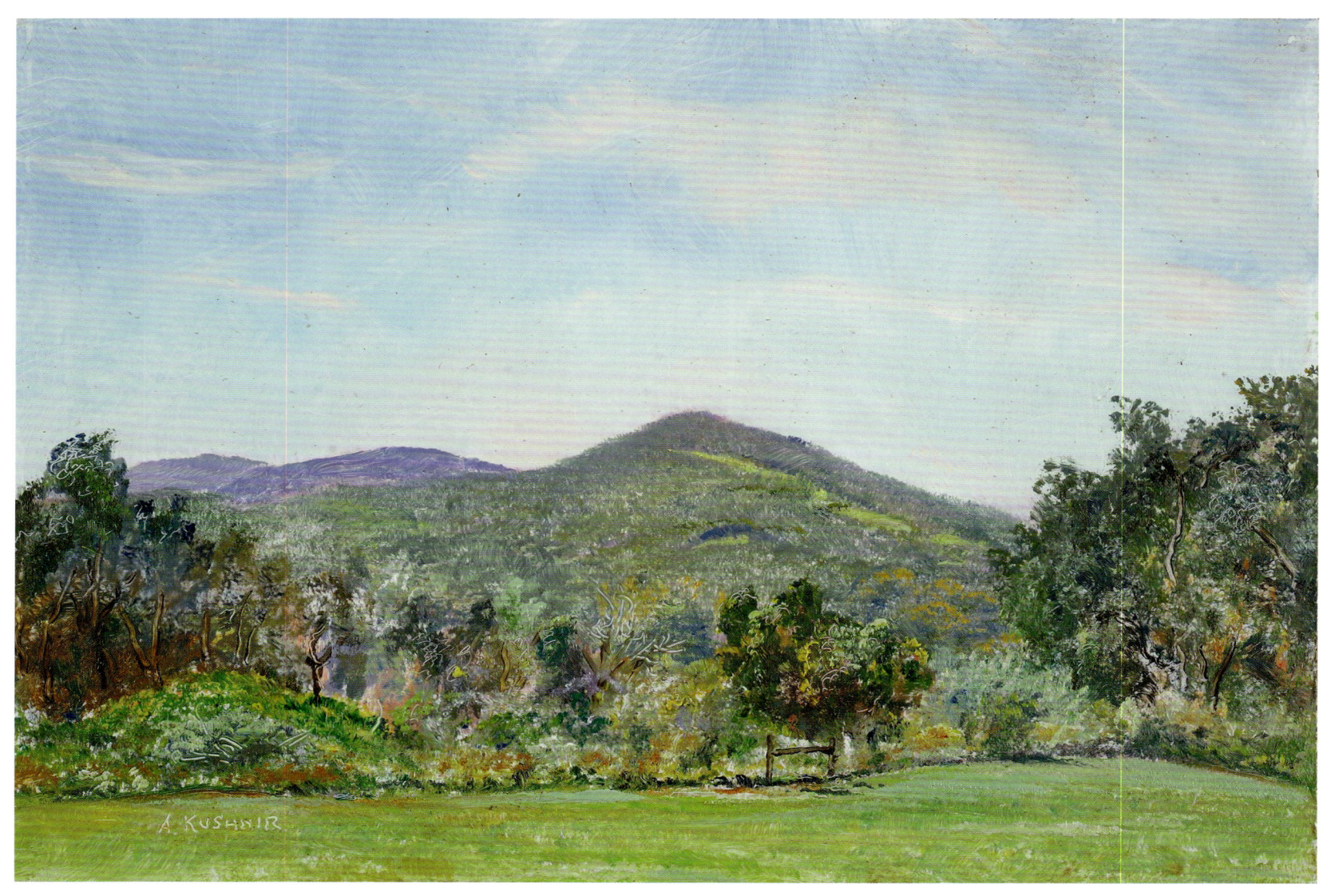

View East of Manassas Gap from Father Tranquil's Cottage at St. Dominic's Monastery near Exit 13 at I-66, Linden, oil on panel, 9" x 6," October 19, 2018.

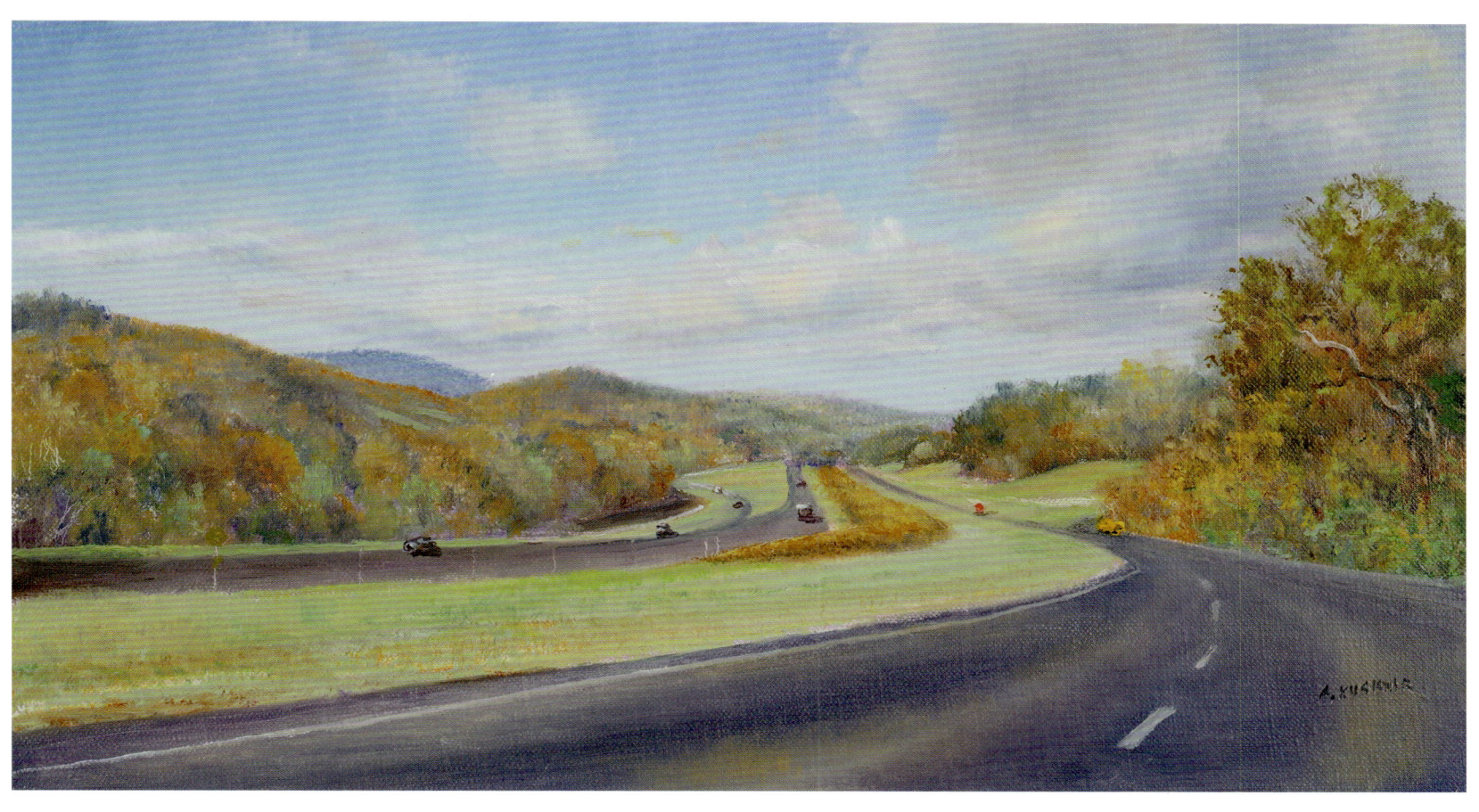

View West of the Blue Ridge Mountains, from Exit 13 on I-66, Linden, oil on panel, 7½" x 13½," October 11, 2020.

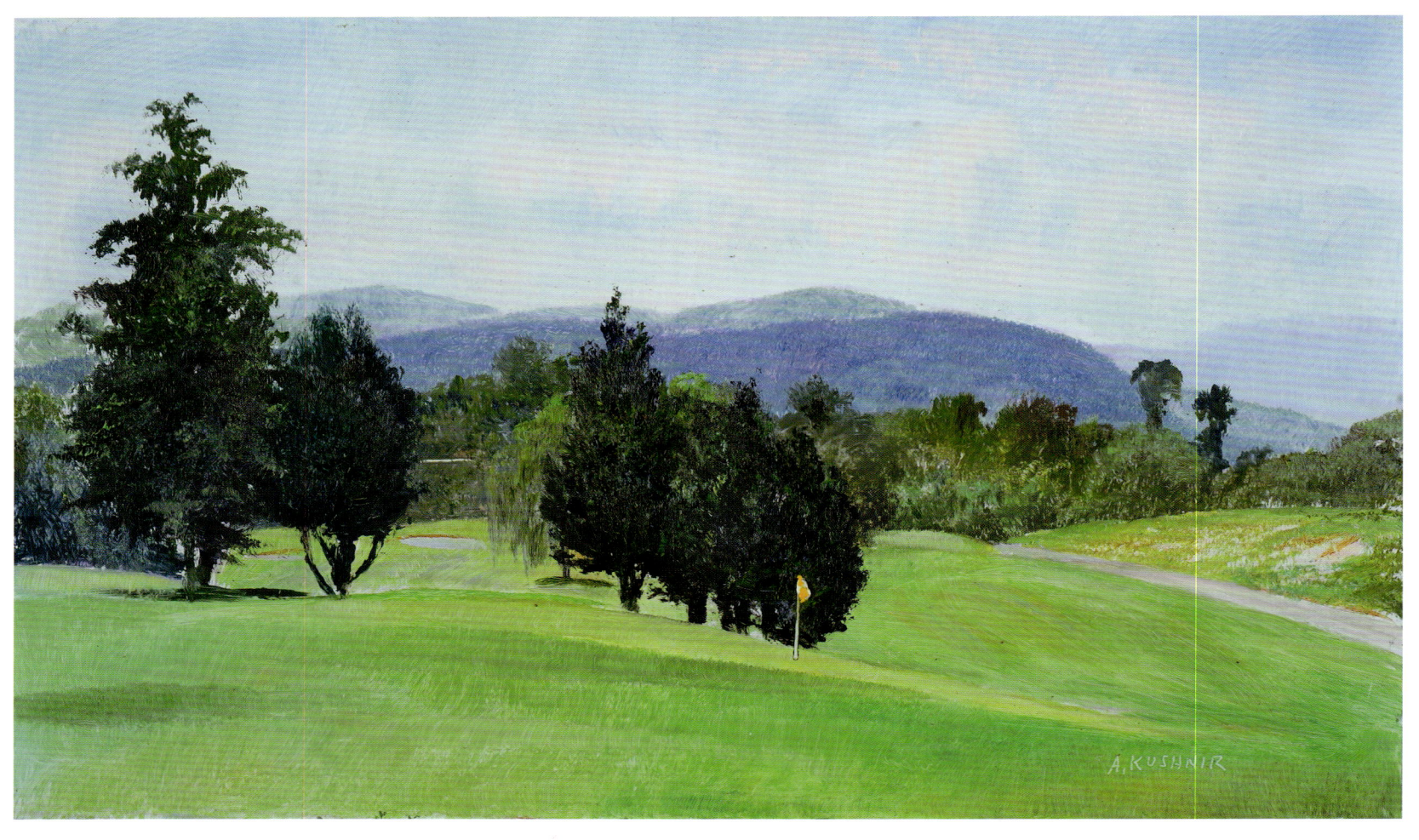

View South from the Front Royal Golf Club along the Shenandoah River at Exit 6 on I-66, Front Royal, oil on panel, 7" x 12," August 5, 2018.

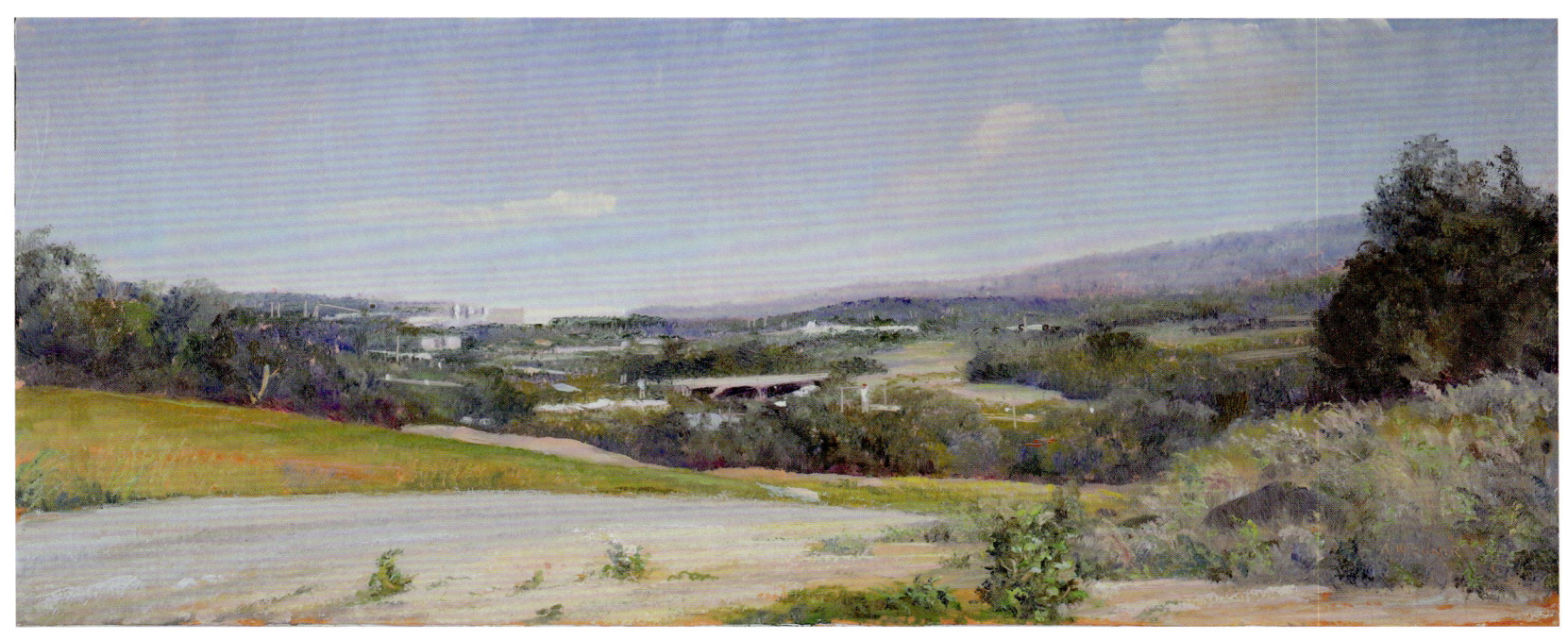

Inland Port and Riverton Commons at Exit 6 on I-66, Front Royal, oil on panel, 8½" x 21½," October 27, 2021.

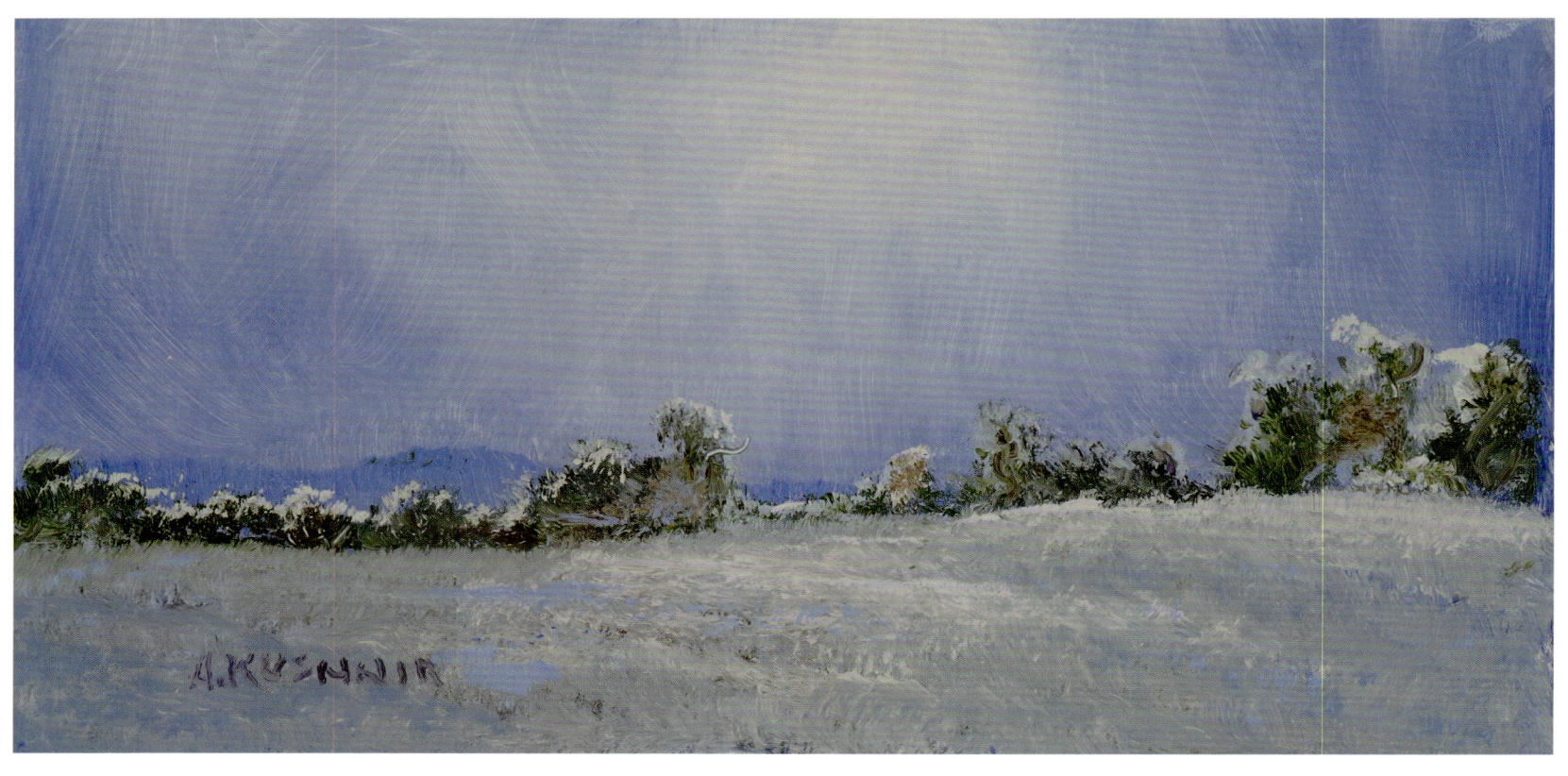

Snowy Fields, Montvue Farms, MM1 on I-66, oil on panel, 4" x 8," January 16, 2022.

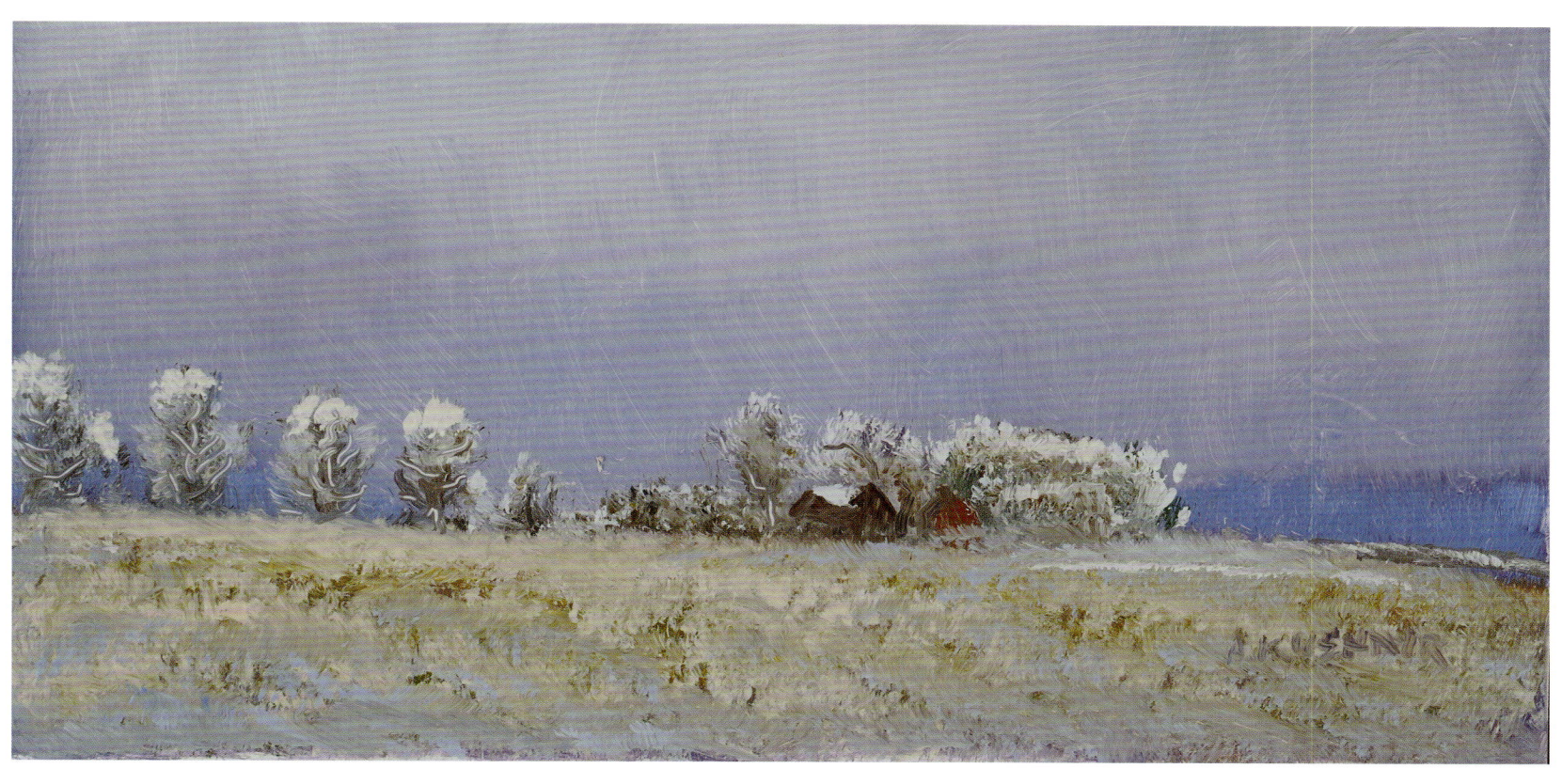

Winter in the Valley, Montvue Farms, MM1 on I-81, oil on panel, 4" x 8," January 16, 2022.

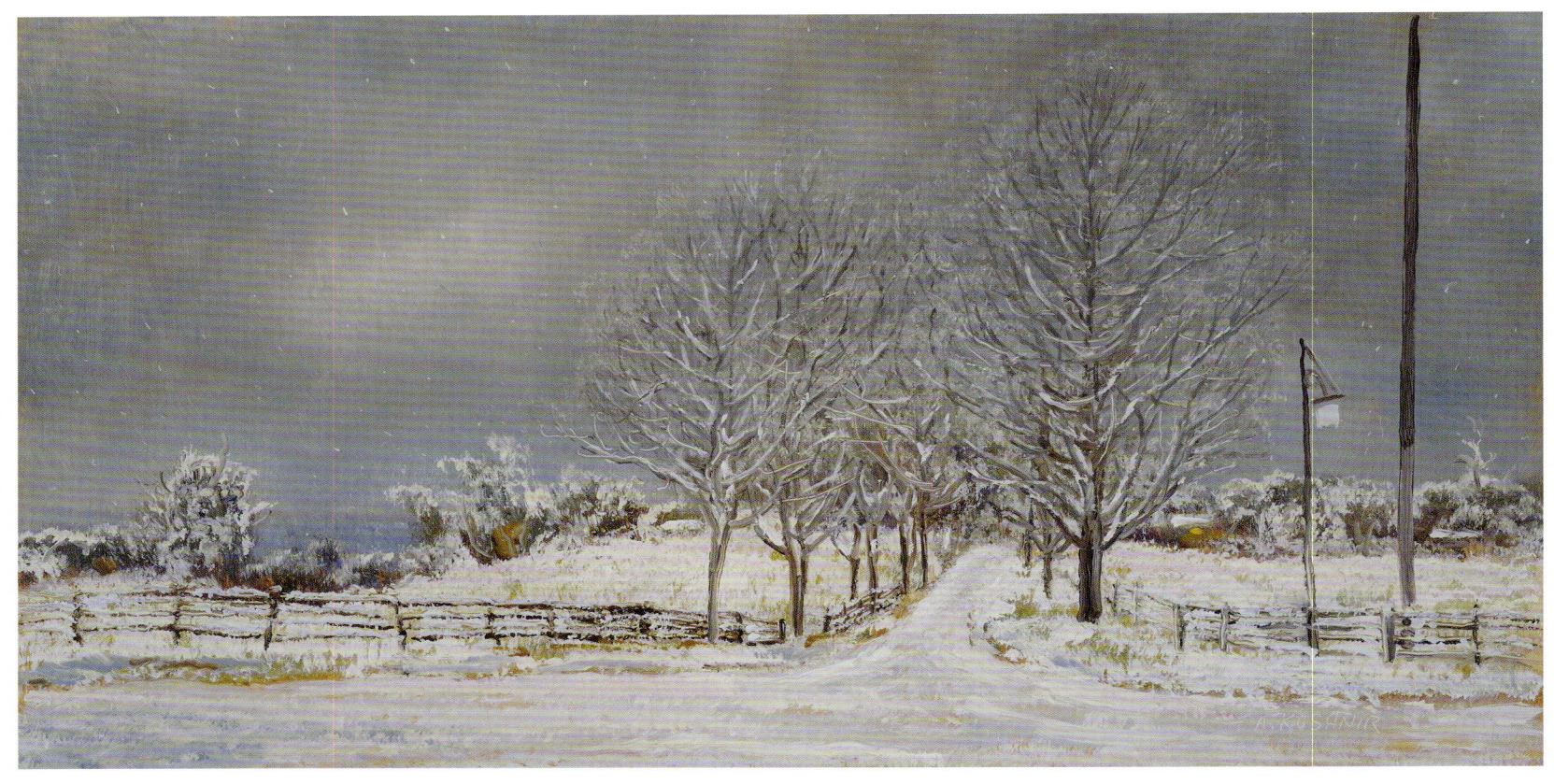

View South of a Winter Storm at Montvue Farms, MM1 on I-66, oil on panel, 8" x 16," January 16, 2022.

Note: I-66 intersects with (and terminates at) I-81 one mile east of here.

PORTFOLIO III: Interstate 64

Note to the traveler:

All paintings in *Portfolio III* follow I-64 West, from pages 99 to page 107. For those who are driving I-64 East, your visual journey begins on page 107 and ends on page 99. Note that I-64 joins I-81 (for some 31 miles/50 kilometers) from Staunton (pages 68–72) in the north to Lexington (pages 79–80) in the south.

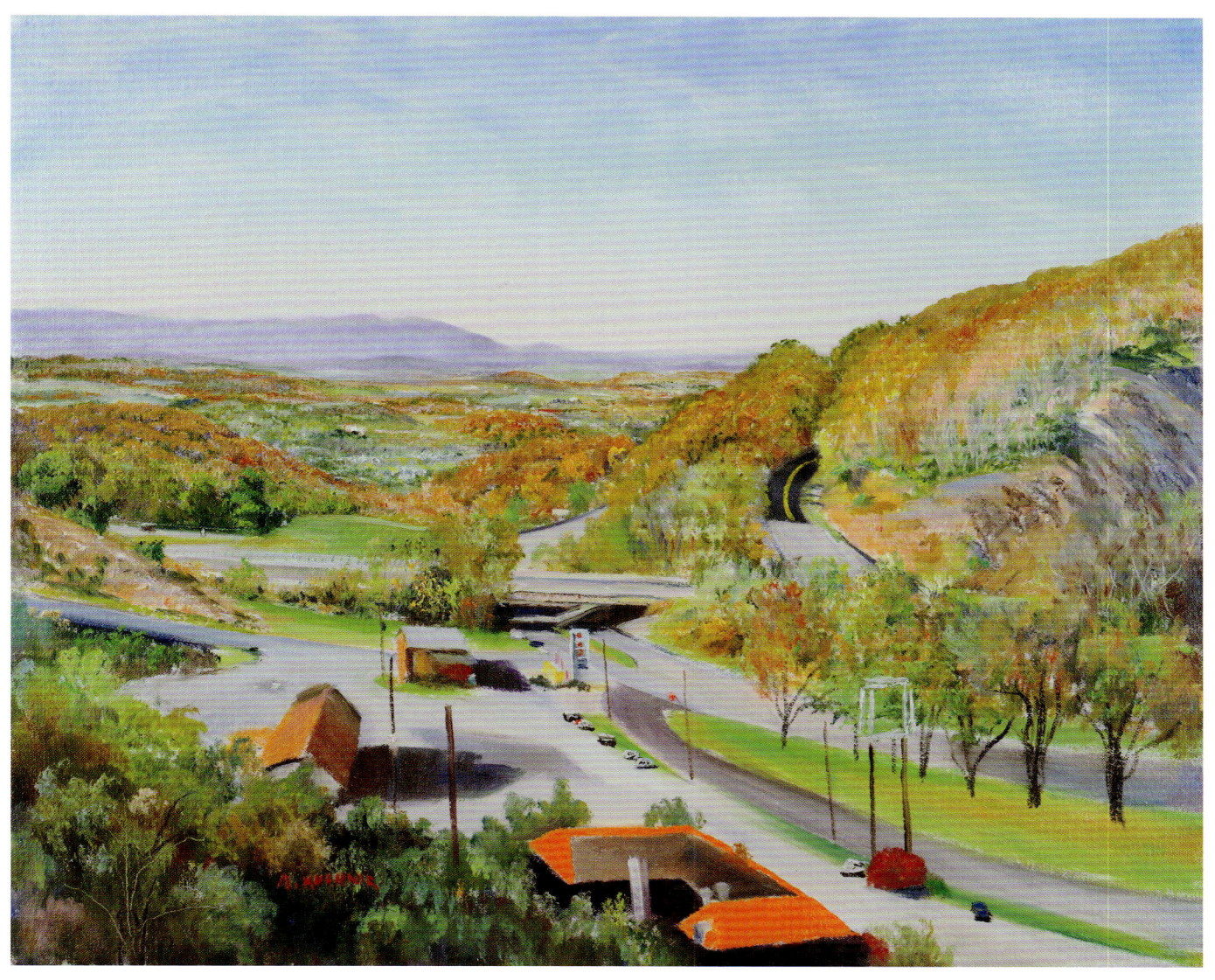

View West of the Shenandoah Valley from Afton Mountain at Exit 99, where I-64 intersects with U.S. 250, the Skyline Drive (upper right), and Blue Ridge Parkway (lower right, not pictured), oil on canvas, 16" x 20," October 28, 2019.

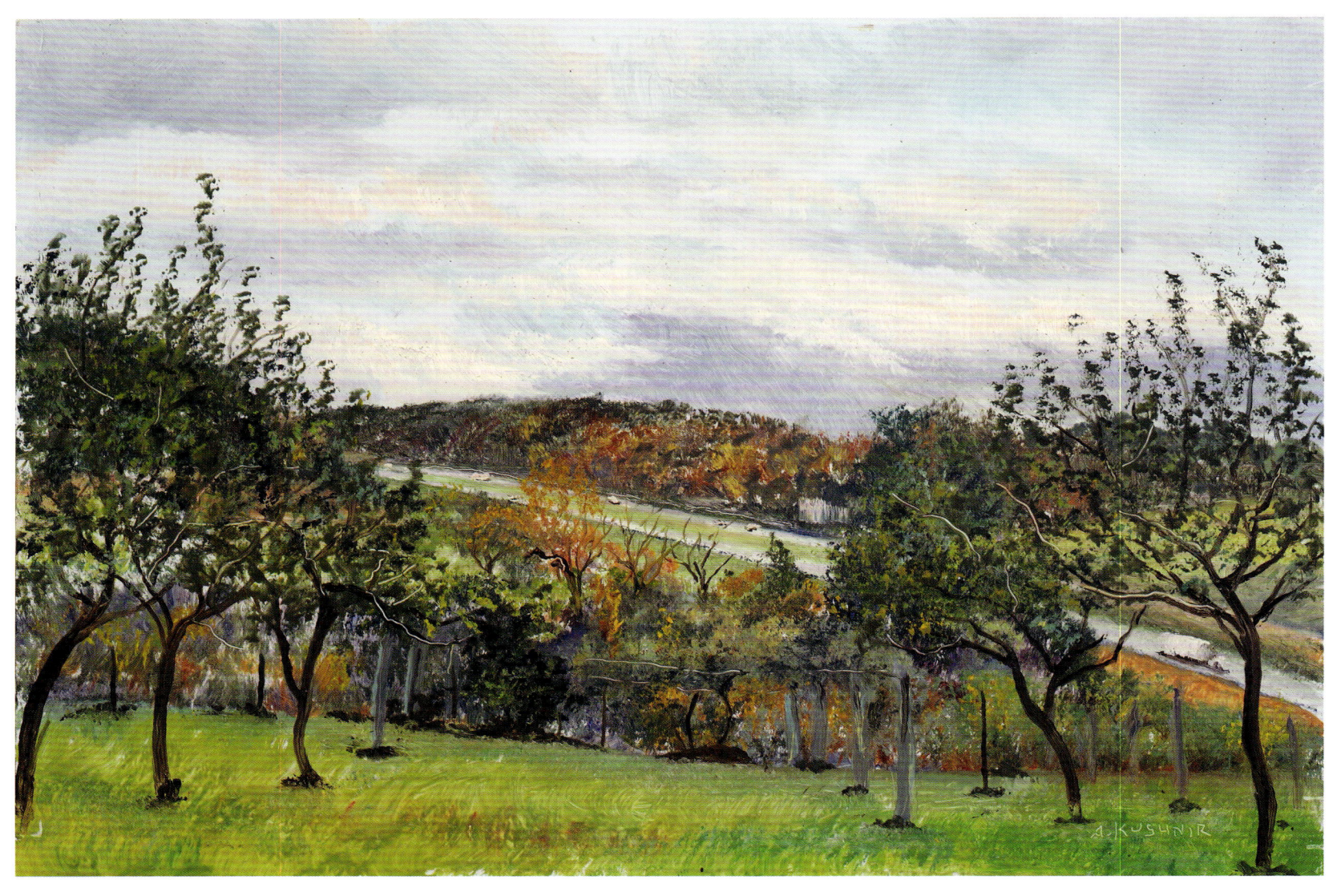

The Orchard at the Christian History Society of America I, looking east at I-64 from Exit 91, Fishersville, oil on panel, 8" x 12," October 29, 2019.

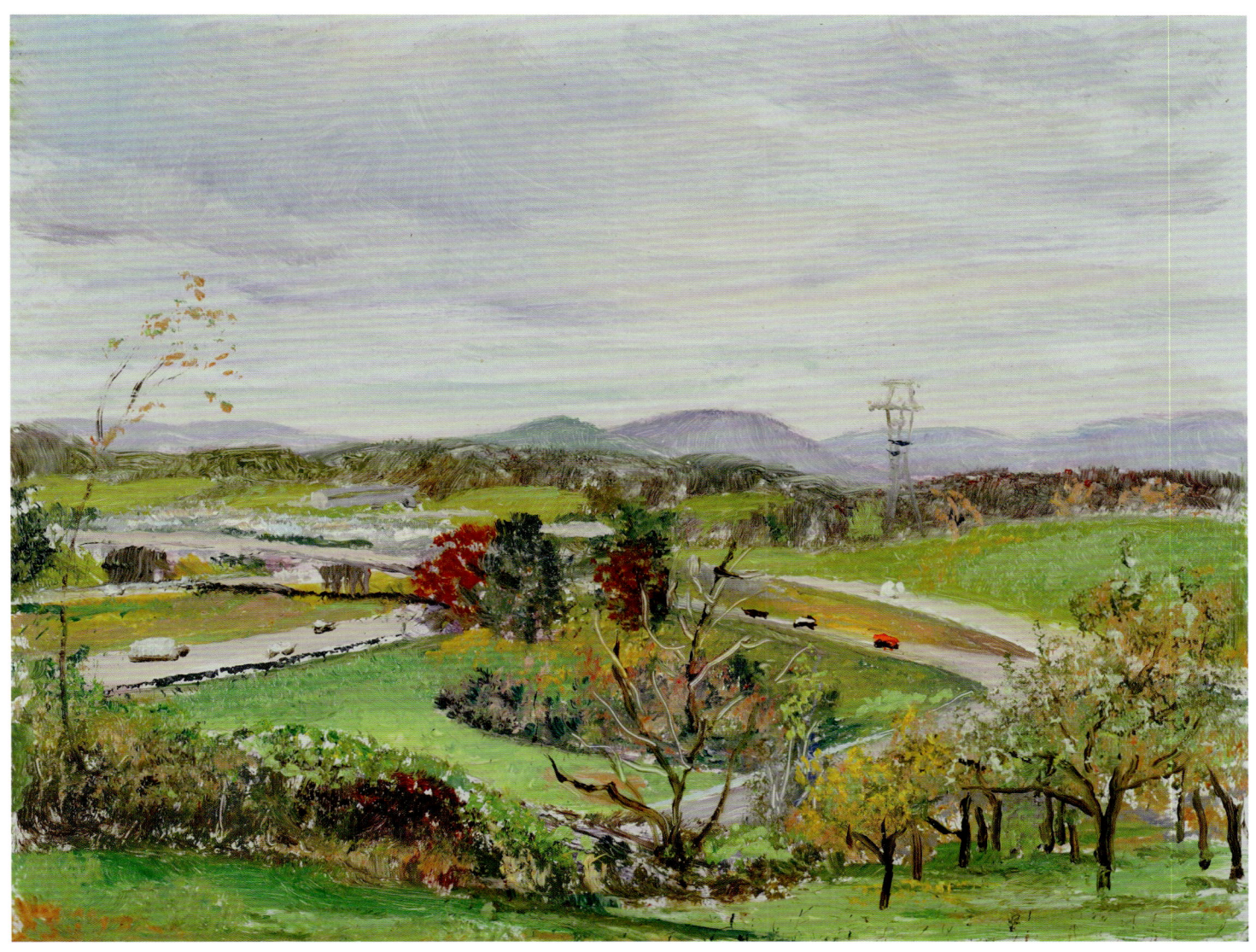

The Orchard at the Christian History Society of America II, looking west at I-64 from Exit 91, Fishersville, oil on panel, 6" x 8," October 29, 2019. Note: I-64 joins I-81 (for some 31 miles/50 kilometers) from Staunton (pages 68–72) in the north to Lexington (pages 79–80) in the south, where I-64 continues west toward West Virginia and Kentucky.

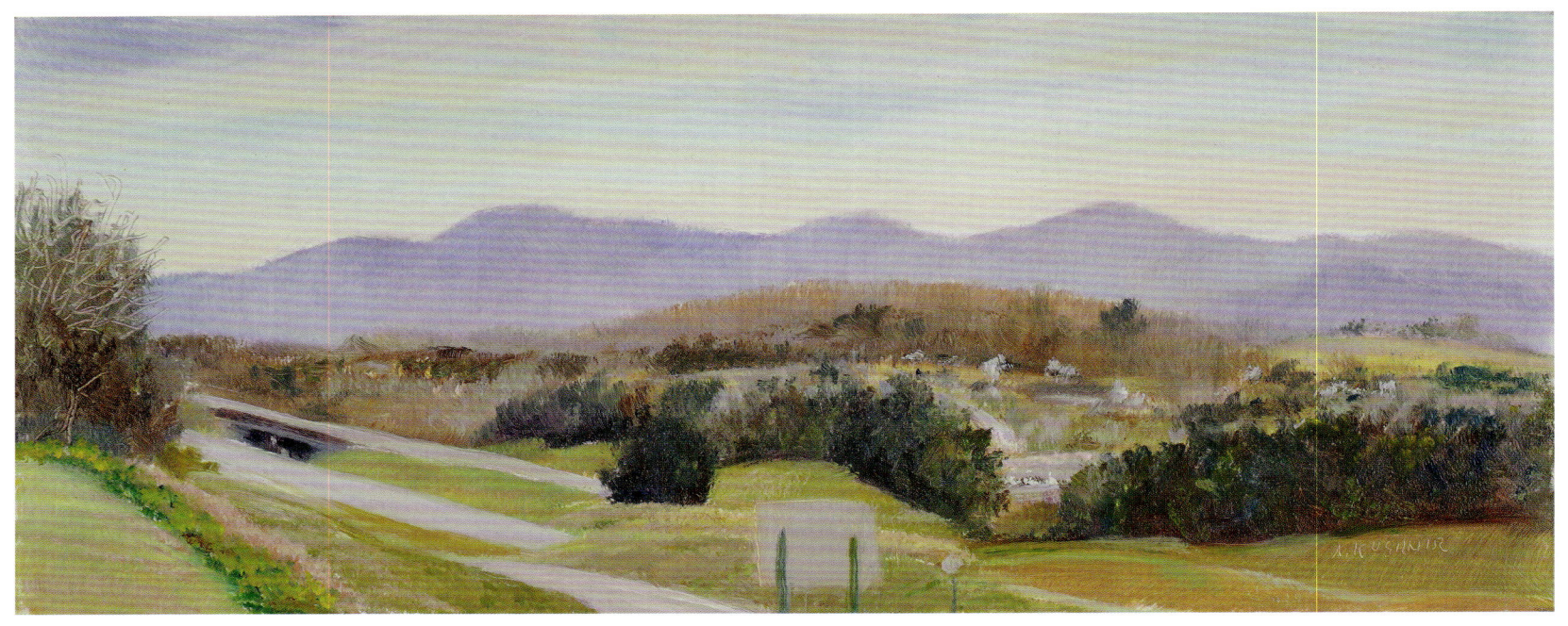

View East from U.S. 11 at Exit 55 on I-64, Lexington, oil on panel, 4¾" x 12," March 2, 2020.

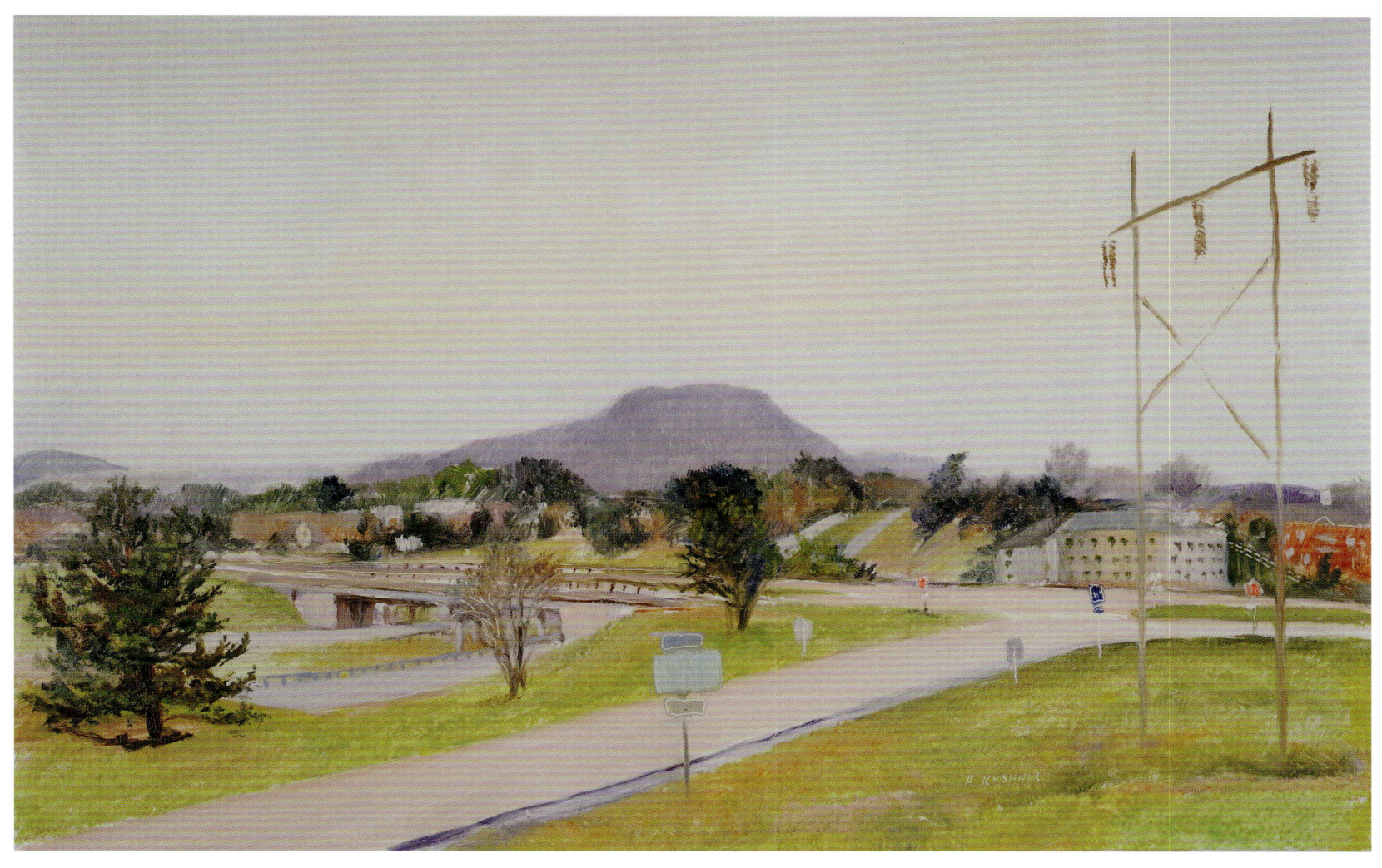

View West of Brushy Hill from U.S. 11 at Exit 55 on I-64, Lexington, oil on panel, 10" x 16," March 2, 2020.

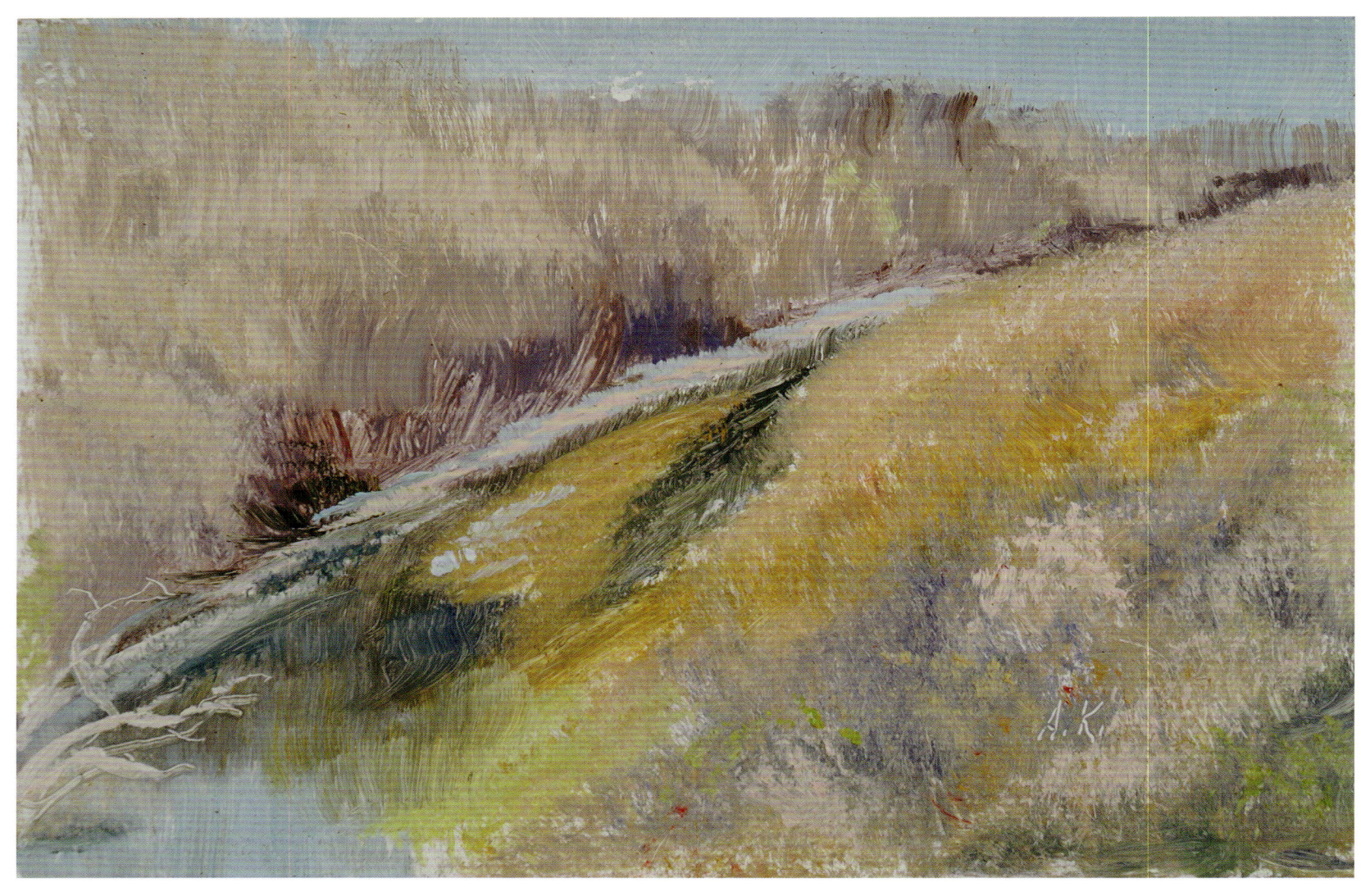

View South of the Maury River from the I-64 West Bridge, MM 54.4 near Exit 55, Lexington, oil on panel, 4" x 6," March 1, 2020.

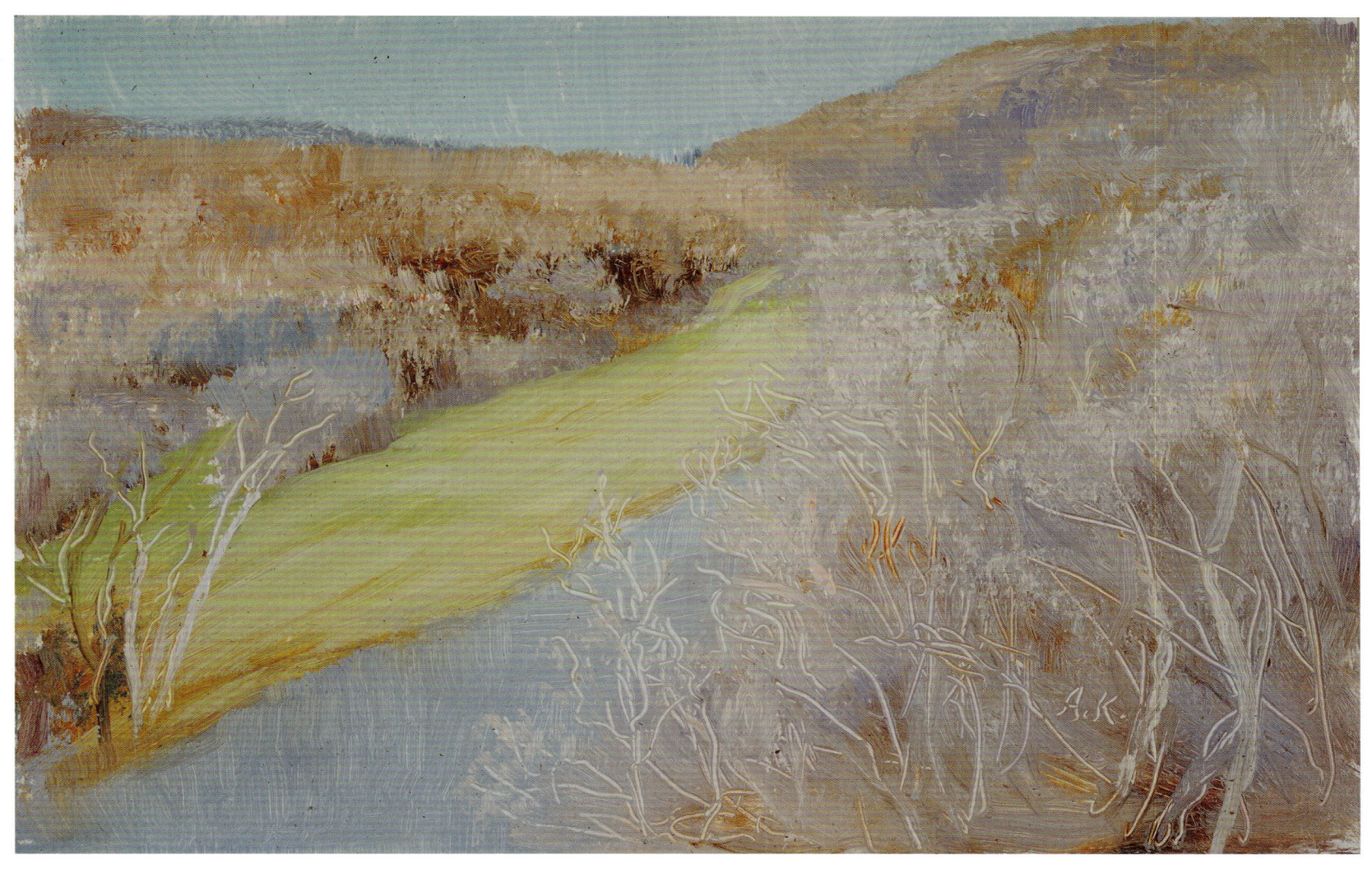

View North of the Maury River from the I-64 West Bridge, MM 54.4 near Exit 55, Lexington, oil on panel, 4" x 6," March 1, 2020.

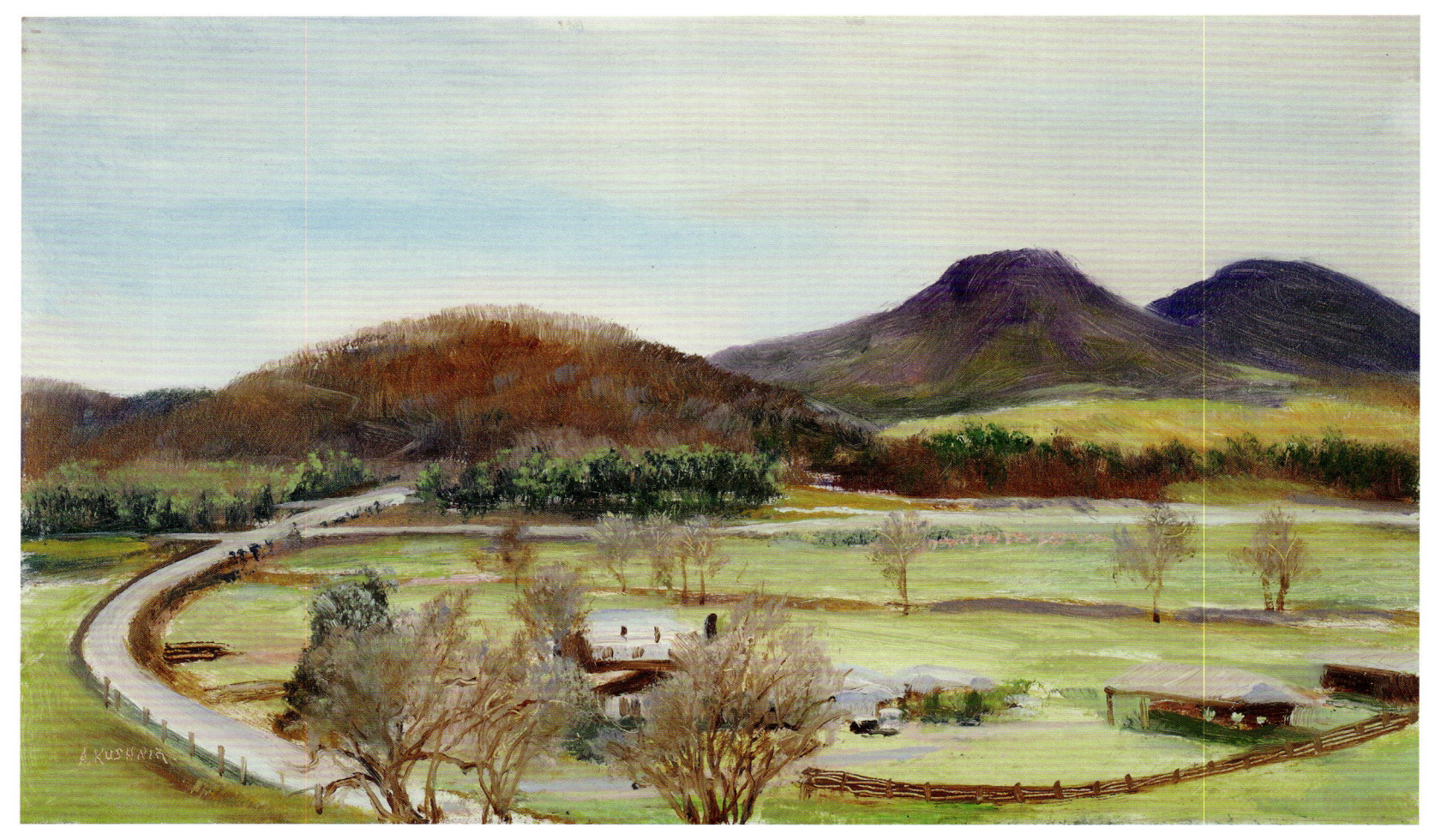

View South of Environs Around Big Spring Farm and Hogback Mountain, I-64 at Exit 50, oil on panel, 7" x 12," March 1, 2020.

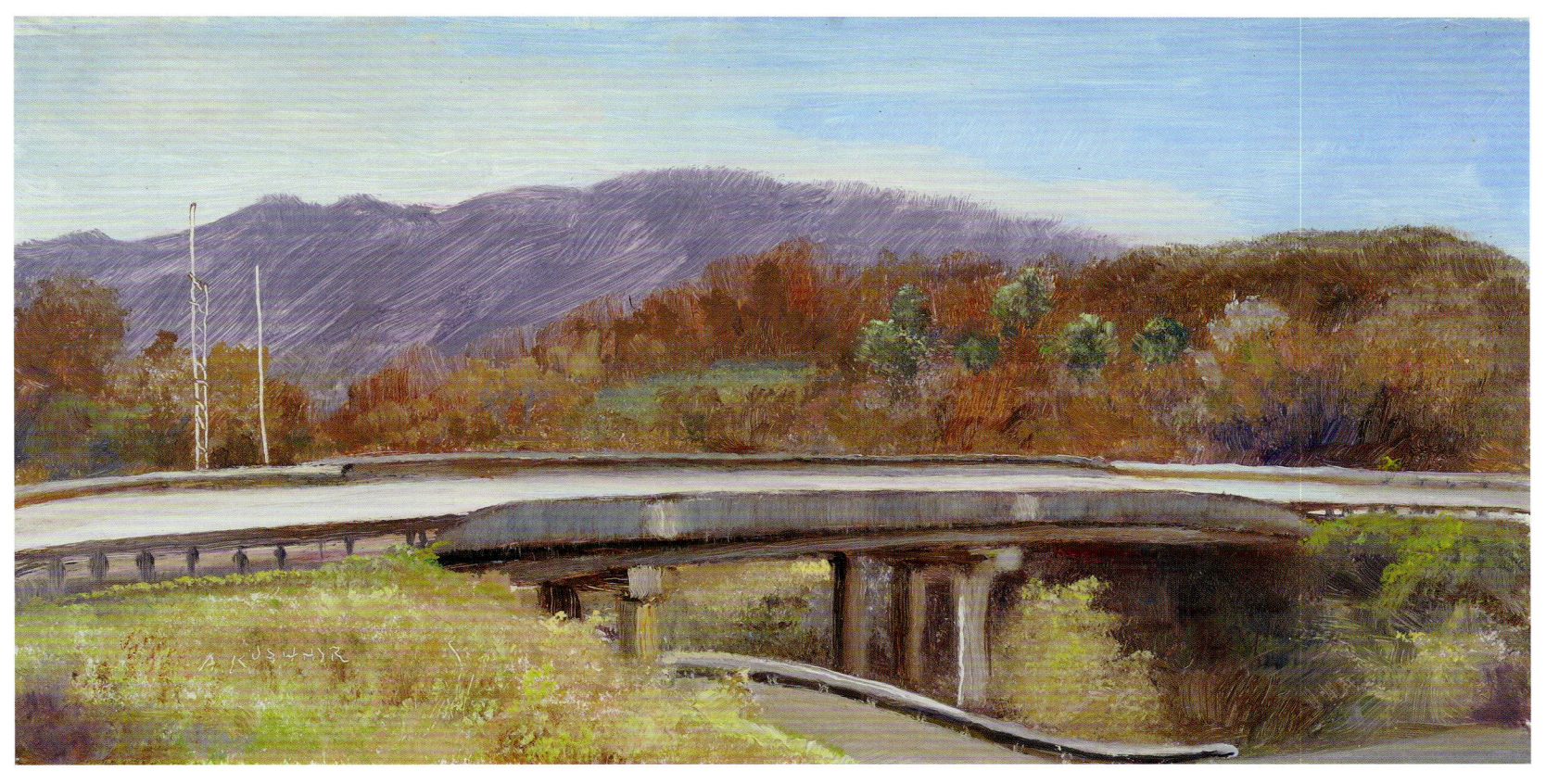

View South of I-64 and Environs from VA 629, west of Exit 50 on I–64, oil on panel, 6" x 12," March 1, 2020.

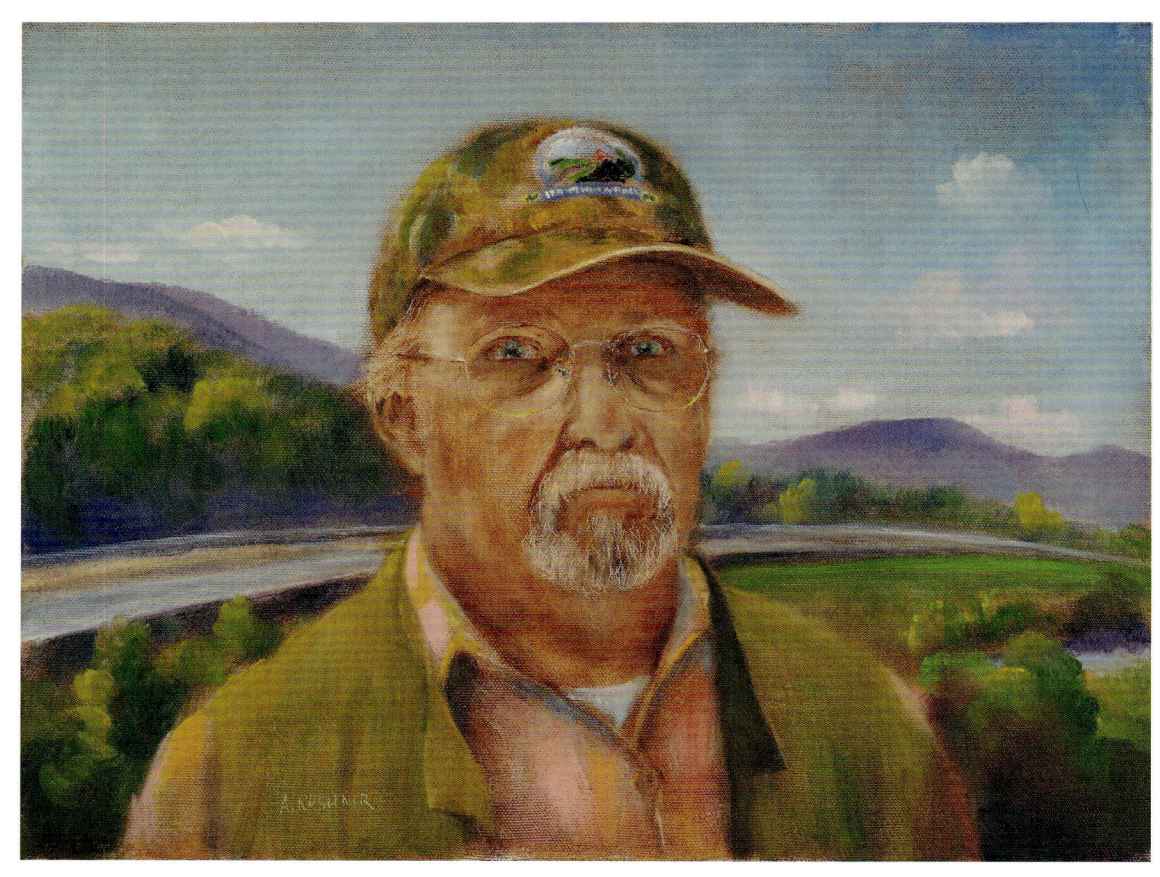

Self-Portrait, oil on canvas, 12" x 16," May 2022.

Acknowledgments

I express my sincere thanks and deep gratitude to George F. Thompson, my publisher, for his vision for and development of this project. Also my heartfelt appreciation to Mikki Soroczak, George's assistant, for the many editorial challenges faced and accomplishments achieved; to David Skolkin, for his amazing book design on this and my previous book, *Oh, Shenandoah*; and to Morgan Pfaelzer, for her maps. The GFT Publishing team made this book possible, from its inception to its current content and gorgeous presentation.

In his introduction, historian Warren Hofstra, aside from making me blush, endows the reader with a most accurate understanding of my artistic goals and the particular concepts and categories of the art world within which my work might fit. His deep understanding of Virginia's history and the place and importance of the interstate highways that run though the Shenandoah Valley makes a boon companion to the paintings.

I also convey my appreciation to both Warren and George, for traveling with me on those road trips in search of appropriate—and safe—sites to limn. And special thanks to photographer Gregory R. Staley, whose talent and expertise has captured the essence of my painted creations.

Very importantly, I acknowledge the friendship and patronage of particular champions of my artistic efforts, whose encouragement and faith in me has been fortifying and empowering: Carl J. Arbes, Esquire, Tacey Battley, Alain J. Cohen, Hall and Betsy Johnstone, Linda Ksansnak, John and Linda Sillin, Michele Martin Taylor, Dr. William N. and Ms. Laura Ellen Wade, and Betty Williams.

My last note of appreciation goes to my family, who stuck by this itinerant artist through thick and thin: my beloved wife, Raissa, our intrepid children, Basil and Larissa, and my loyal brothers, Anatolij and Walter.

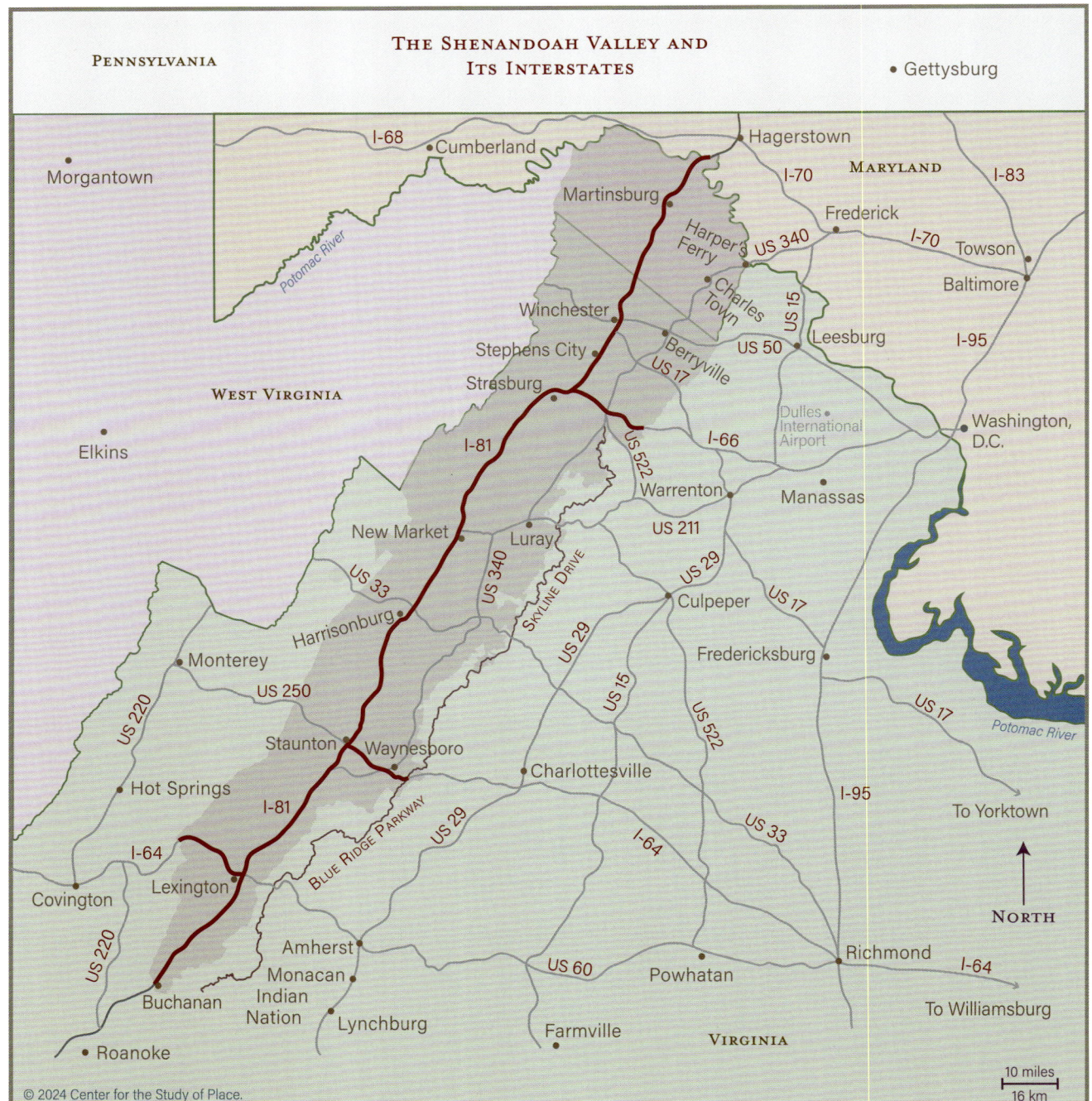

A Portfolio of Maps

by Morgan Pfaelzer

110

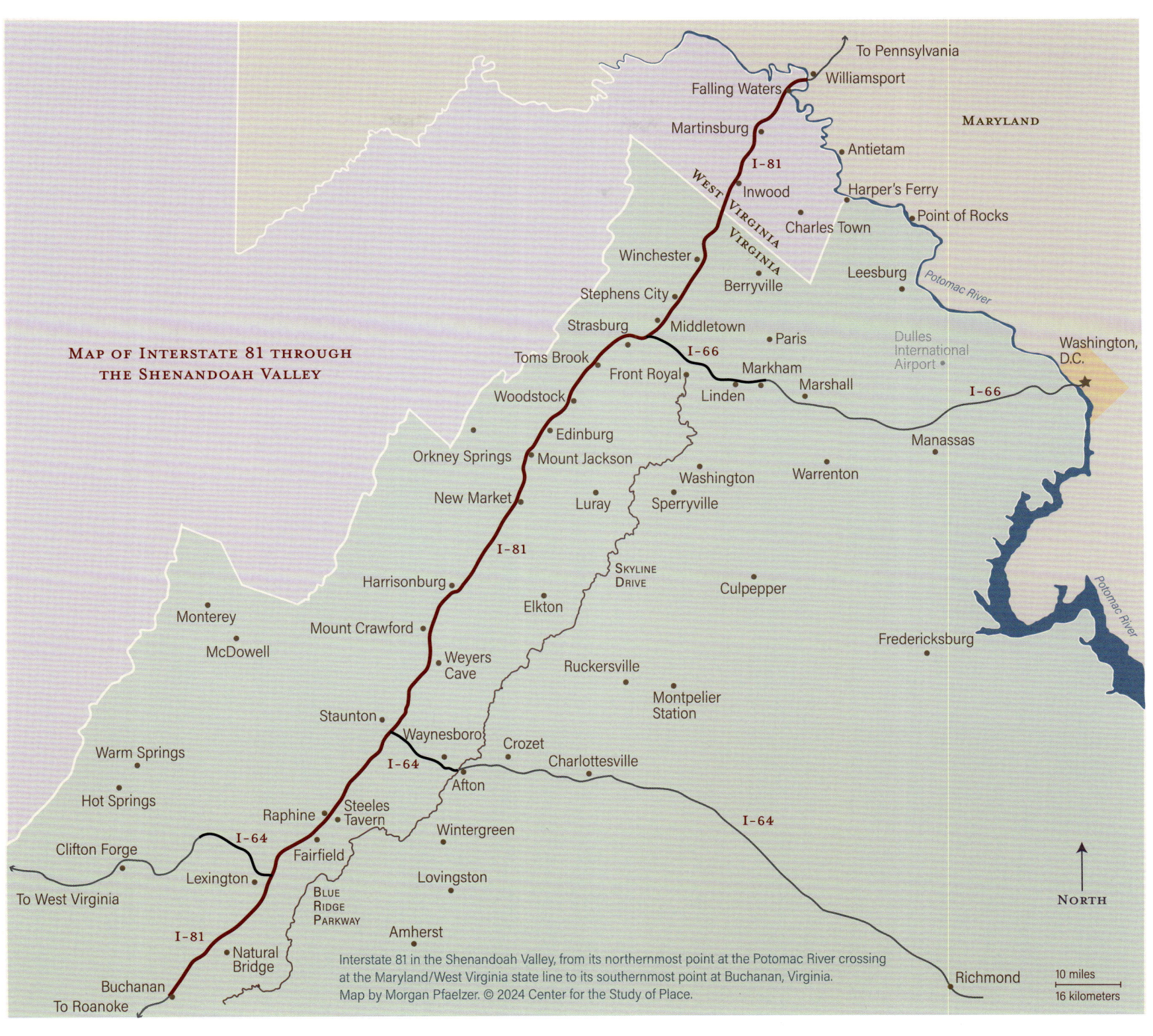

MAP OF INTERSTATE 81 THROUGH THE SHENANDOAH VALLEY

To Pennsylvania

Williamsport

MARYLAND

Falling Waters

Martinsburg

I-81

WEST VIRGINIA

Inwood

Antietam

Harper's Ferry

Charles Town

Point of Rocks

VIRGINIA

Winchester

Leesburg

Potomac River

Stephens City

Berryville

Strasburg

Middletown

Paris

Dulles International Airport

Washington, D.C.

I-66

Markham

Toms Brook

Front Royal

Linden

Marshall

I-66

Woodstock

Edinburg

Orkney Springs

Mount Jackson

Washington

Warrenton

New Market

Luray

Sperryville

Manassas

I-81

SKYLINE DRIVE

Culpepper

Harrisonburg

Elkton

Mount Crawford

Fredericksburg

Weyers Cave

Ruckersville

Staunton

Montpelier Station

Waynesboro

Crozet

Warm Springs

I-64

Charlottesville

Afton

Hot Springs

Raphine

Steeles Tavern

Wintergreen

I-64

Clifton Forge

I-64

Fairfield

NORTH

To West Virginia

Lexington

Lovingston

BLUE RIDGE PARKWAY

I-81

Amherst

Richmond

Natural Bridge

Buchanan

10 miles

To Roanoke

Interstate 81 in the Shenandoah Valley, from its northernmost point at the Potomac River crossing at the Maryland/West Virginia state line to its southernmost point at Buchanan, Virginia.
Map by Morgan Pfaelzer. © 2024 Center for the Study of Place.

16 kilometers

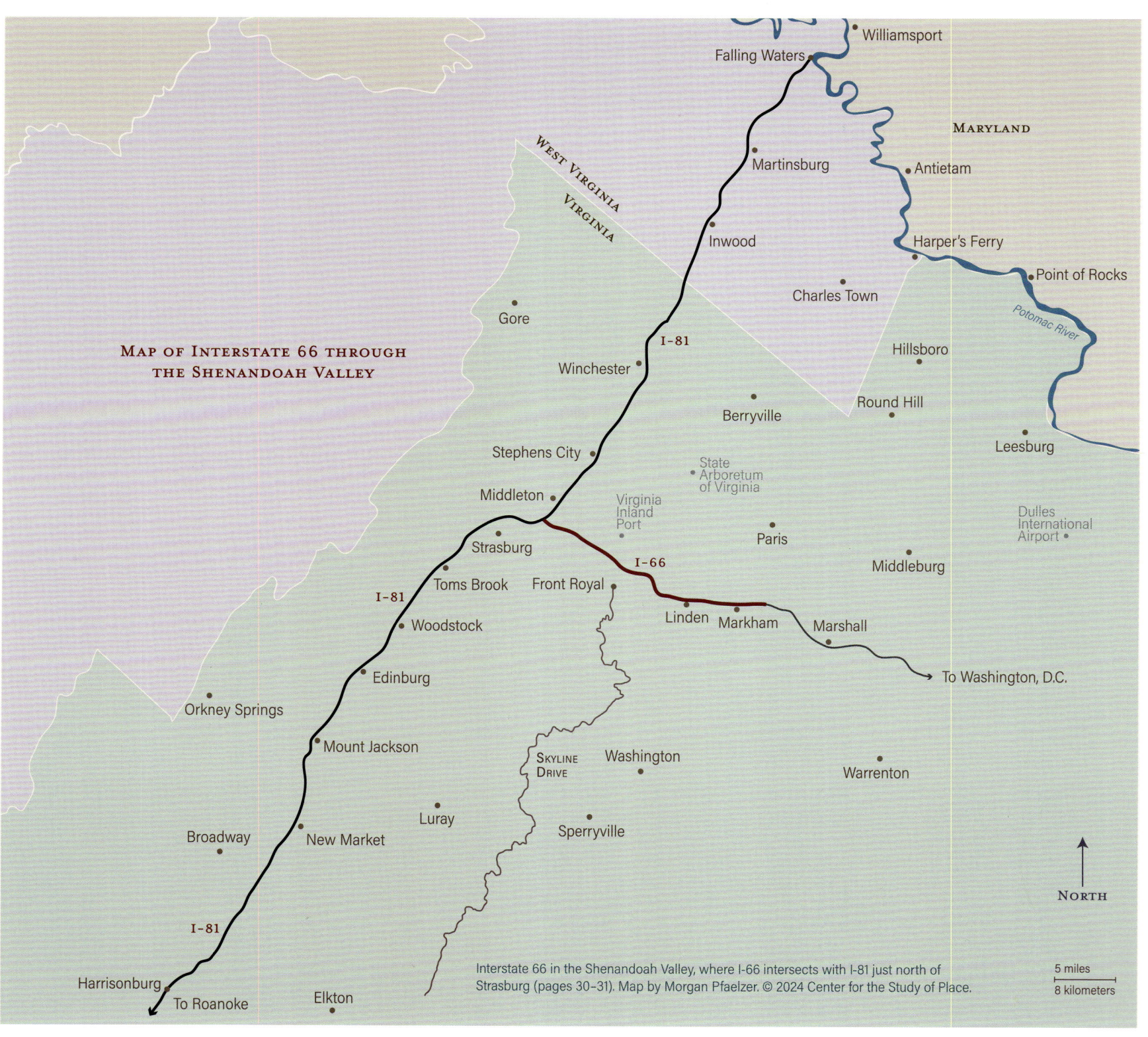

MAP OF INTERSTATE 66 THROUGH
THE SHENANDOAH VALLEY

MARYLAND

WEST VIRGINIA

VIRGINIA

Williamsport

Falling Waters

Martinsburg

Antietam

Inwood

Harper's Ferry

Point of Rocks

Charles Town

Potomac River

Gore

Hillsboro

I-81

Winchester

Round Hill

Berryville

Leesburg

Stephens City

State
Arboretum
of Virginia

Middleton

Virginia
Inland
Port

Dulles
International
Airport

Strasburg

Paris

I-66

Middleburg

Toms Brook

Front Royal

Linden Markham

Marshall

I-81

Woodstock

To Washington, D.C.

Edinburg

Orkney Springs

Mount Jackson

SKYLINE
DRIVE

Washington

Warrenton

Broadway

New Market

Luray

Sperryville

I-81

NORTH

Harrisonburg

To Roanoke

Elkton

Interstate 66 in the Shenandoah Valley, where I-66 intersects with I-81 just north of
Strasburg (pages 30–31). Map by Morgan Pfaelzer. © 2024 Center for the Study of Place.

5 miles

8 kilometers

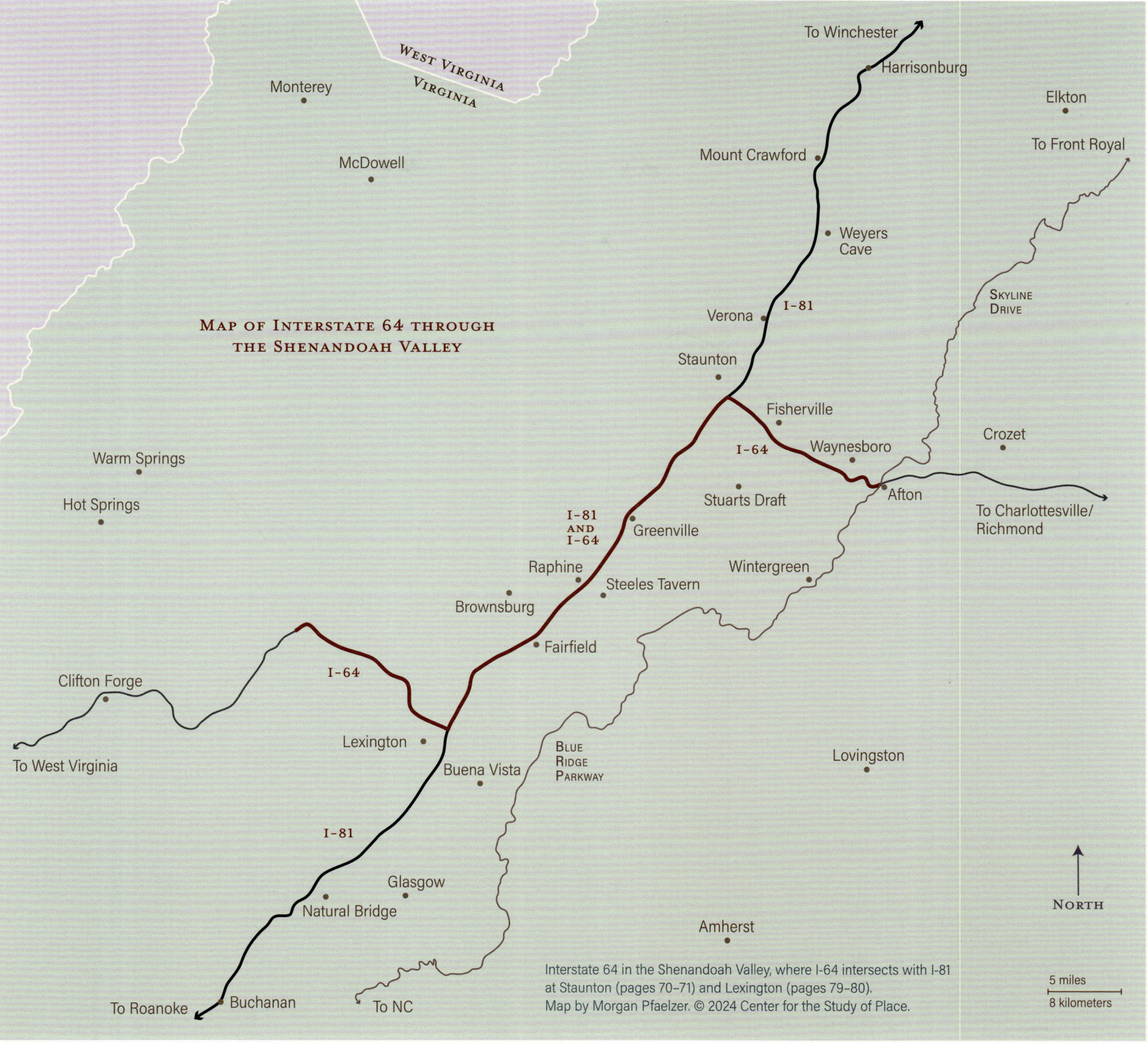

MAP OF INTERSTATE 64 THROUGH
THE SHENANDOAH VALLEY

WEST VIRGINIA
VIRGINIA

Monterey

McDowell

To Winchester

Harrisonburg

Elkton

To Front Royal

Mount Crawford

Weyers
Cave

I-81

SKYLINE
DRIVE

Verona

Staunton

Fisherville

Crozet

Warm Springs

Hot Springs

I-64

Waynesboro

Stuarts Draft

Afton

To Charlottesville/
Richmond

I-81
AND
I-64

Greenville

Raphine

Wintergreen

Steeles Tavern

Brownsburg

Fairfield

Clifton Forge

I-64

Lexington

Lovingston

To West Virginia

Buena Vista

BLUE
RIDGE
PARKWAY

I-81

Glasgow

Amherst

Natural Bridge

NORTH

To Roanoke   Buchanan

To NC

Interstate 64 in the Shenandoah Valley, where I-64 intersects with I-81
at Staunton (pages 70–71) and Lexington (pages 79–80).
Map by Morgan Pfaelzer. © 2024 Center for the Study of Place.

5 miles
8 kilometers

About the Essayist

Warren R. Hofstra was born in 1947 in New York and grew up in the Maryland suburbs of Washington, D.C. He completed his B.A. at Washington University, his M.A. at Boston University, and Ph.D. at the University of Virginia, all in the field of history. Hofstra is the Stewart Bell Professor of History at Shenandoah University, where he has taught since 1977. In addition to teaching in the fields of American social and cultural history and directing the Community History Project of Shenandoah University, he has published more than fifty papers and written or edited ten books, including *"Sweet Dreams": The World of Patsy Cline* (University of Illinois Press, 2013), *Ulster to America: The Scots-Irish Migration Experience* (University of Tennessee Press, 2011), *The Great Valley Road: Shenandoah Landscapes from Prehistory to the Present*, with Karl B. Raitz (University of Virginia Press, in association with George F. Thompson Publishing, 2010), and *The Planting of New Virginia: Settlement and Landscape in the Shenandoah Valley* (John Hopkins University, in association with the Center for American Places, 2004). His long-term research program focuses on the regional history of Virginia's Shenandoah Valley as a field of inquiry in a large-scale investigation of American capitalism and material culture. He is also engaged in an effort employing immersive technology to present elements of the debate on electing the president at the Constitutional Convention of 1787 in a virtual-reality format that draws participants into real-time experiential and learning environments and accounts for the creation of the Electoral College. With Kevin Hardwick of James Madison University, he is currently engaged in writing a supporting volume to be entitled *"Perfectly Novel": The Intellectual Origins of the Electoral College*. He resides in Winchester, Virginia.

About the Author

Andrei Kushnir has painted in oils since 1980, with a focus on the American landscape rendered *en plein air* (painting out of doors). His paintings have been exhibited widely in numerous juried and invitational shows throughout the United States, often selected by judges who were curators at the Corcoran Gallery of Art, Hirshhorn Museum, National Gallery of Art, and National Museum of American Art, all in Washington, D.C. These include the Virginia Museum of History and Culture, where he was the first living artist accorded such an exhibit; University Club, Capitol Hill Art League, and Taylor and Sons Fine Art, all in Washington, D.C.; Rehoboth (Delaware) Art League; Museum of the Shenandoah Valley; South Florida State College Museum of Florida's Art and Culture, in Avon Park, Florida; and James Madison University's Duke Gallery of Fine Art. The artist's paintings are also in the permanent collections of the Virginia Museum of History and Culture (formerly the Virginia Historical Society); U.S. Coast Guard; University of Maryland Global Campus; Museum of the Shenandoah Valley; Museum of Florida's Art and Culture; and District of Columbia's Commission of Arts and Humanities, among others.

Kushnir is the author of ten publications of his work: *Painted Boca Grande* (2020), *Small Marine Paintings* (2018), *Blue Ridge Paintings* (2017), *Oh, Shenandoah: Paintings of the Historic Valley and River* (2016), *River Visions* (2013), *Painted Seasons* (2010), *Potomac River School* (2009), *Painted History* (2004), *American Light, 2001* (2001), and *My River* (1999). Articles about Kushnir, his paintings, and his books have appeared in *The Washington Times*, *The Washington Post*, *The Register Guard* (Oregon), *The Nature Conservancy Magazine*, *The Montgomery Gazette* (Maryland), *The Longboat Observer* (Florida), *The Journal* (West Virginia), *Hill Rag* (Washington, D.C.), *Highlander Today* (Florida), *The Gloucester Matthews Gazette Journal* (Virginia), *The Gasparilla Gazette* (Florida), and *élan* Magazine (Virginia), among others.

Kushnir is a signature member of the National Oil and Acrylic Painters Society; an elected member of the Washington (D.C.) Society of Landscape Painters and Miniature Painters, Sculptors and Gravers Society, of Washington, D.C., where he served as a vice president; and an artist member of Oil Painters of America; Capitol Hill Art League; Blue Ridge Arts Council, of Front Royal, Virginia; and Alexandria and Fairfax, Virginia, Art Leagues. He has also served as an Official U.S. Coast Guard Artist.

About the Book

The Shenandoah Valley's Interstates: Plein-air Paintings along I-81, I-66, and I-64 was brought to publication in an edition of 800 softcover copies with gatefold flaps. The text was set in Mrs. Eaves, the paper is Gold East Art, 157 gsm weight, and the book was professionally printed and bound by P. Chan & Edward, Inc, in China. The epigraph on page 4 originally appeared in Charles Slack, "The End of the Pavement," *The Richmond Times-Dispatch* (August 19, 1996). The paintings on pages 26, 34, 35, 45, 46, 48, 49, 60, 68, 76, 77, 78, and 79 originally appeared in Andrei Kushnir's *Oh, Shenandoah: Plein-Air Paintings of the Historic Valley and River* (George F. Thompson Publishing, in association with the Museum of the Shenandoah Valley, 2016).

Publisher and Project Director: George F. Thompson
Editorial and Research Assistant: Mikki Soroczak
Manuscript Editor: Purna Makaram
Book Design and Production: David Skolkin

Published in 2024. First softcover edition.
Printed in China on acid-free paper.

George F. Thompson Publishing, L.L.C.
217 Oak Ridge Circle
Staunton, VA 24401–3511, U.S.A.
www.gftbooks.com

32 31 30 29 28 27 26 25 24   1 2 3 4 5

The Library of Congress Preassigned Control Number is 2023951283.

ISBN: 978-1-960521-00-2